THE
FAMILY
BUCKET LIST

First published in English in the United States of America in 2023 by
Universe Publishing
A division of Rizzoli International Publications, Inc.
300 Park Avenue South
New York, NY 10010
www.rizzoliusa.com

Conceived, designed, and produced by The Bright Press,
an imprint of the Quarto Group
1 Triptych Place, Second Floor
London SE1 9SH, United Kingdom
T (0)20 7700 9000
www.quarto.com

Publisher: James Evans
Editorial Director: Isheeta Mustafi
Managing Editor: Jacqui Sayers
Publishing Operations Director: Kathy Turtle
Publishing Assistant: Jemima Solley
Art Director: James Lawrence
Senior Editors: Caroline Elliker, Izzie Hewitt
Project Editor: Kath Stathers
Design and Picture Research: Anna Gatt

ISBN: 978-0-7893-4417-5
Library of Congress Control Number: 2023933604

2024 2025 2026 2027 / 10 9 8 7 6 5 4 3 2

Printed in China

Visit us online:
Facebook.com/RizzoliNewYork
Twitter: @Rizzoli_Books
Instagram.com/RizzoliBooks
YouTube.com/user/RizzoliNY

Front cover credit: Jim Mallouk/Shutterstock
Front cover: The Grand Canyon, Arizona, US
p. 1: Sawa-i-Lau Caves, Fiji
pp. 2–3: Madikwe Game Reserve, South Africa
pp. 4–5: Lake Garda, Italy
p. 7: Venice, Italy

THE
FAMILY
BUCKET LIST

1000 Trips to Take and Memories to Make
Around the World

NANA LUCKHAM AND KATH STATHERS

UNIVERSE

HOW TO USE THIS BOOK

This book is divided into six chapters—North America, South America, Europe, Africa and the Middle East, Asia, and Oceania. Within each chapter, entries are arranged by country, with a more specific location, such as town or area, provided at the beginning of each. Specific locations can also be searched for using the index on page 406.

COLOR CODE

Each entry number in the book has been given a color that relates to one of eight categories, as shown below, allowing you to select activities based on the type of experience you're interested in.

■ Spectacular place to sleep   ■ Sport and recreation

■ Wildlife and nature   ■ Epic journeys

■ Food and culture   ■ Exploring history

■ Festival and celebration   ■ City break

CONTENTS

INTRODUCTION

Whether your ideal vacation involves a trek through a windswept wilderness or soaking up the sun on a beach, some of life's greatest pleasures are found away from home. But as anyone who has traveled with family knows, things look very different after kids enter the picture. From keeping little ones safe on the road to dealing with temperamental teens, there are challenges involved even for the most seasoned travelers.

But these challenges don't mean that travel is less fun or that it's time to put adventure aside—quite the opposite in fact. With patience, flexibility, and a sense of humor, your family travels will be some of the best adventures you'll ever have. With that in mind, for this book we've researched and selected one thousand amazing experiences around the globe to suit families of all kinds. First timers traveling with young children, single-parent families, families bringing the grandparents along for the ride—whatever your dynamic, you'll find something that fits.

While we've included many once-in-a-lifetime experiences, such as visiting Santa Claus in Finnish Lapland, snorkeling Australia's Great Barrier Reef, and watching the great wildebeest migration, we also celebrate some simpler travel pleasures. After all, telling ghost stories around a fire, building sandcastles on a beach, or spending a night under canvas can be equally magical and memorable.

From my perspective, the best thing about traveling with kids is getting to see the wonder in the world anew. Whether you're delving into ancient history, introducing kids to different cultures, or sparking a passion for wildlife and the environment, these shared experiences will broaden their horizons, strengthen family bonds, and create memories that will last a lifetime.

We hope this book provides ample inspiration and wish you and your family many happy adventures!

NANA LUCKHAM

PS The world is a turbulent place. Some of the destinations in this book might have recently been, or still are, in conflict zones. But one day, they will be safe to visit again. We didn't want to overlook a place's cultural or historical value based on its political present, but it does mean some entries might not be accessible—or advisable—at the moment. Please check all government guidelines before traveling to countries where there is ongoing war or insurgency.

1
NORTH AMERICA

WHITEHORSE, YUKON

1 Take a kid-friendly hike through the Alaskan wilds

The vast wilderness of the Yukon is made for outdoor exploration. Challenging hikes abound, but there are gentler ways to experience these landscapes if you've got kids in tow. The wheelchair-accessible Whitehorse Millennium Trail is a 2.8 mi. (4.5 km) stretch through towering pine forests, past snow-covered peaks, and along the banks of the mighty Yukon River. Come after dusk from September to April and you might be lucky enough to spot the northern lights.

VANCOUVER, BRITISH COLUMBIA

2 Swap homes for a holiday

Experiencing the true spirit of Vancouver is easy: sidestep the hotels and arrange a home swap in one of the city's diverse neighborhoods. You'll save a bundle on accommodation, experience the city's legendary cultural scene, and still be within easy reach of mountains, beaches, and rain forest walking trails. Plus, there's the bonus of a family-friendly base when you return. Agencies like Love Home Swap and Home Exchange can make it happen.

1 HIKING IN THE YUKON

VANCOUVER ISLAND, BRITISH COLUMBIA
3 Orca safari, whales guaranteed

There's a troublesome side to spotting whales in their natural environment: there's always a chance that they won't show up. When you're managing children's expectations, that's a big risk to take—which is why going to look for orcas off Vancouver Island is such a must-do activity. Between May and October, huge pods of resident orcas, as well as humpbacks, and even shyer minke whales, are pretty much guaranteed.

LAKE LOUISE TO JASPER, ALBERTA
4 Drive the Icefields Parkway

Winding through the Canadian Rockies, between Lake Louise and Jasper, is one of the most beautiful roads on Earth. The Icefields Parkway is 145 mi. (232 km) of towering peaks, waterfalls, and ancient glaciers that will blow the mind of even the weariest traveler. Just off the highway are all manner of walks, from leisurely strolls for preschoolers to challenging hikes for teens. Walking out on the Athabasca Glacier will get the thumbs up from all ages.

3 WHALE WATCHING

5 TOTEM POLES

HAIDA GWAII ISLANDS,
BRITISH COLUMBIA
5 Wonder at the splendor of timeworn totem poles

Rugged, remote wilderness is what the Haida Gwaii island group is known for. But this British Columbian hotspot has another big draw—the huge totem carvings of the Haida people. See the evocative remains of nineteenth-century memorial poles and longhouses on the island of SG̱ang Gwaay, then visit the Haida Heritage Center, where you can learn about Haida culture and see new totem poles being carved.

GOLDEN, BRITISH COLUMBIA
6 Get to know a pack of wolves

You'll learn all about wolf conservation at the Northern Lights Wolf Center, a wildlife refuge that's home to a small pack of rescued wolves. Family tours offer ample opportunity to watch them play and feed, as well as hear their haunting howls. For the ultimate thrill, over-sixteens can walk alongside a wolf in the beautiful Blaeberry Valley.

GREAT BEAR RAINFOREST,
BRITISH COLUMBIA
7 Search for rare spirit bears

Deep in the Great Bear Rainforest, the Kitasoo/Xai'xais people live alongside ethereal spirit bears— black bears with a rare recessive gene that turns their fur white or cream. From the Indigenous- owned Spirit Bear Lodge, head into the rain forest in a guided group in search of these elusive creatures, though you'll also have the chance to spot black bears, grizzlies, and coastal wolves. These hardy hikes are best suited to teens.

NORTH VANCOUVER, BRITISH COLUMBIA
8 Test your mettle on the Capilano Suspension Bridge

You'll need sure footing and a head for heights as you tackle the gently swaying Capilano Suspension Bridge. Set high up in the tree canopy in a coastal rain forest park, this 449 ft. (137 m) long walkway sits a heart-pumping 230 ft. (70 m) above the Capilano River and has been pulling in visitors since the late nineteenth century. Further adventures come in the form of a cliffside walkway and a treetop adventure trail.

SIMILKAMEEN VALLEY, BRITISH COLUMBIA
9 Spot a lake of delightful dots

As the summer heat evaporates the water of Ktlil'x (Spotted Lake), in the Similkameen Valley, the water forms into hundreds of circular colored pools, all ringed by a salty mineral deposit. The area is protected, so you can't dip your toes in the water, but it is a strange and beautiful sight from the slopes above.

8 THE CAPILANO SUSPENSION BRIDGE

COLUMBIA ICEFIELD,
ALBERTA

10 Walk on ice at the Athabasca Glacier

The ancient Athabasca Glacier is a draw for adventurers of all ages who come with one mission—to get out onto the vast expanse of ice. Guided walking tours and all-terrain vehicles take you far along the glacier, where you'll see dramatic ice formations and learn about the impact of climate change. A water bottle comes in handy to taste the fresh glacial water.

WANUSKEWIN HERITAGE PARK,
SASKATCHEWAN

11 Explore ancient First Nations culture

Some six thousand years ago, Wanuskewin was a meeting place for nomadic tribes, who came to gather food, hunt bison, and hide from the harsh winter. Now a cultural heritage park, it's a fantastic place for budding archeologists, who can see ancient tipi rings, stone cairns, and animal bones, and find out what life was like in the old days. Sleepovers in a tipi add to the fun.

CRINKLAW MAPLE, LONDON,
ONTARIO

12 Taste maple syrup straight from the tree

March and April is maple season in Canada. Many farms, such as Crinklaw Maple, invite visitors in for weekend festivals when you can see the syrup collecting process in action, take wagon rides through the "sugar bush," and taste the delicious results with pancakes, waffles, and more.

10 ATHABASCA GLACIER

DINOSAUR PROVINCIAL PARK, ALBERTA

13 Hunt for signs of dinosaurs

Paleontologists have discovered hundreds of dinosaur skeletons in the parched, rocky landscape of Dinosaur Provincial Park. Sign up for the Family Dino Stomp Tour and you can dig for fossils, see a hadrosaur leg bone, and imagine what life was like millions of years ago. To continue the adventure, bed down at the park's campsite.

SUTTON, QUÉBEC

14 Pedal through the treetops

If you enjoy the views from up high and you're over twelve years old, you can tackle the world's highest suspended bicycle ride at VéloVolant. The details? You ride a recumbent bike, suspended 100 ft. (30 m) above ground and attached to a mile-long cable. Once you catch a glimpse of the waterfalls, ravines, and towering maple trees, any fears will go out of the window.

THROUGHOUT NEWFOUNDLAND AND LABRADOR

15 Build your own igloo

The Inuit have been building igloos for centuries, and Newfoundland winters provide you with the goods to get creative. First, you'll need a basic plan and structure, then some flat ground. Next, hard-packed snow that can be cut and shaped into blocks. After a good half day's work, you'll have a sleepable igloo that's an ideal den for kids.

13 DINOSAUR PROVINCIAL PARK

14 PEDAL IN THE TREETOPS

16 Marvel at ice sculptures

The subzero temperatures don't stop families coming out in droves for the Québec Winter Carnival, the largest winter carnival in the world, held in late January or February each year. There's everything from night parades to ice-canoe racing, but it's the fantastical ice carvings that capture kids' imaginations. Sculptors come from all over the world to carve ice palaces, battle scenes, horses, and giant chessboards, and you can get active on several carved ice slides.

MONTREAL, QUÉBEC

17 Sample a Québécois delicacy

Canada has given many gifts to the world, but
poutine is one of the most delicious. The ultimate
Québécois comfort food, it consists of three things
most kids will love: crispy fries, gravy, and cheese
curds. Crowds gather early outside legendary
restaurant La Banquise, in Montreal, where over
thirty varieties include pepperoni, guacamole,
and bacon.

MONTREAL, QUÉBEC

18 Introduce the kids to jazz

The smooth sounds of the Montreal International
Jazz Festival aren't just for grown-ups. Attracting
the world's best performers, this granddaddy of jazz
events is the best place to get young people hooked.
Many performances are free, and the Rio Tinto
Musical Park is an interactive, kid-friendly zone,
where banging drums, strumming guitars, and
jumping on a giant piano is actively encouraged.

18 MONTREAL INTERNATIONAL JAZZ FESTIVAL

MONTREAL, QUÉBEC

19 Bug out at an insectarium

Take your kids' love of creepy crawlies to the next
level at the Montreal Insectarium, one of North
America's largest insect museums. You'll learn how
bugs move and negotiate tight spaces as you explore
a range of habitats. And the butterfly room, where
thousands of colorful wings gently flap, adds to the
feeling of wonder.

19 INSECTARIUM

THROUGHOUT NOVA SCOTIA

20 Go loopy for lobster

People have been pulling lobsters out of Nova Scotian waters for centuries, from the Indigenous peoples of Atlantic Canada to the hardy fishermen of the nineteenth century, who turned it into a profitable industry. Luckily, there's now a Lobster Trail you can follow to lead you to the best lobster action in the province. You could find a no-frills spot serving lobster on the beach, attend an authentic lobster boil, or join the Great Canadian Lobster Fishing Feast and head out to sea with a local crew, returning to cook your catch over an open fire. Kids of all ages will adore the eating part. Cracking open the shell, smothering the meat with buttery sauce, and sucking the remnants out of the tail is the perfect excuse to get messy. Or, for something different, there are lobster rolls, lobster tacos, lobster macaroni cheese, lobster risotto…

20 NOVA SCOTIA

CAPE BRETON HIGHLANDS, NOVA SCOTIA

21 Hike the Cabot Trail after dark

The rugged landscapes of the Cabot Trail are dramatic enough by day, but as darkness falls, they take on a different character. Sign up for a tour and walk by lantern light, with costumed guides telling stories from the past. The sound of crashing waves and distant bird calls heighten the eerie atmosphere. One for adventurous kids aged eight and up.

THROUGHOUT PRINCE EDWARD ISLAND

22 Meet Anne of Green Gables

For young fans of Anne Shirley, Prince Edward Island's bluffs, fields, and rust-red sand are literary heaven. There are visits to Avonlea Village and tours of author Lucy Maud Montgomery's home, but best of all is Green Gables Heritage Place, where you can walk down Lovers Lane, drink raspberry cordial, and see one of Anne's famous puff-sleeved dresses.

TORONTO, ONTARIO

23 Eat lunch in the sky

As memorable family meals go, lunch atop Toronto's iconic CN Tower—once the world's tallest tower—is up there with the best. Alongside local, sustainable cuisine, the rotating restaurant serves 360-degree views across the city from 116 stories up. If you've a head for heights, kids over thirteen can tackle the EdgeWalk outside for dessert.

SIGHTS ALONG ROUTE 66

ILLINOIS TO CALIFORNIA

24 Drive across a continent (almost) on the legendary Route 66

Stretching from Chicago to Santa Monica, Route 66 was carved out by Americans fleeing the drought of the 1930s to the land of plenty in California. Inspiring everyone from John Steinbeck to the Rolling Stones, it is a stalwart of popular culture, and an ever-popular two-week-long road trip that leads you through the stunning and varied landscapes of the US. Small children might get restless, but it's a great way to spend side-by-side time with teenagers, who can be charmed by the tiny gas stations, awed by the Chain of Rocks Bridge across the Mississippi, entertained by the opportunity to spray-paint half-buried Cadillacs in the middle of the Texan desert, and impressed by the Grand Canyon, which is just a short detour from the route.

Classic diners

Half-buried Cadillacs

Field Museum of Chicago

Meramec Caverns

The Grand Canyon

ANCHORAGE, ALASKA

25 Travel by dogsled

The winter wonderland of Alaska is exciting
enough for children, but add traveling through
that wonderland on a dogsled and it takes the
picture to a whole new level. Dogsledding has
a long tradition in Alaska, and many of the
tours will take you to trails that form part of
the prestigious Iditarod Trail Sled Dog Race—
a 938 mi. (1,510 km) long race in which your
"musher" (from the French *marcher*, meaning
"to walk") might even have taken part.

TOTEM BIGHT STATE HISTORICAL PARK, ALASKA

26 Explore Alaskan Native culture

An 11 ac (4.5 ha) patch of rain forest scattered with
mysterious totems, Totem Bight State Historical
Park is a place to wander, explore, and learn about
Alaskan Native culture. An interpretive guide tells
you the story behind the structures, which were
created to pass stories from generation to generation
and either restored or recarved by Haida and Tlingit
artists. At the center of the park, you can visit a
colorful replica clan house and cultural center.

25 DOGSLED RIDE

27 NĀ PALI COASTLINE

KAUAI, HAWAII
27 Swim with tropical fish

From the harbors of Kauai, explore the exotic Nā Pali coast by boat. This jagged, green coastline has been the star of many favorite family movies, including those featuring dinosaurs in an amusement park. Where these impressive mountains meet the sea is an ideal place for kids and adults to snorkel surrounded by a rainbow of tropical fish. It's a great place to teach the kids some underwater photography too.

KAUAI, HAWAII
28 Dip into a dormant volcano

Known as the Garden Island, Kauai was formed, like the other Hawaiian Islands, from ancient volcanos. Wow the kids—and yourself—by exploring the depths of these dormant volcanos by helicopter, dipping down vertically inside the jungle-covered rocks, where you'll see waterfalls, flowering tropical plants, and colorful birds that would be impossible to see from any other vantage point. It's beautiful and thrilling in equal measure.

29 Create flower garlands on Lei Day

Celebrated on May 1 since 1928, Lei Day is an explosion of Hawaiian culture centered around the *lei*—a traditional flower garland or wreath. Kids can listen to folk tales and take part in lei-making competitions and *luaus* (Hawaiian feasts). Find family-friendly workshops at Maui's Bailey House Museum.

MAUI, HAWAII

30 Take a dip in the Seven Sacred Pools

At the very end of a curving jungle road, past the distant town of Hāna, lie the Seven Sacred Pools. Here families can scramble across smooth rocks, dip into cool waters, and enjoy a fun picnic lunch. Nestled in a valley green with jungle growth, these ancient pools have important meaning to Indigenous Hawaiians. A chain of dramatic waterfalls and streams leads down from the mountains above to fill the pools all year long. More adventuresome visitors can also explore local flora and fauna along nearby hiking trails, some leading through bamboo forests to striking waterfalls and higher vistas overlooking the ocean below.

30 SEVEN SACRED POOLS

MAUI, HAWAII
31 Cycle down a volcano

Rousing the family in the predawn hours may be
the hardest part of this adventure, but well worth
the effort. An early morning start allows you to
witness the sun rising from atop a gigantic volcanic
crater. From there, jump onto your bikes and whizz
your way down the hill from 10,000 ft. (3,000 m)
to sea level. Twists and turns along the road provide
breathtakingly beautiful views of Maui landscapes,
the ocean, and other Hawaiian islands beyond.
A delicious garden breakfast greets riders at the
bottom as a reward for early rising.

O'AHU, HAWAII
32 Learn to surf in Waikiki

What better place to learn how to surf than the
famous waves at Waikiki Beach in Honolulu? There
are huts all along the beachfront, with boards for
hire and instructors experienced enough to teach
both eager children and their less quick-to-learn
parents too. Learning something together as a
family is lots of fun and a great bonding experience,
and when you're done, enjoy a fresh coconut-and-
pineapple smoothie on the shore.

32 WAIKIKI BEACH

34 KUALOA RANCH

Ride quad bikes

Go fishing

Visit movie sets

O'AHU, HAWAII
33 Learn about history at Pearl Harbor

The horrors of World War II come to life at Pearl Harbor, where kids of all ages can hear stories told and memories revisited. The harbor and exhibits are hands-on, approachable, and interesting, including historic boats to board, dozens of different missiles and torpedoes to compare, and even a spot where you can choose an oyster and bring home the real pearl inside. Make sure to visit the USS *Arizona* Memorial and the Battleship *Missouri* for a deeper experience while you're there.

O'AHU, HAWAII
34 Channel *Jurassic Park* at Kualoa Ranch

The landscape at Kualoa Ranch is pure prehistoric magic—so much so that it featured in *Jurassic Park* more than once. Kids aged three and up can take part in the Jurassic Adventure Tour, where they'll bump across the cinematic landscape in an open-air vehicle, visiting movie sets including the famous paddock that imprisoned *Indominus rex*.

SEATTLE, WASHINGTON
35 Wander through a glass garden

An otherworldly collection of 3D glass sculptures in unusual shapes and sizes dots the landscape at the Chihuly Garden and Glass. Sitting in the shadow of the iconic Seattle Space Needle, these colorful and whimsical creations will tempt your family's imaginations. Play a fun game during your visit to describe what you each see in these free-form exhibits. Is that a rabbit or a circus clown? A school of jellyfish or bowls of spaghetti?

HOOD CANAL, WASHINGTON
36 Forage for your dinner

Pull on your waterproof boots, pack a pair of waterproof gloves, check the tide times (and obtain a valid license), and head down to the beaches of Hood Canal, a fjord off Puget Sound, to harvest fresh oysters. Who doesn't love foraging for their food—especially when it's food at the luxury end of the menu?

CANNON BEACH, OREGON
37 Take part in a sandcastle-building competition

Over twenty thousand visitors head to Oregon each June to check out the wonderful sand creations on Cannon Beach. Choose to take part and you'll be given your very own patch of sand on which your family can create its masterpiece. As well as sandcastles, you'll see everything from dragons and whales to recreations of Mount Rushmore.

FLORENCE, OREGON
38 Watch sea lions in America's largest sea cave

If you thought your kids were noisy, wait until you hear the racket in this vast sea cave. The height of a twelve-story building, the Sea Lion Cave, situated 11 mi. (18 km) north of Florence, is home to a huge herd of Steller sea lions. Visit in summer to see the pups taking their first swim, and possibly gray whales too.

CLATSOP SPIT BEACHES, OREGON
39 Race against razor clams on the beach

Digging for razor clams is a race against time because they burrow into the sand so quickly. Once you spot the "shows"—dimples in the sand that betray the clams' location—either team up as a family to pluck them out or see who can catch the most for lunch.

FORT BRAGG, CALIFORNIA
40 Sift through glass pebbles on a beach

On an isolated stretch of northern California coastline, Glass Beach is made from a combination of sand and polished sea glass. Visitors can sit for hours sorting through multicolored pieces of sea glass, smoothed over time by the pounding surf. Nearby, there are some impressive tidepools filled with shells, anemones, crabs, and other sea life.

FORT BRAGG, CALIFORNIA
41 Pedal along a railroad track

Pedal along historic railroad tracks through the redwood forests of Mendocino County on specially designed rail bikes. Electrically powered, the bikes glide along the forest rails beside a stream, through fern gullies, and across wooden trestle bridges. Spy enormous bird nests, jumping frogs, colorful wildflowers, and communities of bunnies along the way.

41 FORT BRAGG

YOSEMITE NATIONAL PARK, CALIFORNIA

42 Tell ghost stories round a campfire

Sitting round a campfire as the sky darkens and the forests come alive is a timeless childhood experience, and the vast wilderness of Yosemite is the perfect venue for a chilling tale. Spooky local happenings include a wailing ghost at Grouse Lake, strange disappearances at Tenaya Canyon, and a wandering spirit at the nearby Ahwahnee Hotel, whose interior inspired the sets of *The Shining*.

YOSEMITE NATIONAL PARK, CALIFORNIA

43 Get a taste of wilderness in Yosemite

Famously captured in the black-and-white photography of Ansel Adams, Yosemite National Park is wild and majestic. The park is peppered with hiking options for all different stamina levels. As well as fantastic views, there's also plenty of wildlife to look out for, from chipmunks and gophers to bighorn sheep and black bears—several hundred of which call the park home. It's quite something to see them in the wild, ambling around their natural habitat. Park ranger talks provide kid-friendly insights into bear behavior.

43 YOSEMITE NATIONAL PARK

SAN FRANCISCO, CALIFORNIA

44 Walk across the Golden Gate Bridge

One of the most iconic structures in the world, the Golden Gate Bridge is recognizable at once by its design and color. With the city of San Francisco in the background and the wide-open Pacific Ocean beyond, a stroll across the Golden Gate frames the area from a multitude of viewpoints. Along these vantage points, spy out key points of interest, including Fisherman's Wharf, Alcatraz Island, and Coit Tower, while watching the sailboats and container vessels moving through the water underneath. Hint: dress for windy weather.

SAN FRANCISCO, CALIFORNIA

45 Climb some of the world's steepest steps

You'd develop strong calf muscles living in San Francisco. This is a city built on hills, some of them famously steep. Put your stamina to the test with a family hike up the Filbert Steps, which lead from Levi's Plaza up to Coit Tower. They've appeared in numerous movies and TV shows over the years, and they offer spectacular vistas of Telegraph Hill and across the San Francisco Bay. Who will be first to the top? There are more than four hundred steps in all, so take your time and make sure you stop for a breather at Napier Lane. This charming stretch of urban foliage is maintained as a public garden by local residents. Listen out for the chatter of a troop of feral parrots that have made Telegraph Hill and the Filbert Steps their home.

44 GOLDEN GATE BRIDGE

46 ALCATRAZ ISLAND

47 PRIDE MARCH

SAN FRANCISCO, CALIFORNIA

46 Explore the prison on Alcatraz Island

Is any prison more legendary than Alcatraz? Positioned precariously in the middle of San Francisco Bay, with surrounding waters so rough they are virtually unswimmable, the prison closed in 1963 but is now open for tours. Feel what it's like to be behind bars, while hearing chilling stories about attempted escapes. Then explore the view of the Golden Gate Bridge and downtown skyscrapers from the prison's old exercise yards.

SAN FRANCISCO, CALIFORNIA

47 Take to the streets on a Pride march

Whether an LGBTQ+ family or not, show your children how to support inclusivity and visibility in this gleeful parade full of rainbows, live music, and celebration along San Francisco's Market St. Although it's not the oldest Pride march in the world, the city is synonymous with the advancement of LGBTQ+ rights, acceptance, and equality.

JAMESTOWN, CALIFORNIA

48 Pan for gold in the Californian foothills

Explore authentic gold rush legends in the rugged California foothills, where gold miners once worked to find their riches. In Jamestown, grab a pan and trowel in town and set out for one of the many streambeds nearby for the chance to find real gold nuggets. Kids delight in getting wet and muddy in the process and, who knows, someone in the family might find their fortune in the pay dirt.

SANTA CRUZ, CALIFORNIA

49 Thrill seek on a wooden roller coaster

Scream with delight while riding the twisting tracks of the historic Giant Dipper roller coaster. Since 1924, this coaster has carried excited passengers to heights of 70 ft. (21 m) and speeds up to 50 mph (81 km/h), making it one of the most popular wooden roller coasters in the world. After your ride, hit the beach for a swim, or grab some saltwater taffy at the nearby arcade.

SAN SIMEON, CALIFORNIA

50 Wonder at the opulence of Hearst Castle

Your eyes will pop at the excess of this modern castle, nestled in the hills of central California. Newspaper magnate William Randolph Hearst collected antiques, art, and historic artifacts from throughout the world, bringing them back to San Simeon as he constructed Hearst Castle. A gold-tiled swimming pool, human-height fireplaces, herds of zebras, and flocks of peacocks are all part of the tour. The main house has 165 rooms jammed full of curiosities.

49 WOODEN ROLLER COASTER

MONTEREY BAY, CALIFORNIA
51 Kayak with sea lions

Paddling the calm waters of Monterey Bay in colorful kayaks allows up-close views of this ocean treasure, brimming with sea otters, sea lions, starfish, and more. Sea lions bark and frolic from their perches on rocks and wharfs as you wind through moored sailboats and yachts. Look for adorable and curious otter families, who often swim up to peer at the strange human creatures floating by.

SAN LUIS OBISPO, CALIFORNIA
52 Contribute to Chewing Gum Alley

Kids love to visit Chewing Gum Alley in San Luis Obispo because it's both gross and beautiful. The colorful walls of this small alley are covered with pieces of chewing gum placed by previous visitors. This kaleidoscope of various colors and textures is sure to wow some and disgust others. The best part is leaving your own contribution to this growing, sticky mural.

SOLVANG, CALIFORNIA
53 Visit Denmark —in the US

Complete with old-country windmills and European architecture, this quirky Danish village, the "Danish Capital of America," is best known for its sweet and delicious Danish pastries. After enjoying a plateful with homemade jam and powdered sugar, you can burn off some energy exploring Solvang's shops, or riding tame ponies in nearby pastures.

51 SEA LIONS

53 SOLVANG

LOS ANGELES, CALIFORNIA
54 Hike to the Hollywood sign

A symbol known around the world, the famous Hollywood sign makes for a fun hiking destination in the LA area. Pack a picnic lunch and set out along the hillside, with views across downtown skyscrapers and all the way to the sea. Hikers can reach the sign by several approaches, some easier than others. Families with younger kids can enjoy a view of the sign from nearby Griffith Observatory.

LOS ANGELES, CALIFORNIA
55 Watch the stars from a world-famous observatory

Forget the movie stars of Hollywood—LA's Griffith Observatory is more concerned with the stars of the cosmos. Families can get all the big questions answered at the most visited public observatory in the world. Questions like: Will we ever live on Mars? Could astronauts land on the Sun if they went at night? Don't miss the enthralling shows in the planetarium.

54 THE HOLLYWOOD SIGN

PALM SPRINGS, CALIFORNIA
56 Stand on a fault line

California is renowned for its dramatic earthquakes, and the strongest have been felt along the San Andreas Fault. Now you can visit the fault on an open-air jeep tour out of Palm Springs, venturing into the desert hills to put your feet on the ground near its origin point. Visit the bubbling waters of a real palm oasis, and walk into a rock crevice formed by the shifting tectonic plates. It's a spooky kind of fun with some geology facts thrown in.

PALM SPRINGS, CALIFORNIA
57 Snowball fight in the desert

The thermometer in sunny Palm Springs can top 100°F (38°C), while the majestic mountains that surround the valley are still white-capped with snow. Let the kids play in the swimming pool for a while, and then blow their minds by taking the Palm Springs Aerial Tramway from the desert floor up to an elevation of 8,500 ft. (2,591 m) in less than ten minutes. Have a snowball fight in your shorts and sandals while gazing down at desert sands, golf courses, and movie stars' homes.

GIANT FOREST, SEQUOIA NATIONAL PARK,
CALIFORNIA

58 Feel the majesty of the world's biggest trees

The giant sequoias of northern California are magnificent trees. As you wander through this grove of eight thousand towering sequoias, many over one thousand years old, with their rich, red bark stretching up around you to heights of 300 ft. (91 m) and more, you feel the true power of nature. The world's largest living tree is here, General Sherman, with a trunk that's 100 ft. (30 m) wide.

DANA POINT, CALIFORNIA

59 Spy whales and dolphins close up

Board a cabin cruiser in Dana Point Harbor and head out to sea from the "Whale Watching Capital of the World." On a good day, passengers can spy waterspouts from the blowholes of migrating whales. Visitors report regular sightings of blue, gray, and humpback whales, while schools of dolphins often swim alongside the boat. Marine biologists accompany tours to provide information and background on what is being seen.

CATALINA ISLAND, CALIFORNIA

60 Run alongside a bison herd

Originally brought to Catalina Island as part of a 1920s Hollywood movie set, this bison herd has prospered on protected land. Marvel at the bisons' size and sheer power as you see them up close on a Bison Expedition. Then tour the island in an open-air biofuel vehicle as you enjoy the history of Catalina, its wildflowers, and its shorebirds.

58 GIANT SEQUOIAS

CARLSBAD, CALIFORNIA
61 Wander in flower fields

Stroll garden paths through a dizzying array of colors at the Flower Fields at Carlsbad Ranch®, where acres of blooming flowers form a massive rainbow, visible from the sky. Alternatively, if walking's not appealing, choose to ride the tractor wagon as it rumbles around the rows of colorful ranunculus blossoms. Whether you walk or ride, the sight of flowers for acres and the smell of springtime is fun for all ages. Not into flowers? Then visit the on-site blueberry patch and grab a basket to fill as you pick ripe berries (of course, you must taste a couple to make sure they are sweet and ready). Other activities include a Sweet Pea Maze, orchid greenhouse, poinsettia display, food trucks, and games.

JULIAN, CALIFORNIA
62 Pick apples and eat pie

Julian is a picturesque, gold rush-era mountain town with a haunted hotel and a penchant for apples. You can pick your own in nearby orchards or wander into the village, where local bakeries line Main Street serving up apple pie in many variations. Whether you prefer traditional, crumb, à la mode, or perhaps mixed with berries, the apple pies here are legendary.

61 CARLSBAD RANCH

BIG SUR, CALIFORNIA

63 Take a road trip along the Big Sur

Big Sur is a rugged stretch of coastline in northern California. Mountains rise steeply out of the Pacific, with Highway 1 carving its way along the edge. Epic views and wildlife-watching opportunities abound, including California condors soaring above and gray whales diving in the sea below. The Big Sur Coast Highway is only 90 mi. (145 km) long—which is perfect for little ones who prefer shorter journeys—and if you make your vehicle of choice a classic RV, it's the stuff children's road-trip dreams are made of. Along the route there are many well-known (and much-photographed) sights, such as Bixby Bridge, with its arch stretching across a canyon, national parks with hiking routes, and stunning beaches and coves. Oh, and it's so remote that there's hardly any phone reception. It's no surprise that it was the featured destination in the Red Hot Chili Peppers' song "Road Trippin."

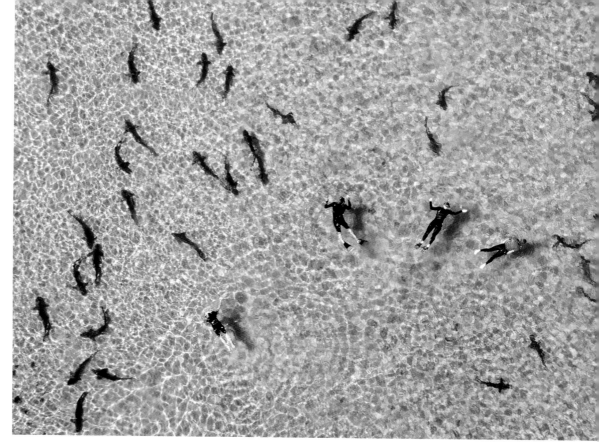

64 LEOPARD SHARKS

LA JOLLA, CALIFORNIA
64 Swim with leopard sharks

Spotted leopard sharks live in the waters off
La Jolla Shores Beach all year round, but in the
summer months, the warmer waters lure them
toward the beach. These docile visitors wow locals
and visitors, who wade or swim with them in the
shallow waters. Marine biologists deem them
completely harmless to humans, and sharing the
water with schools of sharks makes kids (and
adults) screech with excitement.

CORONADO, CALIFORNIA
65 Hunt for sand dollars

Splash in the shallow, calm waves along a stretch
of beach in Coronado where a species of sea urchin
called "sand dollars" wash up with the ocean waves.
The trick is to hit the sand early, starting at Silver
Strand State Beach in the morning, before the
beach becomes crowded. Look along the surf line
at the water's edge for the sand dollar shells, some
bleached white by the sun or half-buried in the sand.
Be gentle if you find a live one and leave it be.

66 SAN DIEGO COMIC-CON

68 OMEGA MART

SAN DIEGO, CALIFORNIA

66 Dress up for Comic-Con

Once a one-day event for hardcore comic fans, San Diego Comic-Con is now a family-friendly, multiday extravaganza, where you can go nuts over everything to do with fantasy, comic books, and superheroes. Dress up in your most outlandish costumes, turn up as early as possible, and revel in memorabilia, gaming, and celebrity appearances.

LAS VEGAS, NEVADA

67 Stay at an over-the-top Vegas hotel

An extravagant playground in the middle of the desert, Vegas isn't just for adult indulgence. Kids will be equally wowed by the city's bright lights and bombastic nature, especially if you book a themed hotel. You could ride a gondola at the Venetian, go back to the Roman Empire at Caesars Palace, or see wandering medieval minstrels beneath the turrets of Excalibur Hotel.

LAS VEGAS, NEVADA

68 Discover art that makes you smile

For families looking to blow the minds of their teenagers, Omega Mart in Las Vegas is an interactive and immersive art installation like no other. Begin with a walk through what appears to be a supermarket full of surreal products and find hidden messages along the way.

69 GOBLIN VALLEY STATE PARK

70 BRYCE CANYON

GOBLIN VALLEY STATE PARK,
UTAH

69 Make friends with goblins

With its valley floor full of small but weird rock formations, it's easy to see how Goblin Valley State Park got its name. The tiny clusters (made of sandstone deposited during the Jurassic period) are perfect fodder for the imaginations of younger children or the geological insights of older ones.

BRYCE CANYON NATIONAL PARK,
UTAH

70 Take a walk between the hoodoos

Resembling delicate fingers of rock that stretch into the sky, the hoodoos of Bryce Canyon National Park tower up to ten stories high, and glow beautifully at sunrise. Family hikes around them can make you feel as if you're on another planet.

MCGINNIS MEADOWS, MONTANA

71 Work on a real-life cattle ranch

Some jobs feel more like fun than work, and joining cattle ranchers as they round up their cattle on horseback in the stunning Montana scenery is a whole lot of fun. Beginner riders over twelve years old are welcome, and you'll leave with oodles more expertise than you came with.

HULETT, WYOMING

72 Enjoy a close encounter at Devils Tower

Fans of Steven Spielberg's *Close Encounters of the Third Kind* will recognize Devils Tower instantly as the mysterious rock formation where aliens land. There are many oral histories from the Lakota people about the rock, with one tale being that the crevices down the red-rock sides were left by the claws of a giant bear as it chased a group of wily children. You can think up your own stories while tackling a short hiking trail around the base.

THROUGHOUT COLORADO

73 Cook dinner over an open fire

It's a truth all campers know: food tastes better cooked on an open fire and eaten in the fresh air. Find a campsite that allows fires—there are plenty in Colorado, but regulations change with wildfire risk—pack up your sausages or veggie burgers, tease that fire into being, and enjoy one of life's great pleasures as a family, surrounded by beautiful Colorado views and clean air.

73 CAMPING IN COLORADO

MESA VERDE NATIONAL PARK, COLORADO

74 Explore the cliff dwellings of Mesa Verde

Mesa Verde National Park is a treasure trove of ancient dwellings, built by the Ancestral Puebloan people more than 800 years ago using the shelter of overhanging cliffs. For scale, explore Cliff Palace—a complex of 150 rooms, towers, and circular spaces—and for adventure, take a tour to Balcony House, which can be reached via a 32 ft. (10 m) ladder and a short crawl through a tunnel.

GLENWOOD SPRINGS, COLORADO

75 Soak up views—and minerals

While adults will love the luxury of a hot spring with a view over the Rockies, children will love the fact that unlike many resorts, Iron Mountain Hot Springs actively welcomes children. It has a dedicated family pool that is kept at a slightly cooler temperature than the more private adult soaking pools.

77 GRAND CANYON RAFTING

78 JEEP TOUR

MONUMENT VALLEY, ARIZONA

76 Tour Monument Valley with a knowledgeable guide

It's no wonder moviemakers have flocked to this epic landscape for decades—the sight of vast rock formations rising out of the red desert floor is breathtaking. You could self-drive the scenic loop, but a tour with a Navajo guide takes you into the backcountry, and brings the landscape to life for kids. They'll hear Navajo tales firsthand, see ancient Anasazi rock art, and burn off energy racing up and down the dunes.

LEES FERRY, ARIZONA

77 Travel the Grand Canyon by raft

The scale of the Grand Canyon will take your breath away as you float along the Colorado River, between walls of rock up to a mile deep. Guided rafting trips mean everyone gets involved, setting up camp by the riverside and gathering wood to toast marshmallows around the fire.

SEDONA, ARIZONA

78 Off-road on boulders in Sedona

Sedona is known for its otherworldly beauty and deep-red, rocky outcroppings. Sign up for one of the many jeep tours that traverse the rough terrain, climbing impossible boulders to scale heights unreachable any other way. Guides are very knowledgeable about the geology and rock formations—and how to navigate them in a jeep—and the kids love to sit in the back as they bump along the paths.

SEDONA, ARIZONA
79 See planets in the night sky

Viewing the stars and planets from an officially
designated International Dark-Sky Association
site is nothing like your backyard at home. In the
quiet high deserts of Sedona, book a nighttime
outing when there is no moon, viewing the stars
through an extremely powerful telescope manned
by a former NASA engineer. Set in a grass field,
portable chairs encircle an astronomer who narrates
what is visible in the night sky. Lucky viewers can
look through the telescope at the rings of Saturn,
moons of Jupiter, storm clouds on Mars, and
a multitude of stars hundreds of light-years
away. Spy satellites tumbling across the sky,
and meteors—or shooting stars—streaming into
Earth's atmosphere with a blaze of fire and light.

TOMBSTONE, ARIZONA
80 Descend into silver mines

At the Good Enough Silver Mine, don hard hats
and descend 100 ft. (30 m) below ground to witness
silver mining from the late 1800s. Above ground,
the Wild West town of Tombstone is famous as the
home of the O.K. Corral, where Wyatt Earp, Doc
Holliday, and their cohorts had their doomed
shootout. Wagon rides, gunslingers, saloons, and
restaurants line the streets to entertain visitors.

79 GO STARGAZING

ALBUQUERQUE, NEW MEXICO
81 Take a ride in a hot-air balloon

There's something serenely gentle about the way the basket of a hot-air balloon gently lifts you off the ground and carries you off on a breeze. From Albuquerque, the world capital of balloon flights, rise up over the Rio Grande Valley, and enjoy the views, looking out for widlife below—and the other colorful balloons all around.

81 BALLOON RIDE

ROSWELL, NEW MEXICO
82 Go extraterrestrial at Roswell

The "UFO capital of the world" holds a host of wonders for school-age children. It was just outside the city that an alien spaceship allegedly crashed in 1947, prompting an (also alleged) cover-up by the US government. Miniature sleuths can learn about abductions, crop circles, and UFO sightings at the International UFO Museum, visit quirky attractions like Alien Zone Area 51, or head out into the desert to the infamous UFO crash site.

MURDO, SOUTH DAKOTA
83 Step back into the Wild West

Saddle up for adventure at an authentic reproduction of an 1880s frontier town. In Murdo, you can explore the blacksmith's, the barber's shop, the saloon, and the jailhouse to learn what life was really like in the Wild West. Hire costumes as you arrive for some truly memorable family photographs.

THROUGHOUT TEXAS

84 Load up your plate at a BBQ joint

Texans take their BBQ joints seriously and families are welcome to join the throng. You'll be served ribs, brisket, and other red-blooded meats, smoked low and slow in wood-fired pits for that authentic Texan taste. Want cutlery? Forget it. The best places offer nothing but a hunk of bread, plus napkins for that finger-licking stickiness.

DINOSAUR VALLEY STATE PARK, TEXAS

85 Walk in the footprints of dinosaurs

Millions of years ago, this part of Texas was a veritable dinosaur highway as massive creatures—*Acrocanthosaurus* and *Sauroposeidon* among them—stomped across forests and plains at the edge of an ancient sea. You can still see and walk in their fossilized footprints along the Palauxy riverbed during the summer months when the river is dry.

AUSTIN, TEXAS

86 Tiptoe among the wildflowers

While St. Edward's Park in Austin is one of the best places in Texas to admire the spring wildflowers, it's not very well known. A scenic trail by the creek, ideal for little legs, leads to a trickling waterfall where you can paddle undisturbed. Pose for photos among the delightful bluebonnets, which are the Texas state flower.

AUSTIN, TEXAS

87 Watch bats emerge at sunset

Every evening between spring and fall, crowds gather on the banks of Lady Bird Lake in Austin to witness an incredible natural spectacle take place at Congress Avenue Bridge. The world's largest population of Mexican free-tailed bats roosts under the bridge and, around sunset, hundreds of thousands of them pour out into the sky to devour the city's unlucky insects. Families in the know rent canoes or stand-up paddleboards for a view from the water.

HOUSTON, TEXAS

88 Get wet and wild at the Schlitterbahn

Thrill seekers will love Schlitterbahn on Galveston Island, Houston, and its host of white-knuckle, high-speed water slides and rides. But there are plenty of more relaxing activities to enjoy too, including a traditional lazy river, allowing the whole family to float gently around the entire park without ever leaving the water. For a little luxury, splash out on a private cabana for the day and bring your own picnic into the park.

87 BATS AT DUSK

CHICAGO, ILLINOIS
89 See a real *T. rex*

Chicago's Field Museum holds a wealth of information for curious kids, but there's one icon that pulls in fans from across the country—Sue, the most comprehensive *T. rex* skeleton ever discovered. At 40 ft. (12 m) long and 90 percent complete, she's an impressive specimen. You can also get acquainted with her neighbor, Máximo the titanosaur, the biggest dinosaur ever discovered.

CHICAGO, ILLINOIS
90 Enjoy festival fun at Kidzapalooza

Lollapalooza has been rocking Chicago for years, but it's not just the adults that have all the fun. Kidzapalooza is a festival within a festival, aimed at—you've guessed it—families with younger kids. As well as being schooled in the world of rock, they can get interactive at music workshops, take a hip-hop dance class, or get a (temporary) punk rock hairstyle.

CHICAGO, ILLINOIS
91 Eat Chicago's famous deep-dish pizza

While most people associate pizza with Italy, deep-dish pizza is all about Chicago. It began with Italian immigrants recreating a taste of home, and has morphed into the savory layer cake that Chicagoans love today. Try one at Burt's Place—an independent restaurant dating back more than thirty years.

93 ACADIA NATIONAL PARK

ROMEO, MICHIGAN
92 Get spooktacular for Halloween

Every year the residents of Tilson Street in Romeo, Michigan, create Halloween displays that pull in thousands of visitors from across the state and beyond. Alongside the usual severed limbs, ghouls, and grim reapers are huge, staged scenes that take days of preparation—toxic playgrounds, haunted balls, and creepy castles have all been on the bill.

MOUNT DESERT ISLAND, MAINE
93 Cycle around a national park

Situated on the mid-section of Maine's Atlantic coast, Acadia National Park boasts dozens of cycling routes along well-surfaced roads and paths. Bikes to suit every member of the family can be rented, as well as trailers for little ones. Join a guided tour led by a park ranger, or set off with a map to find your own adventures.

WATERBURY, VERMONT
94 Sample the goods at Ben & Jerry's ice cream factory

Ice-cream groupies can learn how Ben and Jerry turned an abandoned gas station into a frozen dream at their factory tour in Waterbury, Vermont. You'll see the production process, visit the tasting room, and learn about their social activism. There's also a "flavor graveyard," where you can check out outlandish flavors of years past.

MARTHA'S VINEYARD, MASSACHUSETTS

95 Sail over to Martha's Vineyard

Sailing is common in Cape Cod, and the island of Martha's Vineyard is the ultimate port. Hop on a sailboat from the Cape Cod shores, snack on a lobster roll, and ride the wind in style. Experienced sailors rent boats to sail across the open ocean and dock on the island. Or charter a boat with a captain, so you can sit back and enjoy a relaxing cruise around the legendary beaches and inlets. A passenger ferry presents a more direct option from Falmouth to Martha's Vineyard in about thirty-five minutes.

PROVINCETOWN, MASSACHUSETTS

96 Climb a historic lighthouse

Lighthouses are the figureheads of Old Cape Cod, and nine still welcome the public, including six that can be climbed. Imagine scaling the circular staircase 180 years ago to attend to the lights and keep sailing ships safely from the rocky shores. The Chatham Lighthouse has amazing ocean views, towering 80 ft. (24 m) above sea level since 1841 and still in operation today. Landlubbers can always enjoy great views from below.

BOSTON HARBOR, MASSACHUSETTS

97 Reenact the Boston Tea Party

It all started in 1773 with a few loads of tea dumped overboard from a ship docked in Boston Harbor, and the rest is history. Reenact the story of revolutionaries at the Boston Tea Party Ships & Museum, with actors in period costumes, props, and a tour on board a replica sailing vessel. Kids and adults are drafted into service, "helping" prepare the ship for the troubles ahead with an entertaining storyline led by the guides. With downtown Boston skyscrapers in the background, it's a fun combination of modern and historic.

95 MARTHA'S VINEYARD

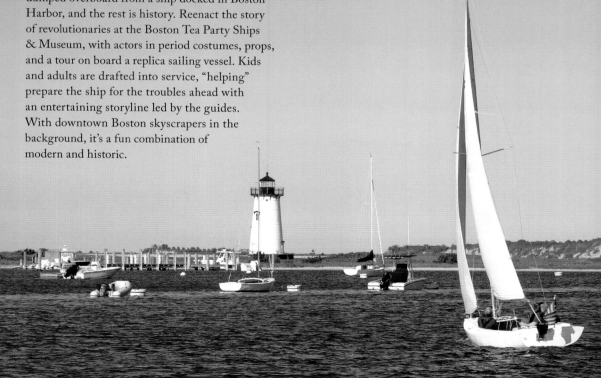

NEW YORK, NEW YORK
98 See the iconic NYC skyline

Step along raised pedestrian walkways as you traverse the length of the iconic Brooklyn Bridge, one of New York City's most well-known sites. It can take about an hour to cross from the Brooklyn side toward Manhattan as you sightsee both historic and modern developments of the city—including the bridge itself, which has been the subject of many movies and photo shoots since it was erected in 1869. Take some selfies and family poses while stopping along the way to ogle at views of the Statue of Liberty, One World Trade Center, the Empire State Building, or the Chrysler Building.

NEW YORK, NEW YORK
99 Trace your family tree

Tracing the journey of your ancestors is fascinating and fun at New York's historic Ellis Island Immigration Museum. Between 1892 and 1954, more than twelve million immigrants passed through the processing center here before pursuing their American Dream. Take the boat out to the island past the Statue of Liberty—for many new arrivals their first sight of America and a life of freedom.

NEW YORK, NEW YORK
100 Catch a baseball game in NYC

As every New Yorker knows, baseball is at its best at Yankee Stadium in the Bronx, and Citi Field in Queens, home of the New York Mets. Even if you don't know your baseball from your softball, cheering alongside passionate fans is a thrilling, quintessentially New York night out. The games are always family friendly, so kids of all ages can join the fun.

NEW YORK, NEW YORK
101 Watch out for ghostly goings-on

Ain't afraid of no ghosts? A visit to the three-story firehouse in Manhattan that served as the Ghostbusters HQ is sure to appeal to nostalgic parents just as much as the kids. Hook and Ladder 8 is a working fire station—the crews here were among the first to arrive at the World Trade Center on September 11, 2001. But if they're not busy, they're always happy to show curious visitors around.

NEW YORK, NEW YORK
102 Take in the iconic Guggenheim Museum

New York's Guggenheim Museum has as much to inspire budding architects as it does budding artists. Frank Lloyd Wright's white spiral design (based on the nautilus shell) leads you through a permanent collection that includes Picasso and Kandinsky, and on to more contemporary work.

98 THE BROOKLYN BRIDGE

104 AFRICAN AMERICAN HISTORY

103 Ride the world's tallest roller coaster

It lasts less than a minute, but a ride on the Kingda Ka, in Six Flags Great Adventure Theme Park, is fifty seconds you won't forget. To get to the top of the roller coaster—the height of a forty-five-story building—the cars are rocket-boosted to reach 128 mph (206 km/h) in less than four seconds. And then it's all downhill. You have to be 4 ft. 6 in. (137 cm) or taller to get on.

WASHINGTON, D.C.
104 Celebrate African American history

A striking, bronze-wrapped building standing proudly on the National Mall, the National Museum of African American History and Culture is a must for understanding the US. As well as celebrating Black achievement, the museum includes somber exhibitions on slavery, segregation, and contemporary race relations, so it's best suited to older kids and teens.

WASHINGTON, D.C.
105 Join a march on the National Mall

Martin Luther King, Jr. gave his "I Have a Dream" speech to a packed crowd on the National Mall, anti-Vietnam protesters gathered here in 1969, and the first Women's March turned the place pink in 2017. Join a march that suits your beliefs and relish the atmosphere of being surrounded by like-minded souls.

PHILADELPHIA, PENNSYLVANIA
106 Immerse yourselves in a world of mosaics

As you stand wander into Philadelphia's Magic Gardens and turn full circle, you'll see that every surface is covered in layers of mosaic. It's the work of one artist, Isaiah Zagar, but was created through a rich sense of community. That community feel continues, and there's a varied events program to inspire creativity, including regular Family Jams.

WILLIAMSBURG, VIRGINIA
107 Scare yourselves on a ghost tour

The pretty, historic streets of Williamsburg provide an atmospheric setting for a candlelit ghost walk. Costumed storytellers lead families with kids aged eight and older on a tour full of terrifying tales about Native American burial grounds, confederate soldiers, and the crying children of Peyton Randolph house, one of America's most haunted buildings.

106 PHILADELPHIA'S MAGIC GARDENS

109 MARDI GRAS

NEW ORLEANS, LOUISIANA
108 Cruise on a historic steamboat

Step back in time with a family-friendly cruise aboard a historic steamboat on the Mississippi River (and see who's best at spelling "Mississippi"). Kids will love bopping to live jazz music, tasty Louisiana brunches, and peering down with amazement at the huge paddle wheel as it churns the water below.

NEW ORLEANS, LOUISIANA
109 Party at Mardi Gras

Colorful, creative, and more than a little crazy, Mardi Gras is the ultimate New Orleans experience. And despite its wild reputation, families take part in festivities across the city. Kids can dress up in their outlandish best, dance along to marching bands, and feel a sense of wonder as the magnificent floats go by.

NEW ORLEANS, LOUISIANA
110 Gorge on gumbo

Finding the best gumbo in New Orleans is an impossible task: there's no standard recipe for this rich stew that has no clear definition. From ingredients to cooking techniques, it draws influences from the many cultures that call New Orleans home, which makes it synonymous with the town.

GREAT SMOKY MOUNTAINS NATIONAL PARK,
TENNESSEE
111 See fireflies light up a forest

If you wanted to believe in fairies, stumbling across
fireflies putting on a light show in a forest could
convince you. Magical to watch, the phenomenon
is, in fact, the fireflies' way of attracting a mate and
only happens for a few weeks each year (around
May or June in Tennessee).

CHATTANOOGA, TENNESSEE
112 Admire an underground waterfall

Get ready to be wowed by Ruby Falls which, at
144 ft. (44 m), is the tallest and deepest underground
waterfall open to the public in the United States.
Thundering away inside the Lookout Mountain
just outside Chattanooga, the falls are reached
by a thrilling, glass-fronted elevator that tracks
past many unusual rock formations on the way
down. After admiring the waterfall in all its glory,
adrenaline lovers can indulge in some zip-lining
on the mountain slopes outside.

NASHVILLE, TENNESSEE
113 Record a song

Take those in-car family sing-alongs one step
further by creating a professional song recording
in a Nashville recording studio. Professional
musicians can help you write an original tune,
or you can record a cover version of a family
favorite. One thing's for sure, it will be a regular
hit at family celebrations for years to come.

112 RUBY FALLS

MEMPHIS, TENNESSEE
114 Duck out for afternoon tea

Quackers behavior is guaranteed at the Peabody Hotel in Memphis, where twice a day you can watch the hotel's resident troupe of ducks march through the lobby on the way for a swim in the fountain. Afternoon tea here is a family favorite but—perhaps unsurprisingly—you'll never find duck on the menu.

MERRITT ISLAND, FLORIDA
115 Prepare for a mission to Mars

If you've ever wanted to become a space explorer, now's your chance—without ever leaving Earth. This immersive experience at the Kennedy Space Center has you working in a team, practicing landing on the Red Planet, and experiencing the thrill of a space walk. Kids aged ten and over can take part.

EVERGLADES NATIONAL PARK, FLORIDA
116 See crocs and alligators in one day

American alligators are found all over Florida, and the state's southern tip is the northernmost range of the American crocodile. This means that around Virginia Key or Flamingo Marina in the Everglades, it is possible to see both crocs and alligators in the same day. Keep your distance from both, but play spot-the-difference with nose shape, color, and teeth.

116 EVERGLADES

SANIBEL ISLAND, FLORIDA
117 Find the best shells on Sanibel Island

Scouring the seashore for shells is a beloved childhood tradition; but the breathtaking beaches of Sanibel Island take it to the next level. They're covered in amazing finds, from conch shells to clam shells, often perfectly intact. There are so many people scouring the beach that locals talk of the "Sanibel Stoop"—the bent-over position used when collecting seashells.

DRY TORTUGAS NATIONAL PARK, FLORIDA
118 Introduce children to world-class snorkeling

A boat or seaplane will take you to Dry Tortugas National Park, an archipelago 70 mi. (113 km) west of Key West, known for its shallow waters and beginner-friendly reef excursions. Younger kids can snorkel from the white-sand beaches, and there are boat trips out to pristine reefs for more confident swimmers. Either way, you're guaranteed a plethora of colorful sea life.

TITUSVILLE, FLORIDA
119 Kayak through bioluminescence

Nighttime kayaking through bioluminescence (light created by living organisms) is an otherworldly experience, thrilling and beautiful at the same time. Kayak through gently glowing plankton, every stroke of the paddle creating vivid new patterns. Summer is the best time to witness this amazing natural phenomenon.

118 SNORKELING IN DRY TORTUGAS

CRYSTAL RIVER, FLORIDA
120 Swim with manatees

For an unforgettable wildlife experience, try swimming, kayaking, or paddleboarding alongside a group of manatees in their natural environment. You'll marvel at the slow-moving grace of these beautiful sea cows. Sadly, manatees are threatened in the wild, but tours led by expert guides can help create young conservationists of the future.

MIAMI, FLORIDA
121 Take an art deco tour

Wow older kids with a tour of Miami's unique and fabulous architecture. Many buildings around the city have been built in chic, art deco style, all geometric shapes and eye-popping colors. And the best guided tours don't simply lead you around the finest examples of art deco in Miami— they can also take you inside some of these buildings to admire the interiors, and explain the stories behind them.

121 MIAMI

122 Cheer the action at a jai alai game

Watching a jai alai game is so fast-paced, the energy of the arena is at a fever pitch. Sit in the stands of the Moroccan-inspired Jai Alai Palace in Tijuana, munch on Mexican treats, and watch a game that resembles a mix of handball and field hockey. Players wear scoop-shaped gloves to catch the hard ball and hurl it against a wall, trying to make the player on the opposite team miss the return catch.

125 LA PAZ

LOS CABOS, MEXICO

123 Go sportfishing in the deep blue sea

Heading out into the warm trade winds while skimming the oceans around Los Cabos will put smiles on the faces of the whole family, even if they don't intend to fish. For the anglers in the crowd, throw a line out behind the boat for the chance to hook a marlin, sailfish, tuna, or dorado. It's a thrilling moment when someone's line starts that telltale tugging and the action begins.

LA PAZ, MEXICO

124 Mingle with whale sharks

Whale sharks are the largest species of fish in the world, and you can swim with them in the Sea of Cortez, near La Paz. Don't worry—they are harmless, gentle, and slow-moving, despite growing up to 30 ft. (9 m). As you bob in the water with a snorkel and vest, the sharks mill about in groups feeding on tiny plankton. One might brush you as it sweeps by, or come directly over to say hello.

LA PAZ, MEXICO

125 Discover a town through its street art

Colorful murals in La Paz take viewers deep into the culture of the town: the importance of the sea and conservation, the caves of the area's Indigenous peoples, and the rancheros in the desert. It's a wonderful way to learn about a place—like a museum painted huge on the side of buildings.

VALLE DE LOS GIGANTES, MEXICO
126 Pose with giant cacti

A forest of twisted cacti in the parched landscape of Baja California, Valle de los Gigantes looks like something out of a desert fairy tale. It's all thanks to the massive *cardón* cactus, one of the largest species in the world and unique to this area. Most in the valley are over a hundred years old and they grow to a whopping 60 ft. (18 m) tall, making for some fantastic photo ops with little ones.

CHIHUAHUA, MEXICO
127 Be awed by nature in the Copper Canyon

Quite apart from being located in the wonderfully named region of Chihuahua, where tiny dogs come from, Copper Canyon is a spectacular location. Technically made up of six connecting canyons, there are endless views over tree-covered gorges, cut through with peaks and ridges. The canyon gets its name from the green rock of the gorge.

126 VALLE DE LOS GIGANTES

MICHOACÁN, MEXICO
128 Marvel at millions of monarchs

It is a beautiful thing to watch a butterfly gather nectar from a flower, but it is an unforgettable experience to see millions clustered together on the trunks of fir trees in Mexico. Each year, about 20 million monarch butterflies migrate 3,000 mi. (4,828 km) from Canada and the US to overwinter here, and walking through them is a privilege.

PUERTO VALLARTA, MEXICO
Take a taco tour

To many families, tacos are a basic food group, to others, a delightful discovery. In Puerto Vallarta, a walking taco-tour stops at eight different taco destinations along a downtown route. Crunch on your favorites, from outdoor taco stands to mom-and-pop restaurants, enjoying a flavor festival of tacos ranging from meat to seafood to vegetarian. Half the fun is exploring the sights and sounds of this colorful city along the way. Kids can be on the lookout for wild iguanas in the trees.

PUERTO VALLARTA, MEXICO
130 Splash in a jungle waterfall

Take a short hike from the beach on a tropical jungle trail toward a spectacular waterfall and swimming hole in Yelapa. To reach this slice of Eden, enjoy a short boat ride along the coastline south of Puerto Vallarta while sighting dolphins and other sea life along the way. After enjoying the waterfall and splashing in its waters, order lunch back at the beach, or shop for trinkets in the small village.

128 MONARCH
BUTTERFLIES

LORETO, MEXICO

131 Sample incredible popsicles

Mexican popsicles are called *paletas*, and the country is known for producing some of the most interesting and delicious flavors in the world. In Loreto, the *paletarías* (popsicle shops) offer too many flavors to count. Cool down with exotic flavors like tamarind, mango and chamoy, sweet corn, cinnamon chocolate, hibiscus flowers, and more.

MÉRIDA, MEXICO

132 Soak up the music of Mérida

Mérida has music coming out of its every pore. You'll see guitar-playing *trovadores* wandering cobbled streets, street musicians playing in the Grand Plaza, and couples waltzing to the sound of Latin folk music. If you've got teens in tow, they might prefer to feel the beat on a Friday night, when everywhere from cantinas to city parks puts on an impressive show.

MEXICO CITY, MEXICO

133 Feel the inspiration of Frida

The artist Frida Kahlo spent most of her life living in La Casa Azul, in Mexico City. Now open to the public, each room in this bright-blue house reflects her unique, creative essence. You can see some of her paintings, as well as those of her husband Diego Rivera, but it's the Mexican folk art, and handcrafted ceramics and glassware from different Mexican regions, that seem to say the most about the artist.

133 FRIDA KAHLO MUSEUM

135 *DÍA DE LOS MUERTOS*

PUEBLA, MEXICO
134 Eat chicken with chocolate

It's not just cocoa that goes into the famous *mole poblano* sauce, but that's the ingredient that children are most likely to remember. Mole poblano is a rich blend of at least twenty ingredients, including cocoa, chilies, almonds, cinnamon, and pumpkin seeds. The result is a rich, dark-brown sauce that is poured liberally over chicken or turkey, and a must-try on a trip to Puebla.

OAXACA, MEXICO
135 Honor past relatives at *Día de los Muertos*

The Day of the Dead, or *Día de los Muertos*, is celebrated throughout Mexico on November 1 and 2, but none rival the festivities in Oaxaca. Colorful parades, pageants, and concerts are held citywide, while participants dress in skeleton-like costumes with painted faces and flower garlands, and join processions to local graveyards to honor memories of past friends and family.

137 SWIM IN A CENOTE

138 CHICHÉN ITZÁ

COBA, MEXICO
136 Scale Maya ruins

Only a small percentage of ancient Maya ruins allow visitors to climb them, and one such marvel is Coba. Ride bicycles through jungle paths to the base of a stone pyramid, and climb 120 steep steps to the top for an unparalleled view of the jungle stretching for miles. Guided tours educate visitors about this ancient civilization and the meaning of these mysterious, intriguing structures.

YUCATÁN PENINSULA, MEXICO
137 Swim with blind cave fish

The Yucatán Peninsula of Mexico is studded with thousands of cenotes—freshwater sinkholes located throughout the thick jungles. Explore a cenote inside a cave, where you can snorkel in the dark waters with headlamps illuminating blind fish, stalactites, and more. High above near the cave mouth, you might see a bat congregation clinging upside down from the craggy ceiling.

YUCATÁN PENINSULA, MEXICO
138 Explore an ancient civilization

Geek out on ancient history as the kids are drawn into stories of human sacrifices and team sports played with a burning ball. One of the New Seven Wonders of the World, the Mayan ruins at Chichén Itzá are a spectacular example of an ancient culture. Dominated by an enormous and remarkably well-preserved pyramid rising from the jungle, the site includes some carved stone ruins that are both macabre and intricate. Chichén Itzá is a fascinating dip into a culture long gone.

TULUM, MEXICO

139 Go cliff jumping in a water park

A huge marine theme park squeezed between jungle
and ocean, Xel-Há Park will have you swimming,
cliff jumping, and rafting around a safe natural
swimming lagoon. If you want to introduce young
children to snorkeling, this is the place to do it. There
are no swells, and the water is stuffed full of tropical
creatures, including angelfish, parrotfish, and sea
turtles. They come right into the shallows, so even
toddlers can get in on the action. More entertainment
comes in the form of a natural lazy river, an adventure
zone complete with zip lines, and a challenging ropes
course. Looming large above it all is a 131 ft. (40 m)
observation tower, flanked by four spiral waterslides.
Anyone brave enough to try will zip down at high
speed before plunging into deep pools beneath.

ISLA HOLBOX, MEXICO
140 Take things easy on Isla Holbox

With white-sand beaches, warm lagoons, and a low-key vibe, Isla
Holbox is ideal for desert island adventures. Set in the protected Yum
Balam biosphere, this 26 mi. (42 km) long island is car-free, but it's
easy to get around by bike, and extra fun to do so by colorful golf cart,
especially if you've young kids in tow. They're easy to drive, simple to
hire, and once you're out of the main hub, you'll often have the sandy
roads to yourself. In just one day you could take in street art in Holbox
Village, visit thick mangrove forest for some wildlife spotting, and
head to crowd-free beaches on the far side of the island, where you
can spot flamingos in the distance and snorkel clear seas.

CELESTÚN, MEXICO
141 See flamingos dance

With their long, spindly legs and bright-pink coloring, flamingos are one of the natural world's most appealing birds, especially for children. Present all year at the Reserva de la Biosfera Ría Celestún, the colony expands between November and March, when they gather to mate. Time it right and you could catch the elaborate mating dance, when the whole colony moves together displaying their head-bobbing and leg-strutting moves.

ANTIGUA, GUATEMALA
142 Learn how to weave

The textiles of Guatemala are beautiful, with bright colors and geometric patterns. Weaving here is a skill steeped in tradition, which dates back to at least the Maya. In Antigua, families can harness some of that tradition on a course to learn the art of backstrap weaving—where weavers attach their looms to a tree or post at one end, and a strap around their back at the other. Once set up, it's a simple enough task for children to enjoy too.

143 CHICHICASTENANGO CRAFTS

145 BABY TURTLES

CHICHICASTENANGO, GUATEMALA

143 Shop in one of Latin America's oldest markets

High up in the mountains, Chichicastenango has been a thriving market town since Mayan times. Every Thursday and Sunday, its streets fill with market stalls as vendors gather to sell traditional clothing and woven fabrics, handcrafted jewelry and leather goods, pottery, vegetables, livestock, fruit juice, and much more. It is a riot of color and bustle.

SUMPANGO, GUATEMALA

144 See a sky full of kites

As part of its Day of the Dead festivities, the small town of Sumpango in Guatemala makes huge, colorful kites—at least 6 ft. (1.8 m) across—that are flown over the cemetery on the afternoon of November 1. The town fills with visitors who come to watch the show, and there's no better place to buy the children their own kite to take home.

MONTERRICO, GUATEMALA

145 Help baby turtles survive

Between September and January, join the staff of the turtle hatchery Tortugario Monterrico as they release baby turtles into the sea. You can also offer children a real-life treasure hunt, with a nighttime walk along the beach to look for turtle eggs so that they can be protected.

147 FINCA EL PARAÍSO WATERFALL

TIKAL, GUATEMALA
146 See pyramids hidden by jungle

The excavated pyramids of Tikal give a hands-on history lesson about the Maya civilization, but what is equally fabulous about this site is that there are so many structures still covered by jungle. Climb to the top of a pyramid to see how dense jungle can utterly swallow up a city.

RIO DULCE, GUATEMALA
147 Swim under a hot-spring waterfall

A short journey from the waterfront town of Rio Dulce is Finca el Paraíso, a pretty waterfall tumbling over rocks into a pool below. The twist? The waterfall is fed by hot, volcanic water. You can swim in the cooler waters of the pool, or scramble over the rocks to have a hot shower under the spray.

PACAYA VOLCANO, GUATEMALA
148 Eat marshmallows toasted over lava

The goal of toasting marshmallows over lava isn't off-limits to even the littlest legs at the active Pacaya volcano. It's a one- to two-hour hike to get to the hotspot, with the option of traveling on horseback if preferred. There are beautiful views and vivid geography lessons all along the way. And marshmallows as a reward.

CAYE CAULKER, BELIZE
149 Chill out on a Caribbean island

Laid-back island vibes are a given on Caye Caulker. This petite island off the coast of Belize moves at a slow pace thanks to sandy streets, where the only road users are bikes, golf carts, and the occasional rooster. Traditionally a haven for backpackers, Caye Caulker now attracts families with kids of all ages, who come to enjoy its turquoise waters, warm breezes, and spectacular offshore snorkeling.

SHARK RAY ALLEY, BELIZE
150 Snorkel with nurse sharks

Shark Ray Alley, a shallow channel in the Hol Chan Marine Reserve, is a magnet for big southern stingrays and nurse sharks, and boat trips take snorkelers out from Caye Caulker to get up close and personal with these marine giants. The water's calm and relatively shallow, so it's a perfect excursion for kids.

HOPKINS VILLAGE, BELIZE
151 Experience Garifuna culture

The Garifuna people are the descendants of shipwrecked enslaved people and Arawak people, and the friendly, beachside hub of Hopkins—a coastal village in eastern Belize—provides a fascinating introduction to their culture. You can hear Garifuna drumming as you wander the streets, check out traditional Punta dance displays, and sample traditional Garifuna dishes such as *hudut* (coconut fish stew).

ORANGE WALK DISTRICT, BELIZE
152 Take a boat to ruins in the jungle

A group of soaring temples surrounded by jungle and overlooking a vast lagoon, the Lamanai Mayan Ruins are the stuff of childhood fantasies. But so is the means of getting there. You'll journey ninety minutes via riverboat from Orange Walk Town, spotting birds, crocodiles, and monkeys in the jungle along the way.

149 CAYE CAULKER

150 SHARK RAY ALLEY

TORTUGUERO NATIONAL PARK, COSTA RICA

161 Cruise through wildlife-rich reserves

It's the diversity of plants and wildlife that brings visitors to remote Tortuguero National Park, a protected wilderness wedged between lagoon and sea. The best way to see it is by boat, gliding silently along a tangle of waterways, where howler monkeys, sloths, and caiman are regularly spotted as well as smaller delights such as tree frogs in the trees (steer clear of the poisonous ones). You can also enjoy volcanic beaches, where green turtles lay their eggs between July and October.

SAN CARLOS, COSTA RICA

162 Explore a labyrinth of tunnels

A spooky labyrinth of limestone caverns stretching for 2 mi. (3 km), the Venado Caves are not for the claustrophobic. You'll put on helmets and headlamps, and follow underground trails through a series of twelve chambers, which were formed fifteen to twenty million years ago. As well as marveling at stalactites and stalagmites, kids will get a kick seeing bats and the occasional small snake.

LA PAZ WATERFALL GARDENS NATURE PARK, COSTA RICA

163 Watch clouds drift over a cloud forest

Sitting on your balcony at the Peace Lodge, 5,200 ft. (1.6 km) above sea level, is the stuff that meditation tapes are made of: clouds drift over the rain forest, birdsong fills the air, the air is crisp and cool. It's the perfect place for some quiet reflection. Oh, and the children will love the on-site aviary, where they can hand-feed toucans.

QUEPOS, COSTA RICA

164 Volunteer as a family

Helping out at the Sloth Conservation and Wildlife Experience (twelve-year-olds and up are welcome) could involve any number of tasks that are needed to help orphaned and injured wildlife. It will mean trips out into the rain forest, assisting the experts, and seeing amazing species such as sloths and anteaters up close. Now that's a memorable getaway.

161 POISONOUS TREE FROG

165 RAFTING TO PACUARE LODGE

LIMÓN PROVINCE, COSTA RICA
165 Raft your way to your lodge

Set in swathes of ancient rain forest, Pacuare riverfront eco-lodge is so remote that even the journey to get there is an adventure. A two-hour bus trip from San José will take you to your jungle departure point, where adventurous over-twelves can grab a life jacket and a paddle for an adrenaline-fueled charge along the river to their destination. The ninety-minute journey takes you over class I–IV rapids in a six-seater inflatable raft, as monkeys and birds peer out from the towering trees on either side. Once you arrive, you can continue the adventure with canyoning, rain forest hikes, and horseback riding, or sample some of the lodge's pampering perks. Pacuare is also known for its stellar sustainability efforts and close relationship with the Indigenous Cabécar people.

MONTEVERDE, COSTA RICA
166 Pick beans at a coffee plantation

Whether you enjoy the taste of coffee or not, picking beans on a hillside in Costa Rica is as authentic as it gets. Fill your bucket with the red coffee berries, soon to be dried in the sun before being carefully roasted. Perched high in the jungles, Costa Rican coffee plantations set the gold standard for flavor known the world over.

167 SKY WALK

168 HOT SPRINGS

MONTEVERDE CLOUD FOREST, COSTA RICA

167 Take in the wildlife on the world's longest hanging bridge

Cloud forests are so diverse that you'll see different plants and wildlife at ground level than you would high up in the forest canopy. On the Sky Adventures' Sky Walk they've got it all covered, with walking trails that lead up and onto suspension bridges, through the canopy, and above the trees. It's a beautiful way to feel totally immersed in the vegetation, enjoy views over the landscape, and get that extra adrenaline thrill—you'll even cross the world's longest hanging bridge at 774 ft. (236 m). There are two different lengths of walks, so little legs can enjoy a one-hour trail, and longer ones the two-and-a-half-hour loop.

ARENAL, COSTA RICA

168 Relax in volcanic hot springs

High in the cloud forests of Costa Rica stands Arenal volcano, which fuels a network of underwater hot springs perfect for soaking and relaxing. Like natural hot tubs, the pools often form part of spa resorts where visitors can stay as they enjoy the cloud forest. Nearby, jungle creatures like sloths, parrots, leafcutter ants, and monkeys are common sightings. Hiking and rafting day trips give the family plenty of stories to bring home.

MANUEL ANTONIO NATIONAL PARK, COSTA RICA

169 Sleep in a refurbished Boeing 727

From a distance, it looks as if a plane has crashed
into the jungle canopy. In reality, this refurbished
Boeing 727 is a quirky hotel suite, elevated on a
50 ft. (15 m) high pedestal so it appears suspended
in the trees. One of several rooms at the Hotel
Costa Verde, this 1965 Boeing used to fly for South
African Airways and Avianca before being given
a new lease of life. There's plenty of room to spread
out, while wooden decking over the wings allows
you to come eyeball-to-eyeball with treetop sloths,
toucans, and monkeys, as well as gaze out at the
Pacific Ocean. There are more thrills to be had at
the "cockpit cottage," a cozy suite set in the fuselage
section of a McDonnell Douglas MD-80, accessed
by a hanging suspension bridge.

SARAPIQUÍ, COSTA RICA

170 Learn the secrets of chocolate making

Chocolate started life as a delicacy of the ancient
Maya, who used the beans as currency and in
religious ceremonies. At a cacao plantation in the
lush Sarapiquí region, Costa Rica Best Chocolate
will talk you through cutting, fermentation,
drying, and roasting, with plenty of chances to
get hands-on, and taste the goods along the way.
Things end on a high with a cup of thick drinking
chocolate, hot or cold.

169 WAKE UP ON A WING

171 ZIP-LINING

172 SLOTH

MALPAIS, COSTA RICA
171 Take a zip-line canopy tour

The green jungles of Malpais offer an ideal setting for a zip-line canopy tour over waterfalls, streams, and canyons. Thrilling and fast-paced, this zip line safely secures riders in harnesses as they whizz toward platforms that seem impossibly far. Throughout the course, orchids grow wild and bloom in vibrant colors among the branches and vines. It's hard not to yell "Tarzan!" as you jump.

OSA PENINSULA, COSTA RICA
172 Spot wildlife at the Osa Peninsula

Rough roads and river crossings take you to the remote Osa Peninsula, where adventures include gliding over mangroves, following wild coastal trails, or scouring thick rain forest in search of jaguars and sloths. You could bed down in all-inclusive wilderness lodges, or embrace rural tourism and stay in a former mining village, where gold panning and horseback riding add to the experience.

173 GUNA CRAFTS

GUNA YALA, PANAMA

173 Learn about the Indigenous people of Guna Yala

Guna Yala, also known as San Blas, is a self-governing archipelago home to the Guna people, who've lived in Panama since the sixteenth century. Guna Yala's 365 islands are the epitome of pared-back paradise. This isn't the place for fancy, air-conditioned resorts and kids' clubs; it's all about relaxing and reconnecting as a family. With no Wi-Fi and patchy cell phone coverage, time can be spent swimming, snorkeling, and playing beach games before retiring to your simple, thatched cabin, which may or may not be suspended over the water. To spend time with the Guna, you can travel to a community island, where you'll learn about their heritage and daily life, and their beautiful artisanal crafts, while your children make some local playmates. Stay for a few hours, or immerse yourself fully and spend a night with a Guna family.

PANAMA

174 See ships pass through the Panama Canal

Opened in 1913, the Panama Canal's 51 mi. (82 km) waterway connects the Pacific to the Atlantic Ocean, saving ships an arduous journey around Cape Horn. At the Miraflores Visitor Center, you can access viewing platforms to see this industrial wonder in action. The center also houses a huge simulator in which children can navigate their way through the locks.

PANAMA PROVINCE, PANAMA

175 Sleep in a security tower in the jungle

A former radar tower turned eco-lodge, the Canopy Tower invites guests aged thirteen and up to sleep at treetop level, within serenading distance of motmot, toucans, and sloths. Climb through the ceiling hatch in the circular lounge and you'll emerge on a 360-degree observation deck, offering sublime views of the rain forest canopy and Panama City beyond.

PARQUE NACIONAL VIÑALES, CUBA
176 Take a trip through tobacco fields in a horse-drawn carriage

Parque Nacional Viñales is full of lost-world atmosphere, thanks to a lush landscape of green tobacco fields, rich red soil, and *mogotes*—ancient limestone hills that tower over their surroundings. Hiking, climbing, and horseback riding are exciting ways to explore the valley, but for younger kids, little beats a ride in a horse-drawn carriage, stopping off to explore caves and tobacco fields along the way. It's a fascinating introduction to life in rural Cuba.

HAVANA, CUBA
177 Ride in a classic automobile

There are many iconic sights in Cuba, one of which is the huge number of classic American vehicles that still cruise through the streets of Havana. They're there because Fidel Castro introduced an import ban on automobiles in 1963, which meant people made sure that they looked after the ones they had. Cubans have become adept at crafty mechanics— classic car buffs would be horrified. Many of the better-preserved vehicles now line up to take visitors for a ride. Cruising down the Malecón, Cuba's famous beachfront road, at sunset has a particularly movie-star feel.

177 VINTAGE AUTOMOBILES

178 Listen to live music

Music is in the soul of Cubans. If they're not playing it, they're dancing to it, or listening to it turned up loud on the radio. It is the sound of joyful rhythm, soaring melodies, and pulsating beats: son cubano, salsa, danzón, charanga, mambo, rumba—all of them originated here, where the melodies and instruments of the Spanish colonizers mixed with the percussion and rhythms of enslaved West Africans brought over to work in the sugarcane fields. It has inspired some fantastic films, such as *Buena Vista Social Club* and *El Benny*, not to mention been an influence on so many genres of music, such as jazz and Argentine tango. Today no trip to Cuba is complete without enjoying some amazing live music. Wander around Calle Obispo in Old Havana and you're sure to hear the sounds of a band emanating from a café or bar, or even just playing in the street.

TRINIDAD, CUBA

179 Step back into the nineteenth century

There are few more beautifully preserved towns than Trinidad, whose cobblestone streets and grand plazas appear frozen in the nineteenth century. The town was built with the massive profits of the sugar and slave trade, and a visit here is a valuable lesson in history and culture. You'll reap further benefits if you stay with a local family in a *casa particular* (homestay), many of which are housed in old colonial buildings.

DISCOVERY BAY, JAMAICA

180 Explore mystical green caves

Green Grotto Caves—named after the bright-green algae that covers their walls—were once a hideout for smugglers and runaway enslaved people, as well as a sacred ceremonial space for the Indigenous Taíno people. Mini-travelers will love putting on a helmet and headlamp, and descending into the 28 mi. (45 km) complex, where they'll see rock formations and a subterranean lake.

KINGSTON, JAMAICA

181 Feel the spirit of Bob Marley

Bob Marley's hometown, Kingston, is the best place to take children on a reggae pilgrimage. Visit the Bob Marley Museum, a colorful shrine where you can view all kinds of memorabilia, and look out at the landscapes from which he drew inspiration for his songs. Charismatic guides are quick to weave Marley's music into the tour, and will soon have you singing and laughing alongside them. You'll feel Marley's spirit before you know it.

179 STREETS IN TRINIDAD

182 BOBSLEDDING

OCHIOS RIOS, JAMAICA
182 Race through the rain forest on a bobsled

A wild bobsled ride through the jungle, inspired by the movie *Cool Runnings*, is the highlight of a visit to Jamaica's Mystic Mountain. Channeling the Jamaican bobsled team, you'll zip through the trees at high speed, though you can always pull the brakes and take in those panoramic coastal views. You can pay homage to the team that first led Jamaica to the Winter Olympics at the on-site exhibition on Jamaican sport.

MONTEGO BAY, JAMAICA
183 Join the world's biggest reggae festival

The mother of all reggae festivals, Reggae Sumfest is a weeklong music marathon that provides an exuberant introduction to Jamaican music and culture, held by the beach in Montego Bay. Older teens can join the throng for nonstop dancing and singing to some of the most famous names in reggae and dancehall.

MONTEGO BAY, JAMAICA
184 Eat authentic jerk chicken

Jerk seasoning is the taste of Jamaica—if your taste buds can take the heat: the blend of (usually) garlic, onion, chili peppers, cinnamon, ginger, and thyme oozing out of meat which has been slow-cooked over wood. Head to Nyam 'n' Jam in Montego Bay for an authentic taste of Jamaica.

CAYMAN ISLANDS

185 Scuba dive in the Cayman Islands

Scuba diving isn't just for grown-ups. Kids Sea
Camp brings families from all over the world to enjoy
getting under the ocean. Four- to nine-year-olds can
learn basic snorkel and scuba-diving skills in both the
pool and the ocean, while the over-tens can train for
their junior PADI Open Water certificate. Both
options will bring them face-to-face with some of
the most spectacular marine life in the Caribbean.

THROUGHOUT PUERTO RICO
186 Ride horses on a beach

Nobody ever forgets riding a horse along a beach, and Puerto Rico is one of the best places to do it. Join an outfit such as Tropical Trail Rides to discover beautiful beaches with turquoise waters, white sand, and green, palm-fringed backdrops. The Puerto Rican Paso Fino horse has been bred for centuries for its sure-footedness, gentle nature, and comfort, so it's perfect for children and beginners.

PUERTO PLATA, DOMINICAN REPUBLIC
187 Hike between waterfalls

Jumping and sliding your way around the twenty-seven waterfalls of Damajagua is just as fun as any water park. Accompanied by a guide, you'll climb through thick foliage, put on life jackets and helmets, and begin your exhilarating descent, jumping into pristine pools and soaking up the spray. You don't have to complete all twenty-seven, but it'll take about five hours if you do.

CABRERA, DOMINICAN REPUBLIC
188 Join world-schooling families

The Hive in Cabrera offers a slice of alternative education alongside adventurous families from around the world. Six-week programs center around the UN Sustainable Development Goals, but there are plenty of social activities built in too, from yoga classes to beach excursions and soccer—so there's a ready-made community for you and your kids.

CHAMPAGNE REEF, DOMINICAN REPUBLIC
189 Snorkel among bass and bubbles

You'll feel as if you're swimming in a giant glass of champagne at Dominica's Champagne Reef. Thermal springs on the ocean floor release volcanic bubbles into the water, and it's not only bubbly but incredibly warm. This doesn't seem to put off the fish, who come here in colorful swathes.

186 HORSE RIDING

ST. MAARTEN
190 Watch planes land—from very close

It's not just powdery sand and turquoise waters that bring travelers to Maho Beach. It's a huge draw for thrill seekers, who come to see planes fly mere feet above their heads as they approach the neighboring Princess Juliana International Airport. The fear factor means that this one's better for older kids and teenagers.

ANSE LA RAYE, ST. LUCIA
191 Sample street food at a Friday night fish fry

Come Friday night, the colorful streets of Anse la Raye fill up with tourists and locals, who've come for the seafood and the St. Lucian vibes. Choose a food shack, pick up some grilled lobster or snapper, then settle down at a picnic table and dig in. After dinner, dancing is encouraged—and people of all ages can join in.

THROUGHOUT ST. LUCIA
192 Marvel at colorful hummingbirds

The birdlife in St. Lucia is stunning, and you'll see colorful, tropical species wherever you go. The most magical, however, is the hummingbird—fast, silent, and with beautiful, iridescent feathers. Kids will love watching them hover silently as they sip nectar from the flowers, and they'll revel in the knowledge that their wings beat four thousand times per minute.

190 MAHO BEACH

193 EXPLORE IN A SUBMARINE

BRIDGETOWN, BARBADOS
193 Explore the deep in a submarine

You can feel the thrill of going deep underwater even without a wet suit, and even if you're only three years old. Take a short catamaran ride from Bridgetown's dock and you can climb into the belly of the *Atlantis* submarine, where you'll sit in front of huge porthole windows, descend to 150 ft. (45 m), and cruise around the sandy bottom spotting fish, corals, and even a shipwreck.

BRIDGETOWN, BARBADOS
194 Learn about slavery on a walking tour

Older kids can discover the darker side of this Caribbean island—an important counterpoint to its sun, sea, and sand image. Bajan-run Eco Adventures takes you to walk in the footsteps of the island's ancestors, visiting a burial ground for enslaved people, the site of a revolt, and a prison for escapees. It's a sobering but necessary way to honor the island's people.

EAST COAST, BARBADOS
195 Explore the wild side of Barbados

The glitzy west coast of Barbados is lined with upscale resorts, fancy restaurants, and plenty of people. Head east and it's a different story. Quiet roads lead to Atlantic-whipped surfing beaches, dramatic cliffs, and the enchanting Andromeda Botanic Gardens, where children can gaze up in awe at huge cacti, palms, and ferns.

196 UNDERWATER SCULPTURE PARK

MOLINERE BAY, GRENADA

196 Snorkel among sculptures

Snorkel in the waters of Molinere Bay and figures come slowly into view, like underwater spirits. Designed by British artist Jason deCaires Taylor in 2006, the eerie Molinere Underwater Sculpture Park contains over eighty pieces, including a man sat at a typewriter, and a circle of children holding hands. Look closely and you'll see that they're slowly being claimed by corals. Good news, as the park was designed to reverse damage caused by Hurricane Ivan.

CARRIACOU ISLAND, GRENADA

197 Experience the Caribbean quiet life

For some family downtime far from cruise ships and sprawling resorts, you can board the two-hour ferry from Georgetown to little Carriacou Island, along with local commuters and the odd intrepid traveler. Once there you'll find the Caribbean of old—sleepy, laid-back, and unfailingly friendly. You can visit crumbling historical sights, snorkel the reefs around tiny Sandy Island, and kick back on windswept beaches, where all you'll have for company is a few wandering goats.

ST. GEORGE'S, GRENADA

198 Visit an outdoor market

The largest in Grenada and one of the best in the Caribbean, St. George's Market is a teeming, colorful introduction to Grenadian culture. Stalls crammed with yams, breadfruit, plantains, and spices are an arresting sight for young children, and friendly chatter and bartering is all part of the experience.

NOORD, ARUBA

199 Swim over a shipwreck

Board a catamaran in Noord to head out to the wreckage of German cargo ship SS *Antilla*, scuttled off the Aruba coastline in 1940. Explore the shipwreck with snorkel or dive equipment, or simply jump off the boat for a sea-level view in the clear, blue water. All around you, neon-colored fish swim in schools as they dodge and dart about.

BEACHES AROUND CURAÇAO

200 Hop from beach to beach and choose your favorite

This Dutch-Caribbean island has beautifully-preserved colonial architecture and a comfortable position outside the hurricane zone, but it's the beaches that are the big pull. Each one has its own character: strong swimmers can glide alongside turtles at Playa Piskado, teens can try cliff jumping at Playa Forti, and everyone will love the wandering pigs of Playa Porto Mari. Occasionally the island's resident flamingos leave their salt lakes for a stroll along a beach.

200 SEE FLAMINGOS ON A BEACH

LA VEGA ESTATE, TRINIDAD AND TOBAGO

201 Be amazed by fruit

The owner of La Vega Estate, Bert Manhin, is a fruit aficionado who has gathered together all manner of nature's lesser-known fruits: dragon fruit, rambutan, durian, giant peewah, and dongs. A wander through his collection is mind-expanding.

TUCKER VALLEY, TRINIDAD AND TOBAGO

202 Walk beneath a bamboo canopy

Not all cathedrals are human-made. Trinidad and Tobago's Bamboo Cathedral, up a path off the Tucker Valley Road, is formed by towering stands of bamboo, which meet high above your head to form cathedral-like arches. It's beautiful and serene, with butterflies fluttering by and the bamboo swaying in the breeze.

2
SOUTH AMERICA

SANTA MARTA, COLOMBIA
203 Sleep in a hammock open to the sea air

It is the remoteness of Tayrona Park on Colombia's Caribbean coast that makes it so special. You either arrive by boat, or hike in through jungle paths. Once at the beach, rent hammocks in a shared, open-air hut on the top of an outcrop of rock and enjoy the true meaning of sea air.

SANTA MARTA, COLOMBIA
204 Zip-line through the tree canopy

The Mamancana Private Nature Reserve, just outside Santa Marta, is devoted to sustainability. Show your children how that can be fun as they hurtle down the 3,280 ft. (1 km) of zip lines through the treetops, which are also home to monkeys and colorful birds. Suitable for eight-year-olds and over.

SANTA MARTA, COLOMBIA
205 Hike to a lost city

The Tairona ruins of Ciudad Perdida (Lost City), in the Sierra Nevada of Santa Marta, were rediscovered by a band of Colombian treasure looters in the 1970s. While they were out hunting turkeys, they stumbled across the 1,200 stone steps that lead up to the city. It is a stunning hike through pristine jungle, with epic views, and wonderful natural swimming pools to cool down in at the end of a day's walking.

205 CIUDAD PERDIDA

207 CARTAGENA OLD TOWN

ISLA MÚCURA, COLOMBIA

206 Sleep in a hut on stilts

Out in the Caribbean Sea, about 12 mi. (20 km) from Colombia's coast, is the stunning island of Isla Múcura. Its remoteness encourages sea life, so there's excellent snorkeling. By night, the stars are amazing and can be enjoyed with a stay in a thatched hut on stilts overlooking the sea.

CARTAGENA, COLOMBIA

207 Soak up life in Cartagena

Wander the cobbled streets of Cartagena's ancient core and you'll take in almost five hundred years of history. The UNESCO-listed Old Town is crammed full of elegant churches, palaces, grand plazas, and mansions—all enclosed by imposing old stone walls. A day here is best spent slowly soaking up the atmosphere. Gaze up at bougainvillea-draped buildings, watch street dancers and musicians perform, and grab an *arepa* or *empanada* from one of many roadside food stalls. Or, to really bring history to life, sign up for a walking tour and hear guides spin tales of battles, gold smuggling, and pirate attacks. Come sunset, join both tourists and locals on the western ramparts to watch the sky change color as the sun sinks into the sea.

208 MUD VOLCANO

209 COMUNA 13

CARTAGENA, COLOMBIA

208 Jump in a mud volcano

Whether children are still at the age of making mud pies or have moved on to mud face-masks, they will all love a dip in the mud volcano Volcán del Totumo, near Cartagena. Lower yourself in and relax in the thick and viscous mud, before washing it off in the nearby lagoon.

MEDELLÍN, COLOMBIA

209 Take a graffiti tour

Once the most dangerous neighborhood in Medellín, Comuna 13 has transformed into a vibrant outdoor gallery. Explore the colorful wall murals with a local guide and you'll learn about the area's violent past, and the role art has played in its rehabilitation. It's a fascinating and inspirational experience for older children and teenagers.

CARACAS, VENEZUELA

210 Go rock climbing in a city center

There's a huge sense of accomplishment to pulling yourself up a rock face using nothing more than your body strength and tiny finger- and foot-holds. As long as you're over seven, you don't need any previous experience for a day out in Caracas's central park with Climbing Venezuela.

213 ANGEL FALLS

CARACAS, VENEZUELA

211 Eat *arepas* in the street

There's no one way to eat an *arepa*—a bread-like patty made of corn flour. Found all over Venezuela, they can be filled with cheese, folded over a meat or fish filling, or topped with a tomato stew. You'll find your favorite and then you'll probably want more.

MANTECAL, VENEZUELA

212 See the world's largest rodent

Capybaras are the world's largest rodents—they can grow to over 3 ft. (1 m) in length and are more piglike than ratlike to look at, with blunt snouts and no tails. Although no wildlife has guaranteed sightings, you can often see capybaras nibbling the grass as you drive in to Hato Cedral cattle ranch in Mantecal.

CANAIMA NATIONAL PARK, VENEZUELA

213 Canoe to the world's tallest waterfall

The sight of Angel Falls— Kerepakupai Merú to the Indigenous Pemon people— is like no other waterfall on Earth. It cascades 3,212 ft. (979 m) from the flat top of Auyán-tepui down to the forest below. By the time the water is at ground level, it has turned to mist.

PARAMARIBO, SURINAME

214 Spot dolphins at sunset

In Suriname you can see a particular species of dolphin, the Guiana dolphin, that likes the brackish water where two rivers merge and join the sea at Paramaribo. Take a tour in a traditional "tent boat" as the sun sets, and hope for the reward of leaping dolphins in front of golden skies. It will delight all the family.

DANG, SURINAME

215 Bed down in a rain forest hut

Set on a forested island along the Suriname River, Danpaati River Lodge will satisfy your Swiss Family Robinson fantasies. After a day of hiking, wildlife watching, and river swims, follow a candlelit path to your family hut, where you'll be lulled to sleep by the jungle, and wake up to a spectacular sunrise.

SURAMA, GUYANA

216 Join community-based tourism in Rupununi

Adventurous kids will love Surama Eco-lodge—if they can brave the lack of hot water and internet, that is. It's operated by the Makushi people, who'll introduce you to their food and traditions, and take you wildlife watching in savanna and rain forest. You can sleep in basic cabins, or in hammocks under a wooden shelter.

THE GALÁPAGOS, ECUADOR

217 Visit the Galápagos

Wildlife on the Galápagos Islands is like nowhere else on Earth. Take a beautiful, 1.5 mi. (2.5 km) walk through dry, tropical forest to reach Tortuga Bay from Puerto Ayora town. Once there you'll find a dreamy white-sand beach, home to giant marine iguanas, pelicans, and the odd flamingo. For more wildlife adventures, get in the clear water and look out for sea turtles and small sharks.

217 TORTUGA BAY

MINDO VALLEY, ECUADOR

218 Watch hummingbirds from your window

With their iridescent colors, incredible wing speed, and perfectly adapted beaks, hummingbirds are fascinating to watch. You can—and will—see them all over Ecuador, but the Mindo Valley is a beautiful location, with many lovely lodges where they flit around the grounds.

218 HUMMINGBIRD IN THE MINDO CLOUD FOREST

QUITO, ECUADOR

219 Stand with a foot either side of the equator

The imaginary line of the equator has proved to be a tricky thing to pinpoint. As a result, there are two places just outside Quito where you can stand with one foot in the northern hemisphere and one in the southern—Mitad del Mundo and Intiñan Solar Museum. They are near each other, and both offer good museums and great photo opportunities.

OTAVALO TO QUITO, ECUADOR

220 Take the train from the Andes to the Pacific

Take the Tren Crucero as it winds its way 278 mi. (447 km) from the Andean Highlands to the Pacific Ocean over four spellbinding days, spending nights in traditional villages along the way. Head to the viewing car to soak up the views of cloud forest, volcanos, and sugarcane plantations—and spare a thought for the workers who battled years of storms, landslides, and even plague to complete the railway in 1908.

EL ORIENTE, ECUADOR
221 Ride in a dugout canoe

A journey in a dugout canoe doesn't just hark back to how people have traveled since the Stone Age—which children will love—it's also so calm and peaceful that you can get up close to the wildlife of the Amazon. Look out for parrots and monkeys as you travel.

QUILOTOA, ECUADOR
222 Paddle on a volcano's crater

All volcanos hold an element of magic, but upon arriving at the rim of the crater of Quilotoa, this magic is enhanced by seeing the crater filled with a beautiful, blue-green caldera lake. After a hike down to the lake's edge, you can rent kayaks and paddle out into the deep.

221 CANOE DOWN
THE AMAZON

223 SWING AT THE END OF THE WORLD

BAÑOS, ECUADOR
223 Swing over a valley

Although you can enjoy the view of the active
Tungurahua volcano with your feet firmly on
the ground, at La Casa del Arbol you can also
take the playground option of enjoying it from
a swing that takes you out over the mile-deep
valley below. Originally built by a grandfather
to lure his grandchildren to visit, it is now open
to everyone big enough to fit the safety harness
(not for small children).

ANGOCHAGUA, ECUADOR
224 Stay in a traditional hacienda

The Ecuadorean Andes are scattered with historic
haciendas-turned-hotels that make for a fascinating
family stay. At Hacienda Zuleta, a seventeenth-
century estate and working farm, kids can spend
their days riding horses along mountain trails,
learning to milk cows, and hunting for treasure
in the grounds, while evenings bring traditional
Andean music and stories around the campfire.
Rooms adorned with old paintings and antiques
hint at the estate's colonial past.

MACHU PICCHU, PERU

225 Watch the sunrise at Machu Picchu

Built by the Incas in the fifteenth century, then abandoned one hundred years later, the sprawling hilltop citadel of Machu Picchu packs a powerful impact, no matter how many pictures you've seen. Guided tours will teach you more about the history, but you could go it alone and follow one of several hiking paths. Families with older kids or teenagers can tackle Huayna Picchu inside the citadel, or else the Machu Picchu mountain behind it, a tougher and less popular climb that's well worth it for the views. For maximum impact, get the first bus up to the site from Aguas Calientes so you can take in the ruins at dawn before the bulk of the crowds arrive. Watching the sun come up behind the mountains, throwing light on the ruins and valley below, is a once-in-a-lifetime experience.

LIMA, PERU

226 Visit a museum full of gold—and guns

The Inca loved gold, for it held ornamental and religious value—referred to as "the sweat of the sun." They used it for jewelry, to line rooms, and to make offerings to their gods. The Museo Oro del Peru (Peru Gold Museum) has more gold than you can imagine and on the ground floor has an Arms Museum with hundreds of old guns, including one that belonged to Fidel Castro.

225 MACHU PICCHU

HUACACHINA OASIS, PERU
227 Surf on a sand dune

Softer than snow and not as cold, sand boarding on a sand dune is a lot of fun. You don't need to know how to snowboard, and you can come down on your front, sitting down, or showing off those snowboarding skills.

URUBAMBA, PERU
228 Sleep on a rock face

Clinging to a cliff in the Sacred Valley are the Skylodge Adventure Suites—clear sleeping pods with incredible views over the landscape below. Kids aged ten and over can don a hard hat and a harness to climb 1,300 ft. (400 m) up the cliff face, then zip-line back to the valley floor the next morning.

227 SAND BOARDING

SACRED VALLEY, CUSCO, PERU
229 Zip-line across the Sacred Valley

Tackling 8,200 ft. (2,500 m) of zip lines above the Sacred Valley is not for the fainthearted, and neither is the forty-minute climb up a cliff to get there. But the adrenaline rush as you soar past mountains and over the river is worth all the drama—and kids as young as eight can have a go.

228 SLEEP UP A CLIFF

LAKE TITICACA, PERU

230 Sleep on a floating island

Made from buoyant *totora* reeds and anchored to the lake bed with wooden poles, the floating Islas Uros are Lake Titicaca's biggest draw. To experience the magic of these small rural settlements, spend the night in a local home—a simple reed hut without running water. You'll go out in reed canoes, catch fish for your dinner, and listen to songs under the stars with your host family.

NAZCA, PERU

231 Decipher the mysteries of the Nazca lines

At ground level, the Nazca lines are just upturned stones on a sandy desert floor, but go up higher— either onto a viewing platform or in a small plane— and these upturned stones are in fact huge images. There's a condor, a hummingbird, a monkey, a spider, and geometric shapes. The many theories about the lines will fuel family debates for days.

230 FLOATING ISLANDS OF UROS

LAKE HUAYPO, PERU

232 Explore Lake Huaypo by paddleboard

The Incas were stand-up paddleboarding on Lake Huaypo centuries before it was fashionable—only on tightly woven reed boards rather than modern fiberglass contraptions. Older kids and teens can continue the tradition, taking in Andean mountains, spotting rare birds, and watching fishermen bring in their catch, all while paddling this high-altitude lake.

THROUGHOUT BRAZIL

233 Fall in love with *pão de queijo*

There are many foods that every visitor to Brazil should eat, such as rice and beans, or fish stews, but the one that the whole family will crave long after you've left the country is *pão de queijo*—cheesy bread balls. Crispy on the outside, soft, doughy, and cheesy on the inside, they are perfect comfort food.

SALVADOR TO ILHA DE BOIPEBA, BRAZIL

234 Beach hop to Ilha de Boipeba

It's a four- to five-hour journey by road and by boat from Salvador to Ilha de Boipeba. Quiet, unshowy, and ringed by empty, golden beaches and shallow reefs, it's perfect for lazy days spent beach hopping and snorkeling. And the lack of roads means you'll have fun getting around by boat, on foot, or by donkey.

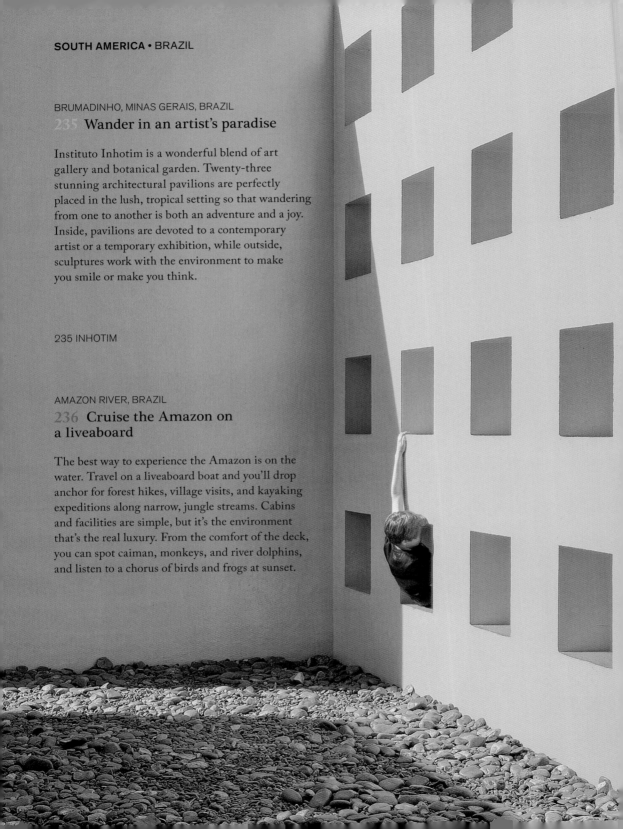

BRUMADINHO, MINAS GERAIS, BRAZIL
235 Wander in an artist's paradise

Instituto Inhotim is a wonderful blend of art gallery and botanical garden. Twenty-three stunning architectural pavilions are perfectly placed in the lush, tropical setting so that wandering from one to another is both an adventure and a joy. Inside, pavilions are devoted to a contemporary artist or a temporary exhibition, while outside, sculptures work with the environment to make you smile or make you think.

235 INHOTIM

AMAZON RIVER, BRAZIL
236 Cruise the Amazon on a liveaboard

The best way to experience the Amazon is on the water. Travel on a liveaboard boat and you'll drop anchor for forest hikes, village visits, and kayaking expeditions along narrow, jungle streams. Cabins and facilities are simple, but it's the environment that's the real luxury. From the comfort of the deck, you can spot caiman, monkeys, and river dolphins, and listen to a chorus of birds and frogs at sunset.

237 PARATY

PARATY, BRAZIL
237 Stay in Paraty

Backed by lush, green mountains and looking out onto a bay full of islands, the historic coastal town of Paraty is a joy to explore whatever your age. Stroll down the cobbled streets, past the white buildings and their colorful doorways. Or take a trip on a boat to one of the surrounding beaches. Teenagers will enjoy paddleboarding on the clear water, and inland you can explore real rain forest with parrots to delight the toddlers.

SALVADOR, BRAZIL
238 Learn the art of capoeira

Devised in the sixteenth century by communities of enslaved Africans, capoeira—a mixture of martial arts and dance—is integral to Afro-Brazilian identity and part of the daily rhythm in Salvador. You'll see dancers on the street throughout the city, particularly in the Pelourinho district, but to really learn a few moves, sign up to formal classes at a studio. It's fun, family-friendly, and a wonderful introduction to Bahian culture.

RIO DE JANEIRO, BRAZIL

239 Visit a samba school

Rio's many samba schools compete for the crown of samba champions at each year's Carnival. Planning of the elaborate floats and costumes can start up to a year beforehand, and dance practice at least three months before the main event in Rio's Sambadrome. Visit one of Rio's samba schools, such as Grande Rio, Salgueiro, or Beija Flor, and learn about the history and rivalry of this fabulously colorful event.

RIO DE JANEIRO, BRAZIL

240 Ride a cable car up Sugarloaf Mountain

Standing at an impressive 1,295 ft. (395 m), Pão de Açúcar, or Sugarloaf Mountain, is a Brazilian icon. You can tackle it on foot, but it's more fun (and easier for kids) to go by cable car, watching as the city's big sights, including Cristo Redentor (Christ the Redeemer) and Copacabana Beach, slowly unfurl beneath you.

239 GRANDE RIO SAMBA AT THE SAMBADROME

240 SUGARLOAF MOUNTAIN

RIO DE JANEIRO, BRAZIL

241 Play ball games on Ipanema Beach

Rio's beaches are always full of life—much of it revolving around playing or watching beach volleyball. If you're a family of four, take a ball, pick a court, and start your own game on Ipanema Beach. If not, join the Cariocas in a game of beach football.

RIO DE JANEIRO, BRAZIL

242 Go to a big soccer game

Whether you're a fan or not, if there's one country where you should watch a soccer game, it's Brazil. They have won the World Cup more times than any other country—five times—and the passion supporters bring to the sport is infectious. Rio's Maracaña stadium is the place to catch the bug.

241 BEACH SPORTS

244 IGUAZÚ FALLS

PANTANAL, BRAZIL
243 Canoe the Pantanal

Young zoologists will be in their element in the
Pantanal, the largest inland wetland in the world.
Move serenely by canoe and you'll better appreciate
the sights and sounds of nature around you.
Whether you're into birdlife, giant river otters, or
the Pantanal's most majestic creature—the jaguar—
there are incredible spectacles around every corner.

IGUAZÚ FALLS, BRAZIL
244 Feel the spray at Iguazú Falls

To introduce your kids to the awe-inspiring power
of nature, there are few better places than Iguazú
Falls, a chain of over 250 thundering cascades
stretching some 1.5 mi. (2.6 km) through the
jungle. You can view them on foot, but it's a bigger
thrill to take a boat trip over the rapids, as close as
possible to the base of the falls. Just be prepared to
get soaked.

LA PAZ, BOLIVIA
245 Commute with a difference across La Paz

Crisscrossing the skies above La Paz is the Mi Teleférico, a cable-car network that serves as the city's main urban transport method. It opened in 2014 and now has ten lines connecting the city to its near neighbor, El Alto. It is a fabulous way to see the city with all its different styles of architecture and it's uplifting to see such a forward-thinking, congestion-reducing transport network.

ALTIPLANO, BOLIVIA
246 See llamas in their natural home

Children—and, let's be honest, many adults—never get tired of spotting llamas out of bus windows. The national animal of Bolivia, llamas are mainly kept for their wool, which is used in clothes and handicrafts. Look out for the bright tags in their ears, which show who their owners are.

SANTA CRUZ, BOLIVIA
247 Inspire new craft projects

The Museo Artecampo was established in 1985 to preserve traditional handicrafts in Bolivia. It brings together the work of five hundred artisans showcasing the traditional craft techniques of ceramics, weaving, woodcarving, and painting. It's a peaceful space, great for inspiration.

AMAZON RAINFOREST, BOLIVIA
248 Wake to the sound of howler monkeys

Bolivia's Amazon is prime wildlife-watching territory, but the sounds of the rain forest are equally thrilling. Sleep in the jungle and you'll never forget the piercing sound of howler monkeys—the loudest primates on Earth. Part-scream, part-bark, their calls can be heard from 3 mi. (5 km) away.

246 LLAMAS

SALAR DE UYUNI, BOLIVIA
249 Cross salt flats in a 4x4

There are few landscapes as mind-blowingly different as that of the Salar de Uyuni—or Uyuni salt flats. Thousands of years ago, a landlocked sea evaporated and left an utterly flat, salty crust covering an area the size of Jamaica. Today you can take a 4x4 tour across this salt crust, watching how it distorts reflections or, after rain, turns into one huge mirror. Visit the cactus-covered islands, the wind-sculpted rock-trees, and the colorful lakes with resident flamingos for a trip that will stay with your children for a lifetime.

COLCHANI, BOLIVIA
250 Sleep in a hotel made of salt

Why save salt for the kitchen when you can use it for the bedroom, bathroom, and living area too—by building a whole hotel from salt blocks? The Hotel Luna Salada is just that. As if children won't be wowed enough to be in a hotel made from salt (dare them to lick the walls), they can even enjoy a game of darts or pool in the games room.

249 UYUNI SALT FLATS

MONTEVIDEO, URUGUAY
251 Drink *mate* Uruguayan style

Everybody drinks *mate* (pronounced ma-tay) in
Uruguay, young or old. And they drink it all the
time—with breakfast, on their way to work, at
work, in the afternoon, driving, always. Pop into
a bakery in Montevideo Old Town and feel truly
Uruguayan as you try this tea-like drink made
from yerba leaves.

251 DRINK *MATE*

SALTO, URUGUAY
252 Soak in hot springs

Oil prospectors discovered hot springs along the
Uruguay River way back in the 1940s, sparking
a tourist boom. These days, everywhere from
campgrounds to fancy resorts to water parks makes
use of their warm, mineral-rich waters, and kids
aged five and up can indulge as well.

PUNTA BALLENA, URUGUAY
253 Stay in an artist's house

Building Casapueblo was a life's work for
Uruguayan artist Carlos Páez Vilaró, who used it
as his summerhouse and workshop. Built of white
stucco, its mazelike design rambles over thirteen
floors. Today it is a hotel and apartment complex
unlike any other, with fabulous sunset views.

253 CASAPUEBLO

SALTOS DEL MONDAY, PARAGUAY
254 See swifts at a waterfall

Paraguay's Saltos del Monday are less well-known waterfalls than the nearby Iguazú, but at 390 ft. (120 m) across and 148 ft. (45 m) high, they are similarly spectacular. The river rushes and tumbles through verdant rain forest, throwing spray and rainbows up into the air. Visit at dusk when thousands of swifts gather at the falls.

CHACO, PARAGUAY
255 Have an offbeat adventure

If you like your family holidays remote and offbeat, head to the wild, melancholy Chaco. Salt pans and marshes attract strange waterbirds; giant anteaters and armadillos wander plains and savanna; and forests come scattered with giant cacti. It's a landscape that will enchant children of all ages.

ASUNCIÓN, PARAGUAY
256 See a city by night

There's no good reason why sightseeing should be limited to daylight hours. By night, cities can take on a whole new quality, as is the case with Asunción. Its seat of government, Palacio de los López, is impressive by day but a twinkling delight by night.

ELQUI VALLEY, CHILE
257 Stargaze in the world's darkest place

By day, the Elqui Valley is a lush strip of vineyards; by night, it's the world's best place for stargazing. The cloudless skies and lack of light pollution led it to be declared the world's first International Dark Sky Sanctuary in 2015. At Elqui Domos, you can stay in a glamping dome with a retractable roof, perfect for counting endless constellations and marveling at the clarity of the Milky Way.

SAN PEDRO DE ATACAMA, CHILE

258 See a landscape turn to gold

Kids will feel as if they're on another planet once they set eyes on the Valle de la Luna—a striking landscape of twisted hills surrounding a parched, valley floor. Come at sunset and they can clamber up a giant sand dune to watch as the sun sinks behind the mountains and the landscape is infused with shades of red and gold.

CHILE TO EUROPE

259 Travel by cargo ship from Chile to Europe

For a water-bound adventure with hardy teenagers, book a berth on a traditional freighter for the journey from South America to Europe. You won't find glitzy restaurants and entertainment, but you'll get to hang out with the crew, dine with the captain, and gain a unique insight into a life lived at sea.

SANTIAGO, CHILE

260 Find your favorite *empanada*

Simple in its concept and delicious in its eating, Chile's national dish, the *empanada*, is pastry filled with either meat, cheese, or seafood. You'll find empanadas in bakeries, restaurants, and food trucks all over Santiago, but head to restaurant Empanadas Tinita for guaranteed joy.

258 VALLE DE LA LUNA

261 VILLARRICA VOLCANO

263 VALPARAÍSO

PUCÓN, CHILE
261 Climb an active volcano

Rising up behind the town of Pucón is the cone-shaped Villarrica volcano. It's a tough four- to six-hour hike to the top (over fourteens only), but worth every grueling footstep. The views over southern Chile's Lake District are stunning, and the 656 ft. (200 m) wide crater is like something from a geography textbook, complete with sulfurous smoke and a lake of molten magma gently bubbling at the bottom.

PUCÓN, CHILE
262 See a forest of monkey puzzle trees

Out of Pucón, toward the Argentinian border, the slopes of the mountains gradually start to be covered in strange, spiky, primordial-looking trees. These are *Araucaria araucana*, Chile's national tree, which is often known in English as the monkey puzzle tree. The tree has been around since the dinosaurs. Its leaves are ferocious spikes, which cover every bit of branch: they would puzzle a monkey—if any lived this far south.

VALPARAÍSO, CHILE
263 Take a funicular in Valparaíso

You can take your pick from twenty-two different funiculars in the coastal city of Valparaíso. Some are beautifully painted, and take you up to the higgledy hilltop streets, with rainbow stairways and street art that charts the political and social moods of the last fifty years.

264 SAN ALFONSO DEL MAR

266 PENGUINS AT SENO OTWAY

ALGARROBO, CHILE
264 Swim in the world's largest pool

San Alfonso del Mar is a swimming pool like no other —it's 3,280 ft. (1 km) long, overlooks the Pacific Ocean, and is so big that as well as swimming in it, you can also sail or kayak on it. There's truly something for everyone, with children's playgrounds and a Teen-Pub too.

FUTALEUFÚ, CHILE
265 Go white-water rafting

The Futaleufú River's name translates from the Mapuche language as "Big River." And that is exactly why it is so popular with white-water rafters. The turquoise waters carve through the mountains, tumbling you across exciting rapids, and leaving you to drift and soak up the views. Quite incredible.

PUNTA ARENAS, CHILE
266 Watch penguins waddle

One outing that delights everyone, from toddlers to grandparents, is to see penguins waddle. Catch these perfect little bundles of black and white at Seno Otway, a short jaunt from Punta Arenas, and watch them look so clumsy on land yet so elegant in the sea.

PATAGONIA, CHILE
267 Hike in the Torres del Paine National Park

The Torres del Paine National Park is one of the world's most stunning wilderness areas. Its hiking paths lead you to three glaciers, several turquoise lakes, and past picturesque views of the three jagged granite peaks that are the Torres del Paine—catch them at sunrise for the best colors. The most popular walking trail is known as the "W" due to the shape it forms, and this would be doable with hardy preteens and teenagers who are happy to carry their food and sleeping gear. However, you don't have to be big hikers to soak up the wonders of the wilderness. There is a driving route around the park, and shorter trails from the campsites still lead to amazing views.

PATAGONIA, CHILE
268 Walk on a glacier

Glaciers, those moving rivers of ice, have a certain allure whether you're young or old, tying us back to the Ice Age as they do, and signaling the worst effects of the climate crisis as they melt away. Feel the allure up close with a hiking trip on to Grey Glacier (one for the teenagers).

267 TORRES DEL PAINE

ANDES, CHILE

269 Ride horses in the mountains

Crossing the high Andes on horseback will thrill most active teens. Take a trip led by gaucho guides through canyons, over high mountain passes, and past ancient ruins, stopping to visit small communities along the way. Nights camping under spectacular starry skies sweeten the deal.

CHILE TO ARGENTINA

270 Take a road trip across the Andes

The road trip from Santiago to Buenos Aires takes you up an unforgettable series of twenty-eight hairpin bends and into a tunnel under the Andes. The scenery is beautiful mountains and valleys—but beware snow in winter (June to August), which can lead to the crossing closing.

PILA, ARGENTINA

271 Learn to play polo

The thundering of hooves, the swinging of sticks, the scoring of goals; there's a lot of excitement around a polo game. Whether you've played before or hardly ridden a horse, El Venado Polo will offer lessons to people of all ages and most abilities (you need to be good enough to handle a horse independently), and once you've tried it, you might be hooked.

SALINAS GRANDES, ARGENTINA

272 Visit Argentina's salt flats

A half hour's drive from the town of Purmamarca are Argentina's salt flats. This huge expanse of crusted salt plains, laid out under a bright-blue sky, formed when a lake dried up millions of years ago. The road to them winds through some impressive mountain scenery and, once there, the otherworldliness will entrance children—and delight the social media feeds of older teenagers.

PUNTA LOMA NATURE RESERVE, ARGENTINA

273 Come face-to-face with sea lions

Children aged seven and up can visit the Punta Loma Nature Reserve to snorkel with curious sea lions. You'll get in the water with these playful creatures as they dive, play, and splash around you. Just remember not to touch them—they may be friendly, but they're still wild animals.

HUMAHUACA, ARGENTINA

274 Marvel at nature's color palette

The steep, angular corrugations of Hornocal mountain range are dramatic enough, but add on to them the strips of color—oranges, reds, golds, and greens—and the sight is phenomenal, especially at sunset. The viewpoint is 13,123 ft. (4,000 m) above sea level (make sure you're acclimatized first), at the side of a snaking road from Humahuaca, past open country where guanacos roam free.

274 HORNOCAL MOUNTAINS

PATAGONIA, ARGENTINA
275 Stargaze from your bed

Set in the dramatic Patagonian landscape, EcoCamp is a collection of domed tents inspired by the ancient shelters of the region's Kaweskar people. Days here are spent hiking, wildlife watching, and biking out in the elements. At night you return to your tent, snuggle under fleece blankets, and look up through the clear ceiling at the starry sky. It's the ultimate camping adventure for kids aged six and over.

EL CALAFATE, ARGENTINA
276 Watch ice fall from a glacier

Take a boat tour to the head of the Perito Moreno Glacier to see—and hear—huge chunks of ice calving and falling into the lake below. This happens as the ice behind pushes forward, and is dramatic seen from the boardwalks on the shore but epic from a boat.

276 PERITO MORENO

LAKE BUENOS AIRES, ARGENTINA
277 Kayak into marble caves

Straddling the border of Argentina and Chile is the glacial turquoise lake of Lake Buenos Aires (or Lake General Carrera if you're in Chile), in the middle of which are spectacular marble caves. Explore them by kayak, getting up close to the columns and arches of swirling, blue-and-white limestone.

277 MARBLE CAVES

279 PALERMO HOLLYWOOD

278 Sample Buenos Aires's best street food

The scent of salt water mingles with barbecued meat as you approach the seaside boulevard of Costanera Sur, a dream for young carnivores. You'll find stalls selling barbecued pork shoulder, flank steak, and Argentina's answer to a hot dog—thick chorizo sausage, crammed into a crusty baguette and topped with chimichurri.

279 Copy a piece of street art

As long as the building's owner agrees, street art is legal all over Buenos Aires. This makes the city colorful in every sense, from its lively streets to the colorfully painted walls. Head to the area of Palermo Hollywood, pick a favorite mural, take out your felt tips, and see how well each family member can reproduce the street art. Memories—and artwork—to take home.

280 Celebrate Latin American Art

Buenos Aires's MALBA (Museo de Arte Latinoamericano de Buenos Aires) is a fabulous journey through contemporary (mainly) Latin American art, showcasing big names such as Wifredo Lam, Frida Kahlo, Diego Rivera, and Jorge de la Vega. It will also inspire younger generations with its commitment to continue acquiring work by today's emerging artists.

283 ONE OF THE SEVEN LAKES

BUENOS AIRES, ARGENTINA
281 Take a family tango lesson

Unleash your family's dramatic side and learn to dance the tango. The stomps, the turns, those leg-swinging kicks: there's a lot to learn but it's a lot of fun doing it. For older children, follow your lesson with an evening out at a *milonga*, where everybody goes to tango.

BUENOS AIRES, ARGENTINA
282 Visit a cemetery

As you wander along the rows of grand mausoleums, styled after everything from Egyptian obelisks to cathedrals, La Recoleta Cemetery can feel more like an eccentric small town than a cemetery. It is the final resting place of Argentinian greats, including Eva Perón. Take a guided tour to hear the tales behind the tombs.

LAKE DISTRICT, ARGENTINA
283 See seven lakes in one day

For road-trip drama that will keep young eyes on the scenery, follow the Route of the Seven Lakes, a one-day journey through Argentina's Lake District. As you drive along narrow, winding roads, the snowcapped mountains, forests, and lakes will keep noses pinned to the windows.

EUROPE

3

284 HOUSES OF THE *HULDUFÓLK*

THROUGHOUT ICELAND

284 Discover the world of the *huldufólk*

All over Iceland, if you look carefully, you can find miniature, perfectly created houses about as high as your knee, or sometimes just a door on a rock face. These are the homes of the *huldufólk*— tiny, elf-like people from Icelandic folklore. They are an intrinsic part of Icelandic life, especially at Christmas and New Year.

GRINDAVÍK, ICELAND

285 When in Iceland... relax in a hot spring

Hot springs are a way of life in Iceland, and the most famous is the Blue Lagoon—a clutch of steaming, turquoise pools surrounded by black lava fields. You can swim, soak, or just rub yourself with healing mud. The 100°F (38°C) water is rich in minerals, so you'll emerge with luxuriously soft skin.

SKJÁLFANDI BAY, ICELAND

286 Whale watch from a traditional sailing ship

Watching wildlife in Skjálfandi Bay is always magical. Do so from a traditional wooden sailing ship and it's even more so. You and your offspring can help hoist the sails and haul ropes, then enjoy the wild landscapes as you look out for humpback whales and seabirds.

AROUND ICELAND
287 Take a road trip around an island

For anyone who loves a circular walk, not out-and-back routes, then to take a road trip that circumnavigates an island is the holiday that dreams are made of. It takes about ten days to drive around the perimeter of Iceland—depending how much you want to stop—and it's best to avoid winter, when roads can be icy and some passes can be closed. The trip is spectacular. Iceland is a smorgasbord of stunning landscapes and views—lava fields, volcanos, waterfalls, black beaches, glaciers, geysers, colorful villages, mountains, fjords, and lakes—the list is almost endless. Add to that the wildlife that you might see, from whales and dolphins, to puffins and Arctic foxes; the stops you can make to swim in naturally heated pools; and the colorful towns and villages you can explore; and it's a trip that has something for everyone, whatever their age.

287 STROKKUR GEYSER

THROUGHOUT ICELAND

288 Swim in a naturally heated swimming pool

Due to the volcanic nature of Iceland—also known as the Land of Ice and Fire—there is geothermal activity bubbling away underneath almost all of the island. This is great news for Iceland's super-clean energy supply—almost 90 percent of hot water and heating comes from geothermal heat and a quarter of the country's energy supplies are geothermal power plants—but it's also good news for swimmers, who will find that nearly all the country's swimming pools are warm all year round, and most of them have hot tubs of varying temperatures too. This has created a nation that loves its pools, whether they are rustic pools in the middle of otherwise-deserted valleys, such as the Secret Lagoon and Seljavallalaug Swimming Pool, or classic, family-friendly pools full of slides and fountains, such as Vestmannaeyjar or Laugardalur.

LANGJÖKULL GLACIER, ICELAND

289 Explore an ice tunnel

You'll have to drive through a stone desert to get to the vast Langjökull Glacier, then board an adapted monster truck to reach its summit. The adventure ramps up even further as you follow the world's largest human-made ice tunnel, going 1,640 ft. (500 m) deep into the glacier. Older kids and teens will be wowed by the caverns, glacial walls, and ice formations, all in varying shades of dazzling white and blue.

288 NATURAL SWIMMING POOL

291 GIANT'S CAUSEWAY

RATHLIN ISLAND,
NORTHERN IRELAND
290 Look out for puffins

Six miles off the coast of County Antrim is Rathlin Island, home to Northern Ireland's largest seabird colony, where puffins, kittiwakes, and guillemots make their temporary homes among the rugged terrain. Come in spring or early summer to see the puffins nest in their thousands on the cliffs. There are telescopes and binoculars on hand at local viewing points for those all-important close-ups of fluffy chicks.

BUSHMILLS,
NORTHERN IRELAND
291 Hop over giant stepping stones

Legend has it that the Giant's Causeway's dramatic basalt formations were built by giant Finn McCool, who constructed a path with huge stepping stones to reach Scotland. This jagged promontory, made up of forty thousand basalt columns spilling down into the ocean, was the result of volcanic activity about sixty million years ago. It's a striking sight—little ones will love taking in the coastal scenery from the cliff top and observing these spectacular rocks up close.

DERRY, NORTHERN IRELAND
292 Learn about politics, through murals

Derry's Bogside neighborhood saw some of Northern Ireland's worst political violence during The Troubles, from the late 1960s to 1998. Twelve murals commemorating the events adorn houses along Rossville Street. One of the most striking is *The Petrol Bomber*, depicting a boy wearing a gas mask as he clutches onto a petrol bomb. Given their shocking, politically charged nature, the murals are best appreciated by teenagers.

294 BELMULLET TIDAL POOL

295 SLIEVE LEAGUE CLIFFS

CASTLEBAR, IRELAND
293 Stay in a hobbit hut

Lord of the Rings fans can channel their inner Bilbo Baggins at Mayo Glamping, where a series of hobbit huts are built into the hillside, complete with grass roofs, rough stone walls, and circular doors and windows. Sit by the fire, gaze up at the stars, and it's easy to imagine you're in the Shire.

BELMULLET, IRELAND
294 Swim laps in a tidal pool

You can swim in salt water without being bothered by seaweed or jellyfish at Belmullet Tidal Pool, a modernist concrete structure jutting out to sea at beautiful Blacksod Bay. Do laps in the main pool, or paddle with little ones in the toddler pool— either way you'll be treated to dramatic sea and mountain views. It's open year-round, so you can even don a wet suit and swim in winter.

TEELIN, IRELAND
295 Walk on some of the highest cliffs in Europe

Among the highest cliffs in Europe, the Slieve League Cliffs dramatically plunge into the Atlantic, the ocean's roaring cold waters painting foamy, white streaks as the waves break into the rock face. Slip your hiking boots on and head for the viewpoint to soak up the panorama, before enjoying a guided walk up the wilds of Slieve League to learn about the local flora and fauna.

298 BRIGIT'S GARDEN

CONNEMARA, IRELAND

296 Visit a smokehouse and taste the produce

If there's one way to get children to try new foods, it's to see it being made. Connemara Smokehouse teeters on the ocean's edge outside Connemara. Inside, it operates an *économusée*, which teaches visitors all about the skills of smoking seafood, as well as offering tastings of their smoked salmon products.

ARAN ISLANDS, IRELAND

297 Explore the Aran Islands

Lying off the coast of County Galway, the desolately beautiful Aran Islands offer jagged coastlines of rocky cliffs, wild beaches, and verdant fields peppered with ancient forts and grazing livestock. The prehistoric stone fort of Dún Aonghasa is a highlight, although take good care—there is no barrier at the edge of the 285 ft. (87 m) cliff.

GALWAY, IRELAND

298 Follow a trail of science-based challenges

The 11 ac (4.5 ha) Brigit's Garden, north of Galway, is a delight, with Celtic-style gardens offering a wealth of fun activities, including nature detective trails, a climbing tower, play area, and Fairy Village, which includes fun nature- and science-based challenges to keep curious minds busy. Refuel at the café with seasonal dishes tastily prepared using herbs from the garden and local produce.

299 KILDARE MAZE

NAAS, IRELAND
299 Find your way out of Kildare Maze

Children and teenagers will test their memory and
perserverance as they try to find their way out of
this maze, with its extensive network of paths and
tall hedges. Once you've reached the viewing tower,
you'll be rewarded with panoramic countryside
views. There's plenty more to keep children
entertained, including an adventure trail, zip
line, and crazy golf.

THROUGHOUT IRELAND
300 Refuel with soda bread

Cross the threshold of any Irish home and you're
bound to come across soda bread, its sweet,
freshly baked smell pervading the air. Made with
bicarbonate of soda and buttermilk, it's delicious
when toasted, dripping with melted Irish butter.
Children will love munching on a slice or two
for breakfast or tea, or as an energizing snack.

CORK, IRELAND
301 Kiss the Blarney Stone for luck

Grab some luck o' the Irish as you climb the stone stairs inside Blarney Castle's tower to kiss the fabled Blarney Stone at the top. Be prepared to lay down and lean backward to smooch the special stone built into the castle wall. And don't worry, handlers disinfect and wipe down the surface before each new kiss.

CORK, IRELAND
302 Check out live music in Cork

Music pumps through Cork's veins, and there are few better places to introduce the kids to Irish culture, spirit, and storytelling. Live venues are everywhere, from tiny pubs to purpose-built concert halls, and the atmosphere matters just as much as the music. Expect racing fiddles, rhythmic clapping, and powerful voices singing traditional tunes.

WATERFORD AND MAYO, IRELAND
303 Cycle on old railway lines

Ireland's cycling routes are a superb way to take in some of the country's dramatic scenery. Mostly flat, the 29 mi. (46 km) long Waterford Greenway follows a historic (now disused) railway line punctuated with attractions, from Norman castles to medieval ruins, while the Great Western Greenway takes cyclists and walkers through bogs and woodlands.

CAHERSIVEEN, IRELAND
304 See the stars at a Dark Sky Reserve

Expect glittering skies and silent nights at Kerry's International Dark Sky Reserve, a vast wilderness squeezed between mountains and the sea. It's protected from light pollution, so there's incredible stargazing on clear nights: you'll catch the Milky Way, faint meteors, and superbly bright stars twinkling over the Atlantic Ocean.

303 WATERFORD GREENWAY

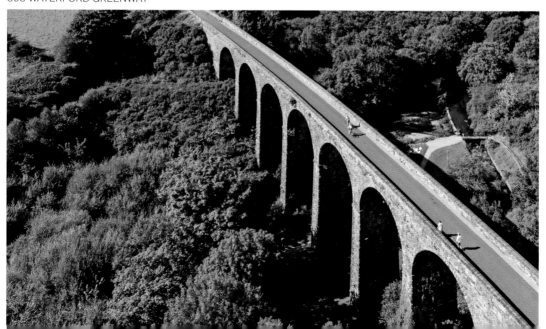

FORT WILLIAM TO MALLAIG,
SCOTLAND

305 Cross a viaduct by steam train

You might recognize the curved arches of Glenfinnan Viaduct from *Harry Potter*. The longest concrete railway bridge in Scotland, it sees plenty of railway traffic, but it's most fun crossed on the Jacobite steam train, which runs from Fort William to Mallaig every summer. Not only can you take in stunning scenery, you can also pretend you're on the Hogwarts Express.

BARRA ISLAND, SCOTLAND

306 Land on the beach in a plane

When you travel to the island of Barra by air, the journey is part of the fun. You'll leave Glasgow in a tiny Twin Otter plane, landing an hour later on a sweep of white sand at the world's only scheduled beach airport—tides permitting, of course. Kids with strong nerves will relish the adventure.

DUNOON, SCOTLAND

307 Experience the Highland Games

Highland Games have been part of Scottish culture for centuries, and they're a fantastic way to experience a slice of the region's community and heritage. At the Cowal Gathering in Dunoon, you can watch the caber toss and the hammer throw, see Highland dancing competitions and bagpipe parades, and get stuck into all sorts of Scottish foods. Older kids can continue the fun late into the night with *céilidhs* and live music.

NORTH COAST, SCOTLAND

308 Drive the NC500

Launched in 2015 as Scotland's answer to Route 66, the NC500 is one
of the world's best road trips—and one that will keep kids' eyes glued
to the scenery. Kicking off from Inverness, it takes in just over 500 mi.
(805 km) of Highland terrain, with single-track roads, steep mountain
tracks, and changeable weather all part of the fun. You'll head first
to the gentle hills and farmland of the Black Isle, before the scenery
becomes progressively wilder. Stop off for hikes around the brooding
peaks and moorland of Assynt; test the waters at powder-white
beaches on the northwest coast; visit Ullapool for boat trips to see
dolphins and basking sharks; or just pull up at the roadside to get
a look at hairy Highland cows. Brave the trails off-season and you
might even catch a glimpse of the northern lights.

308 ROAD TRIP IN SCOTLAND

310 FAIRY POOLS

ISLE OF STAFFA, SCOTLAND

309 Explore a cave with natural acoustics

Take a boat trip to the Isle of Staffa. The area is teeming with legends that children will love; one suggests that Staffa was laid as a stepping stone by a giant. Fingal's Cave is 230 ft. (70 m) deep and beautifully sculpted in hexagonal, basalt columns. Inside, the sound of the waves echoes around, creating a special kind of music: it inspired Felix Mendelssohn to write the *Fingal's Cave* overture.

ISLE OF SKYE, SCOTLAND

310 Swim in fairy pools

It's easy to imagine magical creatures living among the Fairy Pools—a series of mini waterfalls and turquoise pools backed by the soaring Cuillin Mountains. Legend has it that selkies (mythical creatures that resemble seals in water but humans on land) used to bathe in the clear waters. If you don't mind the cold, you can follow their lead and jump in.

CAIRNGORMS AND CENTRAL HIGHLANDS, SCOTLAND

311 Rewild with your child

Spark a passion for the environment while spending time in the wilderness on a short rewilding retreat. Wilderness Scotland organizes trips in the Highlands where you'll work with rangers, learn about ecosystems and land restoration, search for local wildlife, and breathe in the fresh mountain air. It's a wonderful adventure for nature-loving teens.

LOCH ASSYNT, SCOTLAND

312 Soak up the atmosphere of a ruined castle

Set on the shores of Loch Assynt and backed by brooding mountains, the ruins of Ardvreck Castle look like they've jumped from a story book—and a haunting one at that. It's unsurprising that this fifteenth-century relic is said to be home to several ghosts, including the weeping daughter of a MacLeod chief.

BEN LOMOND MOUNTAIN, SCOTLAND

313 Bag a Munro

"Bagging a Munro"—a Munro being a Scottish mountain over 3,000 ft. (914 m)—is a grand Scottish tradition. And Ben Lomond is a popular first climb. It's a 7.5 mi. (12 km) round trip along a well-defined path through oak woods and out into the open, with the views over Loch Lomond and the Trossachs getting better and better the higher you climb. Kids as young as seven can make it to the top.

ELIE NESS, SCOTLAND

314 Wander along a Scottish cliff

A bracing cliff walk is one of life's great pleasures: the wind in your hair, and the waves crashing against the rocks below. The wild cliffs of Elie Ness are great for children, with good paths, the possibility of seeing dolphins out to sea, and a lighthouse as a goal. The lighthouse has been keeping sailors safe since 1908 and its light can be seen 17 mi. (27 km) from shore.

314 ELIE NESS LIGHTHOUSE

ALEXANDRIA, SCOTLAND

315 Go ape in the treetops

The Trossachs National Park undoubtedly offers some of the best views Scotland has to offer, with mountains, moorlands, forests, rivers, and lochs. You and your family (over tens) can appreciate these views in a whole new way as you fly down Britain's longest zip line, or wobble across a rope 72 ft. (22 m) above ground level. If that's too run-of-the-mill, then take the challenge after dark, when atmospheric lighting makes it a whole new experience.

FIFE, SCOTLAND

316 Test your skills at mini golf

Step inside Adventure Golf Island and you'll think you're in sunny Florida. Mini-golfers putt amidst cascading waterfalls, tropical tiki huts, and lush palm trees in a floodlit dome, with fountains and a pirate ship adding to the exotic feel. Head outside for an alfresco experience to test your skills on the Treasure Island course.

EDINBURGH, SCOTLAND

317 Get in on the act at the Edinburgh Fringe

The world's biggest arts festival is sprawling, diverse, and a little crazy, but it isn't just for grown-ups. You can experience everything from puppet shows and toddler discos to comedy for tweens. Or you could just watch the mayhem as the streets fill up with fire-breathers, stilt walkers, and musicians.

317 PUPPET SHOW

DORSET, ENGLAND

329 Hunt for fossils on the beach

It's more than two hundred years since Mary Anning made her prehistoric finds along the beaches of Dorset, an area now named the Jurassic Coast. Book a guided tour in Lyme Regis and you'll hunt for fossils among the shingle, while guides spin tales about the magnificent beasts that once walked these shores.

SOUTH DEVON, ENGLAND

330 Ride the tracks with Thomas the Tank Engine

"Toot, toot, all aboard," shouts a cheerful Thomas. And then, with a puff of smoke everyone's favorite little blue steam train is off, trundling through woodland and riding the tracks down the side of the River Dart. On a sunny day like this even the Fat Controller can't help but smile. Buy a ticket from the Dartmouth Steam Railway for your very own Thomas trip.

CORNWALL, ENGLAND

331 Catch a wave together

You don't have to be able to stand on a surfboard to enjoy all the fun of the waves—fortunately, bodyboarding is just as much fun and involves lying on the board. It's good for young children, who can lark about in the shallows, as well as older teenagers, who can go farther out and teach themselves tricks on larger waves.

CORNWALL, ENGLAND

332 Cycle the Camel Trail

Running alongside the Camel Estuary, from Padstow to Bodmin, the Camel Trail is an 18 mi. (29 km) hiking and cycling route along an old, disused railway line. Railway lines rarely have hills, which makes this a perfect route for little legs. The estuary attracts hundreds of waterbirds such as little egrets, and if you're very eagle-eyed—and lucky—you might also spot kingfishers or otters as you pedal.

331 GO BODYBOARDING

333 Sleep in a country church

A night spent "champing" (church camping) is all about the atmosphere. At St. Dona's, a Victorian chapel overlooking Llanddona Beach, you can bed down between the pews, look for bats in the roof, and wake up to light streaming through the stained-glass windows. Children are free to explore both the church and churchyard.

SNOWDONIA NATIONAL PARK, WALES

334 Go above and below in Snowdonia

Snowdonia National Park is a fantastic playground for adventure-loving families. The park's most famous landmark is Snowdon, the highest mountain in Wales—older kids can make it to the summit and back down in about six hours. Afterward, jump around underground at Bounce Below, a giant trampoline park created in a disused slate mine.

334 SNOWDONIA TRAMPOLINE

336 BRECON BEACONS

SNOWDONIA NATIONAL PARK, WALES

335 Stay in a mountain bothy

You'll have to forgo creature comforts such as water and electricity to spend the night in a bothy (a basic wilderness shelter), so this one's for adventurous older kids. There are around one hundred bothies around Britain. Dulyn, in Snowdonia National Park, offers a wood-burning stove (bring your own fuel) and a sleeping platform. After a long day's hike, you can sit by a fire, dry out your socks, and think of the climbers, hikers, and mountaineers who came before you.

BRECON BEACONS NATIONAL PARK, WALES

336 Stargaze in the Brecon Beacons

Wrap up warm and bring binoculars for a nighttime picnic under the stars that'll fire up young imaginations. The Milky Way, shooting stars, and constellations are all visible on clear nights in the Brecon Beacons, including Draco the Dragon—a long sweep of stars that swirls around Polaris in the northern skies.

MARCROSS, WALES

337 Bed down in a lighthouse

Built in 1832 on a headland overlooking the Bristol Channel, Nash Point Lighthouse is no longer in use, but you can breathe in its history on an overnight stay. Explore windswept beaches, look out for porpoises, and learn about the smugglers and wreckers who'd lure vessels onto the rocks in the days before the lighthouse.

CASWELL BAY, SWANSEA, WALES
338 Go rock pooling

Wandering the coast in search of curious critters and other hidden treasures is an adventure for little kids. Mini beachcombers can find all kinds of creatures at Caswell Bay, a wide, sandy beach near Swansea, with hidden coves and plenty of rock pools. You'll need a net, a bucket, and the patience just to sit and watch.

CARDIFF, WALES
339 Cheer on the rugby in Cardiff

Cardiff lives and breathes rugby, and local enthusiasm for the game is infectious. Whether you're a total newbie or a hardcore fan, watching a hard-fought match at the iconic Principality Stadium is a fantastic night out, and kids are always welcome. Visit when the national team is playing and the atmosphere is electric.

DINEFWR, CARMARTHENSHIRE, WALES
340 Fit the whole family in a tree

Join the children as they scramble up the Castle Oak at Dinefwr Park and Castle, in Wales. Although there are thousands of trees to choose from here, the Castle Oak offers an easy way up with one branch at ground level for novice (or out-of-practice) climbers to start on.

MONMOUTHSHIRE, WALES
341 Build a den

Den-building is a quintessential childhood experience, and Wentwood—part of the largest block of ancient forest in Wales—is a fabulous place to do it. First, you'll need a base tree to secure and weave your sticks and branches around; then once you're happy with your shelter, some heavy logs to keep things in place. To take things a step further, you can customize your hideaway with leaves, moss, and stones.

PEMBROKESHIRE, WALES
342 Test your mettle along the Welsh coastline

If scrambling along the Pembrokeshire coastline, rock climbing, cliff jumping, and wild swimming is your idea of a good time, sign up for a family coasteering trip with an organization such as Celtic Quest Coasteering. Kids as young as eight can join in the fun as you test your limits among jaw-dropping scenery and wonderful wildlife. Wet suits, helmets, and buoyancy aids are provided, so all you need to bring are nerves of steel.

342 COASTEERING

343 SEE 24-HOUR SUNSHINE

TROMSØ, NORWAY
343 Feel the glow of the midnight sun

From late May until late July, the sun doesn't set in Tromsø, a small city 250 mi. (400 km) north of the Arctic Circle. It's the perfect excuse to let the kids stay up late and enjoy the landscape, while bathed in golden light. Find a beach and enjoy a midnight swim, enjoy the silence of the famous Arctic Cathedral, or hike to the mountain plateau and look out over the city.

SVALBARD, NORWAY
344 Drive huskies in Svalbard

For outdoorsy, animal-loving kids, a day spent dogsledding in Svalbard—one of Europe's last great wildernesses—is a dream come true. You'll learn how to harness your own huskies, prepare the sled, then race through remote and snowy wilderness, looking out for winter wildlife including reindeer and Arctic foxes. Kids aged eight and over can take part, while younger kids can join in specially tailored guided tours.

345 CAMP IN THE WILD

345 Go wild camping inside the Arctic Circle

For a summer camping spot with a difference, head for the Arctic Circle. The law of *allemannsretten* (the right to roam) allows you to wild camp almost anywhere in open country, so you can pitch up and enjoy wilderness in its purest form. Just remember to leave the land as you found it.

346 Build a snowman

The experience of rolling snow to build a snowman is one that every family should have—whatever the snowfall where they live. Head to Bergen, which is not only Norway's snowiest city, it also has several public parks where you can find a space and build your snowman. Don't forget a carrot for the nose.

347 Sleep in the trees on a private island

The Island Cabin at Vest-Agder is several childhood fantasies rolled into one: a treehouse, set on its own tiny island, where the only light comes from candles, flashlights, and flames from the fire. Time can be spent swimming, foraging for berries, or canoeing to the mainland for hardy hikes.

NORWEGIAN FJORDS, NORWAY
348 Backpack around the fjords

Backpacking isn't just for students. It's huge fun for families, too, especially if the kids are old enough to carry their own bags. The Norwegian fjords are a great place to start, and not just because of their dramatic beauty. You'll also find excellent transport links and a strong network of family-friendly hostels, so all you'll have to worry about is where to go next.

FLÅMSDALEN, NORWAY
349 Ride The Flåm Railway

Widely regarded as one of the world's most scenic railway journeys, the iconic Flåm Railway runs through the wild and dramatic valley of Flåmsdalen, western Norway. Taking in stunning views of lush, green meadows, steep cliffs, cascading waterfalls, deep fjords, and snowcapped mountains, this one-hour train ride also passes through twenty tunnels, including a horseshoe tunnel through a mountain, making it especially exciting for young children.

GUDBRANDSDALEN, NORWAY
350 Eat Norwegian *brunost*

Cheese comes in many different forms, depending on where in the world you're eating it, and in Norway they like "brown cheese"—*brunost*. Made from boiled-down whey, brunost is more caramel- than cheese-like, and best eaten on a waffle, or on rye bread with jam. One tip, always cut it with an *ostehøvel*— a metal cheese slicer—which was invented in Norway for this very purpose.

348 FJORDS

NORTHERN NORWAY

351 Marvel at the northern lights

There aren't many natural wonders that capture the imagination quite like the northern lights, or aurora borealis. This colorful, natural light display has fascinated humans for thousands of years, and it's easily worth the effort, cost, and time spent standing around in the cold to see them. Northern Norway is a prime viewing location. You could base yourself in Tromsø, and join the locals in the Lyngsalpene mountain range; in Finnmark, Norway's largest and least-populated county; or in Svalbard, one of the few places in the world where you can see the northern lights in the middle of the day, thanks to the dark Arctic winter. The amount of waiting around involved means you might want to save this for older children. Or travel with a local guide, who'll entertain them with legends such as the Firefox, whose furry tail creates sparks as it runs through the night sky.

OSLO, NORWAY

352 Explore a Viking warship

Do your kids get muddy, like to wear silly hats, and rampage around the house destroying everything? Maybe they've got Viking blood! Take them to Oslo to see a genuine Viking ship and let them learn how the masters of rampage went about their business (though perhaps don't linger on the more grisly bits).

351 NORTHERN LIGHTS

353 STAY IN AN ICE HOTEL

ALTA, NORWAY
353 Spend the night in a room carved from ice

You'll need a thermal sleeping bag, a wooly hat, and a stack of reindeer skins to survive a night at Sorrisniva, the world's northernmost ice hotel. Everything here—as the name suggests—is carved from ice and snow, including your bed, so it feels as if you're sleeping inside a wintry fairy tale.

KLARÄLVEN RIVER, SWEDEN
354 Build a raft and float down a river

There's nothing quite like the rewards of self-sufficiency. Imagine building your own raft using just logs and ropes—and a little bit of expert instruction—and floating down the peaceful Klarälven River. Nature Travels can organize the trip, but you'll choose where to stop to camp depending on how fast your raft travels and wherever the bank takes your fancy.

DALARNA, SWEDEN
355 Wild swim in a lake

Sweden has almost one hundred thousand lakes, so it's no surprise that swimming in lakes here is a popular pursuit. There's something magically refreshing about lake water—no chlorine, no salt—and 360-degree views. Many Swedes swim all year round—taking advantage of waterfront saunas to warm up after a winter dip—but in summer, water temperatures can reach 68°F (20°C). Try Lake Siljan for picturesque views.

BOHUSLÄN, SWEDEN
356 Go on a seafood safari

The cold, clear waters off Sweden's Bohuslän Coast produce some of the best seafood in the world, and you can sample it all on a seafood safari. You'll don waterproofs and join local fishermen on the hunt for the "Big Five": oysters, lobsters, langoustines, prawns, and mussels, before returning to shore to cook your catch over an open fire. It's great fun and a chance for the kids to experience and learn about sustainable fishing.

355 WILD SWIMMING

STOCKHOLM, SWEDEN
357 Interact with Sweden's Fab Four

Stockholm's wildly entertaining ABBA The Museum is crammed full of colorful memorabilia and interactive exhibits. You can try on outrageous costumes, join the band (virtually) on stage, create your own hit song in the mini recording booth, and introduce unsuspecting children to the world of Björn, Benny, Frida, and Agnetha.

STOCKHOLM, SWEDEN
358 Discover the spooky side to Stockholm

There are many ways to see and learn about Stockholm and its history, but one that might especially enthrall teenagers is to go on a ghost tour. Delving into medieval murders, shady secrets, myths, and legends, this tour explores the cobbled old streets and courtyards of the city's Old Town—after dark, of course.

SJÁVNJA NATURE RESERVE, SWEDEN
359 Get to know Sámi culture

Sustainability, cultural connections, and wilderness experiences are at the heart of the Sapmi Nature Camp in the Arctic Circle, run by the Unna Tjerusj Sámi community. You'll sleep in traditional *lavvu* (tipi-like) tents, eat meals of local fish, reindeer, and moose, and spend days ice fishing and exploring the local landscape on snowshoes.

357 ABBA MUSEUM

BERGSLAGEN FOREST, SWEDEN
360 Learn how to howl like a wolf

Learn from an expert guide how to track wildlife such as moose, beavers, and wolves by their prints and droppings; feast on berries and mushrooms you've picked yourselves, then thrill to the haunting sound of wolves as they howl by night. Your guide will show you how to imitate their call—can you get a response?

SKINNSKATTEBERG, SWEDEN
361 Go wild at an eco-lodge

You won't have modern comforts at Kolarbyn Eco Lodge—there's no electricity or running water, and you'll sleep in basic wooden cabins. But what you get in return is a magical back-to-nature experience. Adventurous kids will be in their element hiking in the forest, swimming in the lakes and rivers, and cooking their meals over an open fire.

STOCKHOLM, SWEDEN, TO NARVIK, NORWAY
362 Take the sleeper train to the Arctic Circle

Kids love train travel, and cozying up on the Arctic Circle Sleeper Train as you rumble from Stockholm to the frozen Norwegian north is about as exciting as it gets. You might not get the best night's sleep, but the adventure—and the views through picture windows across the wild, Arctic landscape—is well worth it.

361 KOLARBYN ECO LODGE

364 VISIT MOOMIN WORLD

365 REINDEER

ROVANIEMI, FINLAND
363 Hang out with Santa Claus

Santa may be a world traveler, but his home is Rovaniemi, in Finnish Lapland. At Santa's Village you can visit Mrs. Claus and the elves, before meeting with the big man himself and maybe whispering your wish list into his ear. Visit at Christmas and you'll wave him off as he leaves for his journey around the world.

NAANTALI, FINLAND
364 Meet the Moomins

The quirky, hippo-shaped trolls of Tove Jansson's tales are much-loved around the world, but they are true cultural icons in Finland. At Moomin World, which sits on its own island in the Naantali archipelago, the kids can get hands-on at Snork's Workshop, visit the Moominhouse, and see a purple sea dragon. Hugs from wandering Moomin characters are included.

LAPLAND, FINLAND
365 See reindeer running wild

In the far northern reaches of Finland sit the snowy plains of Lapland, where reindeer range the land in herds. Their antlers are furry to the touch, and can reach 50 in. (127 cm) in length before they fall off and regrow the next year. Surprisingly docile in captivity, reindeer are best visited in the snowy winter months, when the northern lights shine above.

367 STARGAZE FROM BED

LAKE SAIMAA, FINLAND
366 Swim in an ice pool

The alleged health benefits of ice swimming—
lowering stress and blood pressure, improving
circulation, boosting the immune system—are
fueling its growing popularity today, but the Finns
have been cutting holes in the ice and jumping in
since the seventeenth century. It's a great way to
boost children's resilience—but do it with a guide.

SAARISELKÄ, FINLAND
367 Sleep in a glass igloo

You don't have to stand out in the cold to experience
the beauty of northern Finland's night skies. At
Kakslauttanen Arctic Resort, you can sleep under
heated glass domes and gaze up at starry skies from
the comfort of your own bed. If you're lucky, you'll
catch the dancing colors of the northern lights.

THROUGHOUT FINLAND
368 Go snowshoeing in the wilds

Pulling on snowshoes and crossing the frozen wilderness is an environmentally friendly way to experience Finnish winter, and one that teenagers can happily join in. You'll need strong thighs for long days crossing snow-covered plains and forest, but evening soaks in a sauna or hot tub should soothe any aching limbs.

LAKELAND, FINLAND
369 Spend a summer like the Finnish

As sunny days arrive, Finns pack their bags and head for Lakeland, the largest lake region in Europe. Summers spent in a cottage by the water are an essential part of Finnish childhood. You could try Lake Pielinen for hill walking; Lake Päijänne, which is peppered with tiny islands; or Lake Saimaa, Finland's largest lake and home to a medieval castle. Wherever you go, while away your days going for long walks, picking berries, and looking out for birds and seals.

THROUGHOUT FINLAND
370 Experience sauna culture

There's little Finns love more than a sauna, and kids can get in on the action from around six years old (but keep an eye on them as children don't regulate their temperature as well as adults). Many houses have saunas in them, or there are ones at local pools and recreation centers. Then, if you're up for it, take a post-sauna dip in a frozen lake.

NORTH KARELIA, FINLAND
371 Look out for brown bears

Snuggle up under warm blankets and settle down in a cozy wildlife hide, deep in the forests of northeast Finland. Feel the silence and keep an eye out for what wildlife will wander past. If you're lucky, you could have brown bears pacing around just outside.

RANUA, FINLAND

372 Meet Arctic animals

As far as zoos go, Ranua Wildlife Park is pretty special. Set just south of the Arctic Circle and surrounded by thick conifer forest, it's home to a plethora of northern and Arctic animals, including moose, lynx, arctic foxes, and Finland's only polar bear. As the animals live in spacious enclosures, it gives a good feel for how the animals would live out in nature—including sometimes hiding away from visitors' eyes. However, come at feeding time and you have a better chance of seeing these beautiful animals up close.

372 POLAR BEAR

373 LEGO

373 Visit the LEGO® HQ

LEGO fans aged ten and over can learn top secrets on the two-day LEGO Inside Tour. You'll get to meet LEGO designers, visit the factory, and snoop around creator Ole Kirk Kristiansen's original home. A visit to next door LEGOLAND and a stay in the LEGO Hotel sweetens the deal even further.

374 Forage for your dinner

New Nordic cuisine is all about eating regional foods when they're in season. You don't need to go to Michelin-starred restaurants for this though: foraging is popular all over Denmark, and the organization Vild Mad can instruct you on what to pick, and provide guides to show you where to go.

375 Swim in the harbor

Once upon a time, Copenhagen's harbor was a polluted basin of wastewater from sewers and industry. But in 1995, the city said "no more" and invested in cleaning it up. Now, Copenhagen is one of the world's best cities for swimming, with clean water and several "harbor baths." Try Islands Brygge, which has two pools for children.

376 Select your favorite topping for *smørrebrød*

Denmark's unofficial national dish has to be the *smørrebrød*—an open sandwich of buttered rye bread topped with any manner of ingredients, such as herring, cheese, or meat. At Palaegade restaurant they have more than forty options on offer—what will your favorite be?

TØNDER MARSH, JUTLAND, DENMARK

377 Watch a murmuration of starlings

In Denmark, they call the gathering of starlings the "Black Sun," as millions of the birds gather together and appear to dance across the sky before settling down to sleep. It happens around mid-September to October, and will leave you mesmerized as to how they keep in such perfect synchronicity.

FAROE ISLANDS

379 Ride a Faroese pony

Petite Faroese ponies are one of the rarest horse breeds in the world, and they've been living up in the mountains for centuries. Horseback riding company Fjallaross is working to save this endangered breed, and can arrange bareback riding trips through the wilds, where you'll get to hear more about the ponies' history and the challenges facing them.

HIRTSHALS, DENMARK TO TÓRSHAVN, FAROE ISLANDS

378 Travel by boat from Denmark to the Faroe Islands

Board the MS *Norröna* in Hirtshals, northern Denmark, for an epic, thirty-six-hour ride to the Faroe Islands. The journey will take you across the North Sea and past the Shetland Islands, with the chance of seeing seabirds, whales, and far-off oil rigs if the weather is clear. Kids will relish the chance to spend the night at sea, and the cabins suit families of all sizes, as do the facilities: there's a movie theater, a PlayStation room, a pool, and even on-deck hot tubs, which can be booked by the hour so you can soak your limbs while gazing out at the ocean. Most magical of all is your arrival. As you approach the Faroe Islands, you'll follow a narrow channel flanked by mighty peaks as the tiny, colorful capital of Tórshavn comes into view. This is slow travel at its finest.

378 TÓRSHAVN

FLEVOLAND, NETHERLANDS
380 See fields of tulips

Where other countries grow wheat and maize, the Netherlands grows tulips—around nine billion of them every year. From mid-March to the end of May, the flowers transform the countryside of Noordoostpolder into huge swathes of rainbow stripes. Be amazed by all the different colors available—from deep blood reds to jaunty pinks, and stunning two-colored varieties. Visit a "cutting garden," where you can pick the flowers direct from the fields.

WADDEN SEA MUDFLATS, NETHERLANDS
381 Hike across mudflats

There are few things kids love more than getting covered in dirt, and on a walk across the vast mudflats of the Wadden Sea, there'll be ample opportunity. You'll start your journey at low tide, wading through water channels, tramping through slimy marshes, and feeling the ooze of the seabed beneath your feet. Experienced guides are a must to avoid getting trapped by the tide, plus they'll help you spot seabirds and the occasional seal.

AMSTERDAM, NETHERLANDS
382 Pay respects at the Anne Frank House

An important story in history is told inventively and sensitively at the Anne Frank House Museum, where visitors can tour the house and see how the family lived during the Nazi occupation. The space "behind the wall" where Anne and her family hid is exposed for viewing, along with her bedroom and personal items. Very interactive and approachable, the museum tells Anne's story in a way visitors of all ages can appreciate and understand.

380 FLEVOLAND TULIPS

383 VAN GOGH MUSEUM

385 EFTELING

AMSTERDAM, NETHERLANDS

383 Get acquainted with Van Gogh

Book a private tour at the Van Gogh Museum and you'll bring the works of this Dutch icon to life. You'll get to skip the lines and go right to his most colorful and well-known works, while your guide throws in games, treasure hunts, and quirky facts along the way.

AMSTERDAM, NETHERLANDS

384 Navigate the canals

The canals of Amsterdam are world-famous for a reason—they are so charming, with bridges to cross, walkways to traverse, and waterways to explore. Board a boat to view medieval structures, learn about life in the Middle Ages, and listen to guides telling stories about when the canals were the main mode of transportation and tulip bulbs were more valuable than gold.

KAATSHEUVEL, NETHERLANDS

385 Visit a fairy-tale theme park

Every ride at Efteling theme park has a story to tell, whether it's a terrifying roller coaster that's taking you down into the mines, or a talking tree in a fairy-tale forest. There is wonder and magic everywhere in a park that has something for children of every age and which their parents will love too.

THROUGHOUT THE NETHERLANDS

386 Go on a cycling holiday to the Netherlands

With its network of cycle paths, lack of hills, and plethora of easy route guides, the Netherlands is the perfect place for a family cycling holiday. Almost every river, canal, and dyke has a bike path running alongside it, so the choice of routes is endless—and beautiful. Along your route you can stop off to tour windmills, take boat rides along canals, and visit cheese markets that have more cheese than you've ever seen in one place before. And at night, make use of the network of small and farm-based campsites—Minicampings—that are perfect for small children, with playgrounds, animals, and family-friendly activities.

386 CYCLE ALONG CANALS

ABCOUDE, NETHERLANDS
387 Sleep in a windmill

In the seventeenth and eighteenth centuries, the Netherlands developed a system of windmills for pumping water out of its low-lying land and back into its rivers. Today, there are still more than one thousand windmills in the country and, in Abcoude, it's possible to stay in one of these evocative buildings. Spiral stairs will lead you up to the eccentrically shaped rooms with fabulous views over the surrounding land.

AMSTERDAM, NETHERLANDS
388 Let kids rule at Speelsloot

It's all about fostering imaginative play at Speelsloot, a scenic adventure playground on the beach—one of seven beaches in fact—at Amsterdam's Twiske-Waterland. Kids can guide planes in to land from the air traffic control tower, ride the cable car or the ferry across the water, and cool off with a splash around afterward. Bring a picnic, because this is the kind of place where families can happily spend all day.

389 CHRISTMAS MARKET

391 CHOCOLATE WAFFLES

GHENT, BELGIUM
389 Get Christmas sorted

Immerse yourself in the Christmas spirit with a trip to one of Belgium's legendary Christmas markets. Wrap your hands around a warming cup of mulled wine—or hot chocolate for the kids—and wander through the enchanting Christmas stalls; you're sure to pick up something good for on and under the tree.

THROUGHOUT BELGIUM
390 Eat the world's best fries

Belgium isn't known for its fine cuisine but when it comes to fries, they're top of the charts. To sample the goods, head to a local *friterie* or *fritkot*. Hot, crisp, and almost always served with a sauce, they're best eaten standing on a street corner, with a fork in hand to help shovel them down.

BRUGES, BELGIUM
391 Make authentic Belgian waffles

Go one step further than eating a Belgian waffle—take a waffle-making workshop in the charming city of Bruges. Kids can get fully involved, breaking the eggs for the batter and picking out their choice of topping for the finished article. Hmmm, chocolate, whipped cream, or syrup? Or all three?

393 MINI EUROPE

BRUSSELS, BELGIUM
392 Indulge your chocolate cravings

Sampling the best truffles, bonbons, and caramels
that Brussels has to offer is a dream activity for any
sweet-toothed child. Book a tour and you'll visit
the city's chocolate hotspots, such as local legend
Pierre Marcolini and praline specialists Neuhaus.
You might even get to create some yourself in
a hands-on chocolate workshop.

BRUSSELS, BELGIUM
393 Visit all of Europe in a day

The best type of trip for many young children is
where you cut out the travel and just see the sights.
At Mini Europe in Brussels, that's exactly what
you can do, visiting all of Europe's most famous
landmarks in one afternoon—in miniature.
The scale models are about $\frac{1}{25}$th of the original
buildings' sizes, but complete with exquisite details
and just the right amount of information about the
country where they're found.

PICOS DE EUROPA, SPAIN
394 Walk along a rock ledge

The Ruta del Cares through the Cares Gorge is barely 6 ft. (2 m) wide, and clings to the mountainside, often high above the rushing river below. It's not a hike to take with small toddlers, but bigger children will enjoy the thrill, the wild goats, and the stunning views.

SERRA DE OUTES, GALICIA, SPAIN
395 Sleep in a treehouse

Every child wants to sleep in a treehouse, don't they? The thrill of climbing a ladder to get to bed and the treetops outside the window. At Cabanas do Barranco, the adults will love them too. The architecturally designed treehouses use recycled timber for their cladding, and all contain a jacuzzi.

ROUTES TO SANTIAGO DE COMPOSTELA, SPAIN
396 Join a pilgrimage route

Christians have been making the pilgrimage to Santiago de Compostela since the ninth century. It's a well-trodden path, with many beautiful sections and hostels along the way. Nowadays it attracts hikers as much as Christians, and children will love spotting other walkers, with their iconic scallop shells on their backpacks.

394 PICOS DE EUROPA

SAN SEBASTIÁN, SPAIN
397 Learn to make *pintxos*

Pintxos are to northern Spain what *tapas* are to
Barcelona—tiny bar-top snacks using the best local
ingredients. Cooking-class and food-tour company
Mimo offers *pintxos*-making courses for children
and adults, and you can be sure you'll be investing
in the cocktail sticks and recreating these
picturesque appetizers when you get home.

397 *PINTXOS*

BILBAO, SPAIN
398 Visit a Guggenheim gallery

Bilbao's Guggenheim revitalized the city when it
opened in 1997. Its distinctive, shiny, steel structure
sits right on the riverfront. There is a dog to
welcome you too—*Puppy*, an artwork by Jeff Koons
that's nearly 40 ft. (12 m) high and made out of
flowers. Children love him almost as much as they
love a soaking in the pavement fountains below.

FIGUERES, SPAIN
399 Wonder at the Dalí Theater-Museum

Like something from another world, the Dalí
Theater-Museum is a fanciful creation of Salvador
Dalí's design. Grab a ticket and explore the mind
of a true visionary. Labeled by some as mad, Dalí
was also considered a genius for his bizarre views
of form and function. Nothing in his art collection
is as it appears, bending reality when viewed from
different perspectives.

398 JEFF KOONS'S *PUPPY*

BARCELONA, SPAIN
400 Introduce your family to Gaudí

Architect and designer Antoni Gaudí brought so much joy and originality to his buildings that they really are like nothing else you see. Why have straight walls when they could be curved? Why use paint when you could cover surfaces with mosaics? Why play it safe when you could fill the world with color? There are several fabulous Gaudí houses, such as Casa Batlló and Casa Milà in Barcelona, which older children will enjoy. Younger children might prefer to run loose in Parc Güell, letting their hands trace the undulating curves of the 361 ft. (110 m) long mosaic bench around the central square, or playing hide-and-seek around the columns beneath it.

400 PARC GÜELL

BARCELONA, SPAIN
401 Eat your way through a food market

La Boquería market has been famously standing on Las Ramblas, in Barcelona, for nearly one thousand years, serving up delicious tastes for all to enjoy. Take your time as you walk through, sampling fresh fruit, baked goods, meats, cheeses, delicacies, and prepared meals. Collect your favorites for a picnic lunch in one of the city's gorgeous parks.

BARCELONA, SPAIN
402 Revel in quirkiness

From every angle, Antoni Gaudí's unfinished cathedral, the Sagrada Família, offers quirky features and unexpected details. Take the elevator up a tower for views over the city— and an up-close inspection of the eccentricities of the design. Or keep your feet on the ground and record your favorite parts in a sketchbook.

BARCELONA, SPAIN
403 Ride gondolas over the Old City

Enjoy the heights by hanging from gondola buckets over Barcelona's Old City as you take in the gorgeous view from beach to mountains. Heading up to the Montjuïc Castle, the gondolas offer a bird's eye view of the Sagrada Família, Las Ramblas, fortresses, parks, and more.

VALENCIA, SPAIN
404 Learn the lingo

Spending mornings in immersive language classes and afternoons exploring vibrant Valencia is a wonderful introduction to Spanish culture for kids aged four and up. Language schools across the city offer packages for families, and you can arrange to stay in a Valencian home to give your Spanish that extra push.

402 SAGRADA FAMÍLIA

SEGOVIA, SPAIN
405 Visit a real-life Disney castle

Every child knows what a Disney castle looks like, but here's something you might not know—Walt Disney didn't conjure the vision for this place out of his head. It's based on several real-life castles: including the superb Alcázar in Segovia, on Spain's central plateau. In its history, it has been a fortress, a royal palace, a prison, and a military academy, but it now offers an excellent day out for visitors.

JEREZ DE LA FRONTERA, SPAIN
406 Marvel at dancing horses

There's something spellbinding about the footwork of Andalusian horses. Watching the horses and riders of the world-renowned Royal Andalusian School of Equestrian Art perfect high-stepping routines while classical music plays in the background is like watching a ballet show.

TOLEDO, SPAIN
407 Be horrified by torture

The collection of medieval torture instruments at Toledo's Museum of Torture is not for the faint of heart. Dating from the infamous period of the Spanish Inquisition, they include such horrors as the interrogation seat with heated spikes, the thumb screw, and the barbed collar. It's educational but not for small children or anyone prone to nightmares.

SEVILLE, SPAIN
408 Learn to dance the flamenco

The passion and pageantry of flamenco comes alive in Seville, home to Spain's National Museum of Flamenco. Here there are flamenco shows daily on the hour, complete with stomping and clapping, colorful costumes, and soulful music. Guests are encouraged to dance along, and lessons can be arranged for groups or individual experiences.

405 SEGOVIA CASTLE

411 MINI HOLLYWOOD

LANJARÓN, SPAIN

409 Join a town-wide water fight

As part of the San Juan celebrations, at midnight on June 23 each year, the peaceful town of Lanjarón erupts into one massive water fight. Residents and visitors grab any receptacle they can and set about soaking each other. It's a rowdy event, so better for older children.

CARTAGENA, SPAIN

410 Get active at a sports resort

A sprawling family resort on Murcia's Iberian Peninsula, La Manga Club is heaven for sporty kids thanks to tennis, golf, and cricket clubs, and a top-class training program during spring and summer breaks. Sign your kids up for the Junior Football Academy and they'll work on their skills with FA- and UEFA-qualified coaches.

ALMERÍA, SPAIN

411 Recreate a Western

The wood-paneled buildings of Oasys MiniHollywood Theme Park started out as a film set for a Western film in the 1960s. Today, the buildings in the middle of the Tabernas Desert are part of a Western-styled theme park that recreates that Wild West feel with Western shows, cancan dancers, and movie theaters showing the classic movies of the genre.

412 WHITE VILLAGES

ANDALUCIA, SPAIN
412 Stroll between snow-white villages

This is hiking for children.
Easy trails wend gently
up and down the mountain
slopes and link searing-white
pueblos blancos (white villages).
There's lots of time for
refreshment pauses, and
quirky stores to poke around
in the villages, all with the
excitement of not quite
knowing what you'll find
around the corner.

ANDALUCIA, SPAIN
413 Safari in Doñana

Flamingos and lynx, great herds
of deer, and scuffling wild boar:
Doñana National Park is as close
as Europe gets to East Africa.
Take a thrilling jeep safari, or go
for a woodland walk and watch
your child's curiosity for the
natural world turn them into
a budding nature journalist.

IBIZA, SPAIN
414 Try a yoga retreat for mothers

Practice yoga and meditate to the
sound of birdsong at HolyMama,
a peaceful mother-and-child
retreat in Ibiza that's ideal for
single mothers. While you're
focusing on mind, body, and
bonding with your peers, your
kids can get creative under the
supervision of qualified nannies
and nursery teachers.

PORTO, PORTUGAL

415 Stride across Porto's Dom Luis I Bridge

You'll need a head for heights to walk across the 148 ft. (45 m) high, 564 ft. (172 m) long Dom Luis I Bridge that spans the Douro River, in the city of Porto. But the views along the river, which is lined by port distilleries, and across the multi-colored buildings of this hilly city will be enough to overcome any fears.

CASCAIS, PORTUGAL

416 Take a scenic cycle route

After a morning exploring Cascais's charming streets (and eating all the ice cream at the famous Santini's Gelati), go on a family bike ride to the picturesque Guincho Beach, with its towering cliffs and expansive dunes. The seaside cycle path is on flat ground, and at just thirty minutes from Cascais, it's perfect for a mini-adventure.

LISBON TO THE ALGARVE, PORTUGAL

417 Take a road trip from Lisbon to the Algarve

Take a road trip along the coast between Lisbon and the Algarve. Jump on the ferry from Setúbal to Troia (keeping your eyes open for leaping dolphins) before visiting the rice plantations of Alcacer do Sal. The landscapes change dramatically, from eucalyptus forests to the arid plains of Alentejo, and there's plenty of time for a dip along the way.

416 CYCLE FROM CASCAIS

PENICHE, PORTUGAL
418 Surf on a legendary coastline

Peniche, forty-five minutes' drive from Lisbon, is famous for some of the biggest waves in the world, the best-known being the break at Supertubos Beach. After watching the pros tackle these rollers, head to the far quieter shores of nearby Baleal Beach for a family surf course.

MALVEIRA, PORTUGAL
419 Learn how to make *pastéis de nata*

Get the whole family involved with a fun and authentic cookery class learning how to make the iconic Portuguese *pastéis de nata*. In Malveira, near Lisbon, you can join Chef João in his *pastelaria*, and learn the art of making these delicious delicacies with their crispy pastry and creamy custard filling. A popular skill to bring back home.

LISBON, PORTUGAL
420 Take a bus ride into the river

With the Hippotrip tour in Lisbon, kids will be rapt with attention as they wait for the moment that this bus becomes a boat. Halfway through your tour of the Portuguese capital, the driver splashes you straight into the Tagus River. No snorkels necessary though—it floats.

420 LISBON'S HIPPO BUS

LISBON, PORTUGAL
421 Ride a historic tram

Hold on tight as Lisbon's beloved Number 12 tram rattles and shakes its way up from the historic old town to St. George's Castle. Imagine yourselves as guards keeping watch from the battlements, then wander slowly down through the atmospheric, cobbled streets of Castelo and Alfama, two of Lisbon's oldest neighborhoods, custard tarts in hand.

SILVES, PORTUGAL
422 Feast at a medieval banquet

A storybook comes to life at the Silves Medieval Festival, held every August in this Moorish Algarve city. Cheer daring knights as they joust on horseback, be amazed as jugglers toss fiery torches, and enjoy the intoxicating aromas of roasted meat as a huge banquet fills the streets around the castle.

SAGRES, PORTUGAL
423 Stand at the end of the Earth

In days of old, Europeans believed that the cliffs around Sagres marked the end of the inhabited world. While that turned out not to be true, mainland Europe's southwestern tip is still an elemental place, where winds rattle in and mighty swells crash against the cliffs. Enough to inspire thoughts of exploration in anyone.

421 ST. GEORGE'S CASTLE

424 CAVE SPOTTING

ALGARVE COAST, PORTUGAL
424 Take a boat and go cave spotting

Not all family holidays in the Algarve stick to the beach. Lined with towering, golden cliffs, the coast of southern Portugal is easily explored by boat. As you sail the Algarve's warm waters, you can roam through sea caves and observe unique rock formations, do some snorkeling, and if you're lucky, spot a dolphin or two.

LAGOA, PORTUGAL
425 Be inspired by sand sculpture

Kids (and parents) can gain inspiration for their own beach masterpieces at Sand City sculpture park in Lagoa. Their spectacular sculptures, which recreate world-famous landmarks and celebrities, will blow you away with their artistry. For an extra treat, see Sand City by night, when the heat has subsided and the sculptures are beautifully illuminated.

SINTRA, PORTUGAL
426 Explore a fairy-tale castle

Imaginative young minds will be captivated by the landmarks of Sintra, just outside Lisbon. There are romantic royal palaces to explore, with stunning views across land and sea; Moorish castles; secret passageways perfect for playing hide-and-seek; deep wells where you can ponder mysterious symbols carved into the stone; and all of it surrounded by fragrant pine forest, where you can escape the crowds and cool off on peaceful hiking trails.

SISTELO, PORTUGAL
427 Walk among the trees in Sistelo

Little legs will enjoy a walk through this little-known gem of northern Portugal. Sistelo is a quaint mountain village that leads you to a fairyland of lush, mossy woodland, where you can wade through streams (or walk over the medieval bridges) and even enjoy some wild swimming under waterfalls. There are two official and very photogenic trails, ranging from an easy 1.2 mi. (2 km) circular walk, to a slightly longer route suitable for older kids.

AZORES, PORTUGAL
428 Get up close to dolphins

Swimming alongside dolphins in their underwater world is an unforgettable experience, and in the Azores archipelago, you can do so responsibly and on their terms. You'll be given the lowdown on dolphin behavior, before donning masks, snorkels, and taking the plunge. If you're lucky, you'll hear their squeaks, clicks, and whistles as they play around you. Confident swimmers aged eight and over can join in the fun.

426 SINTRA CASTLE

SARK, CHANNEL ISLANDS

429 Enjoy the simple life on car-free Sark

You'll feel as if you've gone back in time on the sleepy island of Sark. There are no cars here, only the odd tractor or horse-drawn carriage, so you're free to explore the woodland, beaches, and single village by bike or on foot. It's a magical, carefree adventure for kids.

ARGENTEUIL, FRANCE

430 Get an adrenaline hit with indoor skydiving

Don your jumpsuit, helmet, goggles, and earplugs, and make for the wind tunnel to enjoy all the thrills of skydiving—without having to jump out of a plane. Instructors teach first-time flyers how to move in the air at Aerokart's indoor skydiving center in Argenteuil, northwest of Paris.

430 INDOOR SKYDIVING

431 Sketch a masterpiece

To view the *Mona Lisa* is one thing, but what your children will really remember from a trip to the Louvre—other than the glass pyramid—is the family all sitting down and recreating their own versions. And remember, there's no wrong or right in art.

432 Try new foods and taste some snails

Snails, or *escargots* in French, can be an acquired taste. Kids are fascinated that people eat them, and it's fun to encourage them to try new foods. Cooked in melted butter, garlic, and herbs, *escargot* can be pulled from the shell and served with bread dipped into the butter mixture. A little bite of heaven.

433 Go underground at the Catacombs

You'll follow a spiral staircase deep underground to explore the Catacombs of Paris, a quarry-turned-subterranean mausoleum. Exhumed bones were laid to rest here in the eighteenth century after the cemeteries of Paris became too full, and today you can take a spine-tingling tour of the skull-and-bone-lined tunnels. Young kids and claustrophobics should probably sit this one out.

434 Climb the stairs of the Eiffel Tower

Few landmarks are quite as iconic as the Eiffel Tower—built by engineer Gustave Eiffel for the 1889 Exposition Universelle. This Paris beacon reaches a height of 984 ft. (300 m), and if you take the stairs (rather than the elevator) to the second floor, you enjoy unrivaled views of Paris from between the metal girders.

435 TUILERIES GARDEN

PARIS, FRANCE

435 Ride the carousel in Tuileries Garden

The carousel originated in seventeenth-century Renaissance Paris, and the merry-go-round in Tuileries Garden closely resembles some of the originals. Kids may not care about the history, but guaranteed they will love riding the ponies on this fanciful rendition. Nearby, kids can command small, motorized boats on a shallow pond while ducks and swans dodge out of the way.

PARIS, FRANCE

436 Gorge yourself on patisserie

The patisserie windows of Paris are a magnet for children, thanks to beautiful displays of cakes, éclairs, and pastries. Top of your hit list should be colorful macarons, classic fruit tarts, and Paris-Brest—choux pastry filled with praline cream. Or there's always the simple croissant, which at Laurent Duchêne in Butte aux Cailles is elevated to perfection.

PARIS, FRANCE

437 Take a ride on the Orient Express

The Venice Simplon-Orient-Express is billed as one of the most luxurious trains in the world. Some would say, "why take the children?" And the answer is because they will never forget the experience, which takes you back in time to the 1920s where "jeans are not suitable at any time," while taking you forward across the continent.

LOIRE VALLEY, FRANCE
438 Cycle through the Loire Valley

Head to the Loire Valley on a family cycling vacation and you can explore medieval towns, vineyards, and over three hundred fairy-tale châteaus via a network of back roads, forested paths, and riverside trails. The cycling paths are usually flat and traffic-free, so it's a top choice for family pedaling. Book an organized tour and you'll have your luggage transferred from hotel to hotel, so all you have to worry about is which château to see next.

THROUGHOUT FRANCE
439 Live like you're in a fairy tale

There are over six thousand châteaus in France. Hire one and you can swan about in your own personal kingdom, while the kids play knights and dragons in the grounds. You'll find everything from intimate castle keeps to sprawling, catered affairs complete with perks such as swimming pools, parkland, and even boating lakes.

LA ROCHELLE, FRANCE
440 Explore the deep seas, from on land

The first experience of La Rochelle's state-of-the-art aquarium is an elevator. But this is an elevator into the deep, and when you step out you're greeted by jellyfish appearing to ballet dance, great toothy sharks searching for a snack, and an entire mangrove swamp ecosystem. And it's all wrapped up in an environmental lesson.

438 LOIRE CHÂTEAU

441 LE GRAND ÉLÉPHANT

NANTES, FRANCE
441 Take a ride on a wooden elephant

At Les Machines de L'Île, Le Grand Éléphant is a majestic wooden elephant, engineered to move so smoothly it is as if the 26 ft. (8 m) high model has come to life. It's possible to take rides inside the elephant—which has a terrace on top and a lounge with French doors to a balcony. Ask nicely and it will even sound its trunk for you.

NOIRMOUTIER, FRANCE
442 Dig for shellfish

An island of salt marshes, sea pines, and grassy dunes, Noirmoutier is ideal for an old-school family holiday, with plenty of local traditions to get involved in. When the tide goes out, grab a bucket, net, and three-pronged trowel, and join the locals digging mussels, clams, shrimps, and cockles from the sand and rock pools.

LES EPESSES, FRANCE
443 Bring history to life

Bring the past to thundering, foot-stomping life at Puy du Fou, a huge historical theme park. It doesn't have rides, but it does have replicas of ancient cities, and a whole host of extravagant shows, complete with stunts and special effects. You'll see everything from marauding Vikings plundering a village to gladiators doing battle.

444 MARAIS POITEVIN

MARAIS POITEVIN, FRANCE

444 Boat through Green Venice

In June, when the trees are blooming with fresh green leaves and the mirror-still waters of the Marais Poitevin, a marshland in western France, has a carpet of water lilies spread over it, it can be hard to work out where land ends and water begins. As you steer a boat through this jungly environment you will understand why it's called Green Venice.

BONNAL, FRANCE

445 Sleep on a lake in a floating cabin

The cabins at Coucoo Grands Lacs, set on Lac de Bonnal in the Franche-Comté countryside, look as if they have been sculpted from nature, with pointy, thatched roofs, and little elf-like windows rising up from a floating platform in the middle of a lake. It's a magical, peaceful place to stay.

THROUGHOUT THE PYRENEES, FRANCE

446 Go on a horse-drawn caravan holiday

Slow down and appreciate the journey, not just the destination, as you travel along rural roads in a horse-drawn caravan; listen for brooks babbling beside you, and watch birds flit through the trees. Each evening, stop in a new village, with castles to see, rivers to swim in, and woods to explore.

MONTIGNAC, FRANCE

447 See paintings done in the Stone Age

Some seventeen thousand years ago, our ancestors crept into the caves of Lascaux, in the Dordogne, and painted scenes of daily life. Today, the handiwork of these early artists is considered one of the planet's greatest collections of prehistoric art, and the stunning depictions of the creatures that once haunted this now-gentle land are a source of wonder for children of all ages.

ARDÈCHE, FRANCE

448 Befriend a donkey

A loveable donkey is a fantastic companion as you cross the forests and valleys of the Ardèche, on a weeklong walking holiday with a donkey arranged by Safran Tours. The kids can brush its coat and feed it hay, and it can even help carry some of your kit. Accommodation is in traditional guesthouses—complete with donkey-friendly stables, of course.

GARD, FRANCE

449 Canoe under the Pont du Gard

With three tiers of arches, the Pont du Gard is an impressive aqueduct by any measure, but the fact that it has been standing since the Romans built it almost two thousand years ago is mesmerizing. Hire canoes and paddle your way under the 160 ft. (49 m) high bridge, it's quite phenomenal looking up from water level.

PROVENCE, FRANCE

450 Take a road trip through fields of lavender

Teenage children who have discovered Marcel Pagnol's books and films, such as *Jean de Florette* or *Manon des sources*, will love a road trip through Provence, where they can immerse themselves in his world. Explore terracotta-roofed, hilltop villages, drive through fields of lavender and sunflowers, and be sure to stop and chat with people, and learn about the local customs which so inspired Pagnol.

CASTELLANE, FRANCE

Paddleboard on a turquoise lake

An alpine breeze comes down the valley to bring a freshness and purity to the air on Lake Castillon. Formed by a dam across the gorge—which doubles as one of the world's largest sundials—this turquoise lake in the heart of the Verdon Regional Natural Park is a perfect spot for a paddleboard. Let the children use one for diving practice while you peacefully explore the lake's perimeter.

450 PROVENCE

TOULOUSE, FRANCE

452 Visit space—on Earth

The exhibitions and interactive displays at Cité de l'Espace (Space City) have been designed with children firmly in mind. Everything is truly hands-on, with opportunities to control a rocket launch pad; create and film weather reports; and carry out tasks faced by astronauts in a life-size reconstruction of the cockpit of a lunar module. It's not just reconstructions though: out in the gardens, discover real-life spacecraft too.

454 FLAMINGOS IN THE CAMARGUE

GOURETTE, FRANCE
453 Sleep in an igloo

Sleeping out in nature is one of the most rewarding things you can do as a family. In the beautiful French Pyrenees, with the help of L'Aventure Nordique, you can take your adventure-loving children out into a snowy winter landscape to sleep in an igloo. If snow conditions are right, they'll also teach you how to build one.

CAMARGUE, FRANCE
454 Spot flocks of flamingos

If your children enjoy feeding ducks in the park, then imagine what they will think when they see flocks of wild flamingos in the salt marshes of the Camargue, in southern France. The pink comics of the bird world are easy to spot here, and the totally flat landscape also makes for nice, easy walking.

CORSICA, FRANCE
455 Snorkel in Europe's Caribbean equivalent

Slide on a mask and snorkel, and slip into the warm, limpid waters off the Îles Lavezzi, a small, uninhabited archipelago hanging between Corsica and Sardinia. The water is crystal clear and full of huge shoals of fish who are so used to snorkelers they'll swim right up to you.

456 MINIATUR WUNDERLAND

HAMBURG, GERMANY

456 Feel like a giant at Miniatur Wunderland

When you're young, it can sometimes seem as if grown-ups are giants. At Miniatur Wunderland, kids can enjoy the feeling of towering over adults at this home to the world's largest model railway, as well as intricate working models of an airport, a motorway system, and a busy port. This unique German theme park is not just a fascinating introduction to the world of transportation, but also a testament to the power of the imagination.

FRIEDRICHSHAFEN, GERMANY

457 Take an extraordinary sightseeing flight

Travel up, up, and away aboard a zeppelin from the lakeside city of Friedrichshafen, as an icon of the golden age of aviation is combined with state-of-the-art technology for a thrilling—and completely unique—sightseeing flight over southern Germany. Just fourteen passengers can sit in the zeppelin's gondola, beneath a vast balloon filled with helium, so everyone gets a window seat with spectacular views. Sail gently through the skies at 44 mph (70 km/h) and enjoy a completely different experience to a plane flight.

BERLIN, GERMANY

458 Admire the artworks on a piece of history

Inspire creative kids with a wander around one of Europe's most unusual—and historically important—open-air art galleries. The East Side Gallery memorial in Berlin is a collection of over one hundred colorful murals, painted by international artists on the longest-surviving stretch of the Berlin Wall. Walking or cycling past iconic works such as Dmitri Vrubel's *Fraternal Kiss*, or Thierry Noir's *Homage to the Young Generation*, is a great way to educate older kids about the story behind the wall, and spark conversations around what they may be learning in school. And, of course, to admire one of the world's great monuments to peace, hope, and reconciliation.

MUNICH, GERMANY

459 Enjoy the best of the wurst in Munich

What's the difference between a *weisswurst*, a *stockwurst*, a *milzwurst*, and a *wollwurst*? Find out in the tastiest possible way by sampling the various types of *bratwurst*, or sausage, the classic Munich street food that is available at stalls, cafés, and restaurants around the Bavarian capital. While you may find that everyone has their own favorite, one thing's for sure: you'll never again be satisfied with a regular hot dog.

458 BERLIN WALL

KRÜN, GERMANY
460 Take a family wellness break

Both kids and grown-ups can find their zen at Schloss Elmau, a wellness retreat high up in the Bavarian Alps. You can have treatments in the family spa, swim in a pool with a mountain backdrop, and go on bracing forest walks. There are babysitters and creative clubs on hand should you want some adult-only downtime.

PFRONTEN, GERMANY
461 Spend the night in a tree

If you're eight or older, you can sleep on a wooden platform high up in the trees at Waldseilgarten Hoellschlucht adventure park. But first, you'll have to swing through the branches to get there. Once you do, you'll crawl into a sleeping bag and drift off to sleep—safely secured with a belt and rope.

KRAUSNICK, GERMANY
462 Splash about at a giant indoor waterpark

No matter how cold it is outside, you'll feel balmy at Tropical Islands Resort. The largest indoor waterpark in the world, it's set inside a huge former airship hangar and has an impressive selection of over-the-top amenities, including a mini rain forest, a beach, a lagoon, a lazy river, and plenty of waterslides. If this is all a little overwhelming, there are smaller (and quieter) play areas for toddlers and young children.

461 SLEEP IN THE TREES

462 WORLD'S BIGGEST INDOOR WATERPARK

BAVARIA, GERMANY

463 Hit the Bavarian slopes

Winter sports don't have to be expensive, and you don't need fancy
equipment either. All you need is a sled, a slope, and a healthy covering
of snow. Plenty of Bavaria's upscale winter resorts have toboggan runs
alongside their ski and snowboard slopes, and sleds are easy and cheap to
hire. Be aware that this isn't like sledding in the local park. These toboggan
runs cover serious mileage, with many reached by chairlift. In the resort of
Bad Hindelang, a 1.8 mi. (3 km) slope winds through a forest; at Zugspitze,
a steep trail allows you to pick up some serious speed; or try Spitzingsee,
where there's a gentle option for newbies and young children, which is
illuminated after dark in case you fancy some nighttime action.

466 PARAGLIDING FROM MÜRREN

MONTHEY, SWITZERLAND
464 Soak up mountain views at an eco-hotel

You'll sleep in a canvas dome complete with a mezzanine sleeping bunk for kids at Whitepod, a back-to-nature resort in the Swiss Alps. You can stare at dramatic mountains (and nighttime starry skies) from the comfort of your own bed, then head outside for snowshoeing, snow-scooting, or whizzing down the private ski slopes.

NENDAZ, SWITZERLAND
465 Explore the Alps by mountain bike

With four valleys, twelve itineraries, 124 mi. (200 km) of trails, and numerous lifts equipped to carry bikes, Nendaz is the ideal spot for family mountain biking. There are trails for experienced riders to beginners, and even one route that is all downhill—perfect for little legs. All surrounded by stunning mountain scenery.

MÜRREN, SWITZERLAND
466 Take the kids paragliding

It doesn't get any closer to the feeling of flying than paragliding over a beautiful Swiss valley. Children as young as five and grandparents as old as 105 can be strapped to a pilot for a tandem paraglide with Airtime Paragliding. Drift over the valley suspended beneath the large glider (like a big kite), enjoying the peace and the view below.

469 ALPINE PLAYGROUND

GRUYÈRES, SWITZERLAND
467 Visit a cheese dairy

Over 160 cheese dairies in
Gruyères follow age-old practices
that have been handed down
from generation to generation
to turn milk into cheese wheels.
Dairy tours shed light on the
cheese-making process, with
interactive displays, the chance
to watch expert cheese makers
at work, and tastings to sample
Gruyère at different stages of
the maturation process.

LES REUSSILLES, SWITZERLAND
468 Hike with a husky

Can't decide between
snowshoeing and dogsledding?
If your kids are aged six or older
you can combine the two and
walk with a husky along alpine
trails. Sign up with Vent du
Nord and you'll don snowshoes
and a waist belt, before attaching
yourself to a loveable sled dog.
Or drop the snowshoes and go
in summer for walks through
beautiful wildflower meadows.

SWISS ALPS, SWITZERLAND
469 Check out awesome playgrounds

The Swiss Alps aren't just about
snowcapped peaks and hiking
trails. They also have incredible
playgrounds. Try out the Brunni
Playground & Waterworld, which
has slides, climbing frames, and
water play; Allmendhübel
Flower Park, which has tunnels
and pretend cheese stores; or
Männlichen Alpine Playground,
home to a giant cow complete
with a slide for a tongue.

LUCERNE TO LUGANO, SWITZERLAND
470 Take the Alps's most panoramic train journey

The Gotthard Panorama Express combines boat and rail travel, with local culinary specialities served along the way to tantalize the taste buds. From Lucerne, a steamboat glides across Lake Lucerne to Flüelen, where passengers board a panoramic train that travels through alpine scenery in a southerly direction toward Ticino, where warmer Mediterranean climes await.

ENGELBERG, SWITZERLAND
471 Take part in a treasure hunt

Swiss cartoon characters Globi and Globine invite children to take part in a treasure hunt in a delightful alpine setting. Armed with a map, children have to find eleven treasure chests, each hiding a question, with the correct answers spelling the solution. There are two routes to choose from, with prizes at the end.

GRINDELWALD, SWITZERLAND
472 Walk into thin air

Wrapped around the cliffside of First Mountain
(7,165 ft.; 2,184 m), the Grindelwald cliff walk is an
elevated metal walkway complete with suspension
bridge. It's suitable for all ages, although if you're
afraid of heights, you may find yourself gingerly
tottering toward the ledge, which stretches 148 ft.
(45 m) out into the void.

THUNERSEE, SWITZERLAND
473 Swim in a mountain lake

Many Swiss children spend long summer days at
the lake, swimming in pristine waters and lazing
on grassy beaches. If you want to join them, the
Bernese Alps is a great place to start. Try
Thunersee, the shores of which are dotted with
pretty towns and family-friendly swimming
beaches; or Seebodensee, a turquoise lake in
the shadow of Stein Glacier.

472 GRINDELWALD CLIFF WALK

THURGAU, SWITZERLAND
474 Cycle through apple orchards

Eastern Switzerland has many apple orchards, and tracing a cycle route through them on quiet country roads and car-free paths is a beautiful way to see the countryside. In spring there's blossom, in fall there are apples that you can taste at the different farms along the way. The Altnau Apple Trail can be incorporated into a longer route, and has information panels with puzzles and jokes. Don't leave without eating apple fritters.

KILCHBERG, SWITZERLAND
475 Learn about the history of chocolate

The Lindt Home of Chocolate offers interactive chocolate tours, along with fun courses to learn how to craft the country's most famous sweet creations. The museum sheds light on the chocolate-making process, from cocoa harvesting to transforming cocoa beans into the irresistible finished product. Little ones will love stocking up on sweet delights at the store, the largest Lindt chocolate shop in the world. Heaven.

TOGGENBURG, SWITZERLAND
476 Follow the Toggenburg Sound Trail

The Toggenburg Sound Trail is a cultural experience that brings together local musical traditions with Switzerland's alpine landscapes. The 5 mi. (7.5 km) route (which can be split into smaller sections) is dotted with twenty-six sound stations, where little ones can take part in fun, interactive musical activities, listening and recognizing different sounds surrounded by stunning scenery.

CHURWALDEN, SWITZERLAND
477 Hurtle down a toboggan run

Swooshing down to the valley in a series of twists and turns, this toboggan run on rails is Switzerland's longest, with a length of 1.8 mi. (3 km). Sit back on the chairlift and soak up alpine views to reach the start of the run, then hop into your toboggan and pelt down the mountainside, reaching speeds of up to 25 mph (40 km/h)—there are brake levers to adjust your speed.

475 LINDT CHOCOLATE MAKING

477 TOBOGGAN ON RAILS

SWISS ALPS, SWITZERLAND
478 Breathe in the alpine air

Scores of gorgeous alpine trails crisscross the Swiss Alps, meandering through shaded woodland and open meadows, where cows graze on rich pastures, the chiming of cattle bells ringing throughout the valley. Themed hiking trails abound, with adventure playgrounds dotting routes. The air is gorgeously fresh. Stock up on local delicacies including sausages, cheeses, and cold cuts sourced from local farms, and refuel with a picnic en route as you soak up the alpine scenery. Enjoy just spending your days outside.

THROUGHOUT EUROPE
479 Take the family interrailing

Crossing Europe with an Interrail Pass in hand is a rite of passage for many students. It's also a fantastic way for adventurous families to explore several European countries in one trip. Kids will love poring over maps and planning the journey; and you can travel as little or as much as you want depending on the age and stamina of your brood. Once the trip gets going, the romance and excitement of train travel takes over as you rumble along between historic cities, beaches, and mountains, with large picture windows to take in the views. Throw in the odd night on a sleeper train complete with pull-down bunks, hot showers, and breakfast delivery, and you've got a family vacation of dreams.

478 SWISS ALPS

480 MONT BLANC

481 CYCLE IN THE ALPS

COURMAYEUR, ITALY
480 Ride a cable car to a mountain top

The revolving floor-to-ceiling glass cabins of the futuristic Mont Blanc cable car whisk passengers up to a height of 11,370 ft. (3,466 m), where they are rewarded with wraparound vistas of the highest peaks in the Alps, stretching from Mont Blanc and Monte Rosa to the Matterhorn and the Gran Paradiso. Connecting the ski resort of Courmayeur to Punta Helbronner, the cable car takes passengers close to the summit of Mont Blanc, home to alpine trails and off-piste skiing routes.

SALZBURG TO GRADO, ITALY
481 Cycle along shaded alpine paths

Stretching a whopping 258 mi. (415 km) from Salzburg to Grado, in northeastern Italy, the delightful Ciclovia Alpe-Adria Radweg cycling route offers thirty hours of leisurely cycling passing through gorgeous alpine scenery and traditional villages bursting with history. There are child-friendly sights aplenty to visit on the route, including a water park, panoramic cable car, and the world's biggest ice cave, Eisriesenwelt.

AOSTA, ITALY
482 Float above the Alps in a hot-air balloon

The landlocked region of Valle d'Aosta, in northwestern Italy, is home to some of Italy's highest peaks, not least Mont Blanc, Europe's highest mountain. Hot-air balloon rides are a thrilling way for older children and teenagers to take in glorious alpine vistas as they float amid snowy peaks at a height of over 6,500 ft. (2,000 m).

TRENTINO-ALTO ADIGE, ITALY
483 Climb a mountain using ladders and cables

The Dolomites are peppered with *vie ferrate*, mountain routes fixed with steel cables, ladders, and bridges to make the mountains accessible to walkers. There are *vie ferrate* suitable for all levels, making them perfect for young outdoor explorers. Older kids will love the thrill of the more challenging routes, with zip lines, vertical steps, and iron ladders crossing rocky ravines.

VERNANTE, ITALY
484 Spot 150 murals of Pinocchio

The small mountain village of Vernante celebrates Italian cartoonist Attilio Mussino, who illustrated the first color edition of Carlo Collodi's *Pinocchio*. Over 150 murals depicting scenes from the story of Italy's famous wooden puppet adorn the facades of buildings, and there's even a museum in the town dedicated to the illustrator's life.

483 CLIMB A *VIA FERRATA*

LAKE MAGGIORE, ITALY
485 Visit Europe's largest toy museum

On Lake Maggiore's southeastern shore sits the eleventh-century Rocca di Angera, which houses Europe's largest museum of dolls and toys. On display are over one thousand dolls dating from the eighteenth century to the present day, with a wonderful selection of wooden toys, furniture items, and toy automatons.

LAKE GARDA, ITALY
486 Soak up lake views that inspired poets

Italy's largest lake, Lake Garda has a hugely diverse topography, with rocky cliffs plunging into deep-blue waters to the north, slowly morphing into gentle rolling hills carpeted in olive groves and vineyards as you travel south. The lake has long been a source of inspiration to artists, writers, and intellectuals, who flock here to soak up its natural beauty. German poet Johann Wolfgang von Goethe spent time traveling through, writing about, and sketching the area (he was even briefly imprisoned in Malcesine), while D.H. Lawrence sought solace in the tranquil lakefront town of Gargnano during the winter of 1912, in the company of his partner Frieda.

486 LAKE GARDA

SGONICO, ITALY

487 Marvel at a huge, underground chamber

The huge, underground chamber of the Grotta Gigante is an awe-inspiring sight, with glistening, creamy stalactites and stalagmites, and a ceiling reaching a whopping 330 ft. (100 m) in height. Rock formations merge to create incredible spectacles, and tunnels reveal smaller openings here and there. A walkway leads visitors around the cave, with tours shedding light on its historical and geographical features.

SISTIANA, ITALY

488 Be a shepherd for a morning

Through Trieste Green, take the opportunity to join shepherd Antonič for a morning as he looks after his flock of two hundred sheep, taking them out to pasture on Mount Hermada, where they graze on the Karst terrain. It's an easy walk for children along a dirt track to join the grazing sheep, revealing what life is like as a shepherd. At the end of the experience, participants can sample goat's cheese produced on the farm.

GROPPARELLO, ITALY

489 Press grapes with your bare feet

Crushing grapes with bare feet is an ancient wine-making practice that dates back thousands of years. Little ones will love getting messy as they stomp and jump in a wooden barrel, feeling plump grapes squidging through their toes at the Castello di Gropparello.

490 ROW IN VENICE

491 BROWN BEARS

VENICE, ITALY

490 Learn how to row Venetian style

Rowing a *batela*, a traditional Venetian watercraft, requires dexterity and much skill—and it's no easy feat. Nonprofit organization Row Venice sees expert *vogatrici* (oarswomen) teach their craft, taking visitors along the city's little-known waterways in handcrafted wooden *batelline* to experience the region's culture and traditions.

CENTRAL APENNINES, ITALY

491 Search for Italy's "Big Five"

The central Apennines are all about dramatic scenery, from rugged mountains to thick, beech forest. But they're also home to Italy's "Big Five": brown bears, wolves, deer, wild boar, and the Apennine chamois. Companies such as Rewilding Europe Travel will connect you with a nature guide, who'll help you get up close to these animals both safely and sensitively.

SIENA, ITALY

492 Stargaze from a private observatory

Tuscany was once home to famed astronomer Galileo, and you can follow in his stargazing footsteps at Villa Fassio, a thirteenth-century farmhouse that comes complete with its own rooftop observatory. Hire the services of a local astronomer to talk your kids through the wonders of the Tuscan night skies.

493 GENOA'S AQUARIUM

494 PESTO MAKING

GENOA, ITALY

493 Sleep with sharks at Genoa's aquarium

Snoozing in the company of sharks may not be everyone's idea of fun, but the Aquarium of Genoa offers just that—the chance to sleep by the tanks of these feared fish to observe their nocturnal behavior. Available for children aged seven to eleven, the experience includes a guided night tour, when kids learn all about the marine world at night, before slipping into their sleeping bags. The adventure ends in the morning with breakfast, and the chance to observe the fish as the day gets underway.

GENOA, ITALY

494 Learn how to make fresh pesto

The maritime city of Genoa is the home of pesto, Italy's celebrated pasta sauce made with crushed basil, garlic, pine nuts, Parmesan, Pecorino cheese, salt, and olive oil. An experienced chef teaches budding young cooks how to make the sauce, using a mortar and pestle to pound the garlic and basil into a paste. Children also learn how to make pasta dough during hands-on cooking classes, and get to tuck into their home-cooked delights at the end of the session.

BOLOGNA, ITALY
495 Make your own gelato

Bologna is Italy's foodie capital, and the city's Gelato Museum is one of the best places to learn how to make ice cream. Following a guided tour of the museum, children take part in a hands-on workshop, where they learn how to make gelato following age-old recipes. The experience, of course, includes a fun ice-cream tasting session.

SIENA, ITALY
496 Experience the Palio di Siena

The atmosphere alone is worth the experience for the historic Palio di Siena. Every inch of the city's central square is full of spectators, with more leaning off the balconies above. The race, three laps of the square, is between ten horses representing the city's different areas—*contrade*—and lasts for about one minute.

UMBRIA, ITALY
497 White-water raft in Italy's green heart

The landlocked region of Umbria is characterized by rolling hills, valleys, woods, and rushing rivers that provide the perfect white-water rafting opportunities. Strap on your lifejacket and helmet, and hop onto your raft to rush down the gentle rapids of the Nera River as you soak up the glorious scenery of this region, dubbed "the green heart of Italy."

495 GELATO WORKSHOP

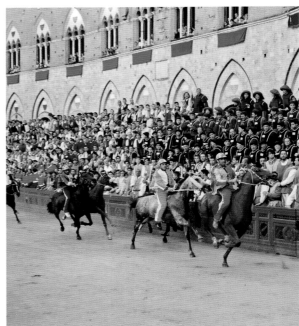

496 SIENA'S PALIO

ROME, ITALY

498 Enroll at gladiator school

You'll feel the power and drama of ancient Rome as you wander around the iconic Colosseum. And you can bring the past roaring back to life with a day at Gladiator School. In the grounds of this two thousand-year-old stadium, you can dress up in Roman costume, attend a combat class, learn how to use a replica sword and shield, and even take on rival families in an epic gladiatorial battle.

NAPLES, ITALY

499 Eat pizza on the streets of Naples

Naples is celebrated for its exquisite street food, catering to those on the go, with scores of *friggitorie* (shops selling deep-fried foods) peppered around the city. As well as deep-fried fish, seafood, and vegetables, there's *pizza a portafoglio*, loosely translated as "wallet pizza," a street-food version of Margherita pizza: fold the sloppy slice in two and satisfy your cravings as you get lost in the city's narrow alleyways.

498 ROME'S COLOSSEUM

500 POMPEII

POMPEII, ITALY

500 Walk through the ruins of Pompeii

It's spooky to think about what happened to the great city of Pompeii when Mount Vesuvius erupted, and covered the city and its inhabitants with ash. Excavated and reborn for visitors to explore, Pompeii is both a somber and fascinating example of everyday life almost two thousand years ago. Walk streets from the year 79 C.E. and imagine life back then, as spectators headed to watch chariot races at the amphitheater, or over to the theater to watch a play. Stone buildings such as fast-food restaurants, residences, baths, and even brothels have been uncovered, along with the ash-encased bodies of people and pets who did not make it. Intricately designed tiles, pottery, and many other treasures continue to be discovered here.

ALBEROBELLO, ITALY

501 Visit a fairy town

Trulli are drystone houses with conical roofs, mainly found in the Itria Valley, in Puglia. The town of Alberobello is famous for them. There's no evidence to link trulli to fairies—the more common explanation links them to tax avoidance as they could be rapidly dismantled—but fairies would approve of their low doorways and pointy roofs.

501 TRULLI IN PUGLIA

503 SNORKELING

SARDINIA, ITALY
502 Enjoy a coastal hike to a secluded cove

Sardinia is famed for its spectacular, white-sand beaches, not least its gorgeous *cale*—secluded, rocky coves that are only accessible on foot or by boat. Hike through endemic vegetation following a pathway that snakes down the cliffside and you'll be rewarded with spectacular views, and the chance to frolic in turquoise seas.

SARDINIA, ITALY
503 Snorkel in Sardinia's crystal-clear waters

With nearly 1,200 mi. (2,000 km) of coastline, Sardinia offers no shortage of snorkeling spots. Its natural reserves teem with marine life, with starfish, sea urchins, crabs, and schools of fish darting through azure waters. There are plenty of shallow beaches that are perfect for children to experience the underwater world for the first time.

MOUNT ETNA, SICILY
504 Hike the slopes of Mount Etna

The gentle slopes of Mount Etna provide perfect hiking opportunities. Down low there are prickly pear orchards and pistachio plantations; as you climb higher you reach barren volcanic landscapes, sometimes still warm underfoot from past eruptions. Children can hop on the back of a donkey if their legs aren't up for the walk.

TAORMINA, SICILY
505 Eat freshly made cannoli

Cannoli are one of the joys of Sicily; a sweet, crunchy, fried-pastry casing with lemon-tinged ricotta oozing from its ends. For the freshest on offer, buy them where they fill them to order, such as at Laboratorio Pasticceria Roberto, and then eat them without delay.

ST. JULIAN'S, MALTA
506 Go on a single-parent adventure

Join a group vacation for single-parent families, organized by Acorn Family Holidays, and you'll find yourself zip-lining, hiking, and sea kayaking along Malta's craggy Mediterranean coastline. Your kids will have instant playmates, and you'll have free babysitting, plus the support of other like-minded parents—so it's a win for all involved.

504 HIKE MOUNT ETNA

505 CANNOLI

507 CHARLES BRIDGE

508 JOHN LENNON WALL

PRAGUE, CZECH REPUBLIC

507 Make a wish on the Charles Bridge

Stroll along this medieval bridge dotted with the statues of kings and martyrs, while listening to street performers playing classical music. Challenge the family to make a wish at the statue of St. John of Nepomuk, by placing a finger on each of the five stars engraved on the plaque below his likeness.

PRAGUE, CZECH REPUBLIC

508 Add your artwork to the John Lennon Wall

Bring your sidewalk chalk and add to the panorama of this famous wall in Prague. Colorful, visually impressive, and moving, the John Lennon Wall in Prague is a great place to explore your creativity. Covered with graffiti and intended to promote peace and love, the wall makes for a lovely photo backdrop too.

PRAGUE, CZECH REPUBLIC

509 Make marionettes in their spiritual home

You'll be blown away by a marionette performance at Prague's National Marionette Theater, but to get really involved, join one of the theater's special workshops. Under instruction from an expert marionette artist, you'll be shown how to make your own puppet.

WAIDRING, AUSTRIA
510 Follow the Triassic Trail

Walk the length of the 2.5 mi. (4 km) Triassic Trail around Steinplatte Mountain and it's easy to imagine a time when it lay under the ancient Tethys Ocean. Along the route there are fossils to uncover, riddles to solve, and a clutch of life-size dinosaur models, who make an arresting sight against the dramatic, mountainous backdrop.

VIENNA, AUSTRIA
511 Sample Vienna's famous Sachertorte

Dreamed up in 1832 for local royalty, Sachertorte is a dark-chocolate cake with a glossy chocolate coating, sandwiched with apricot jam. Finding the best place to sample this Viennese icon is a challenge that most children are up for, and elegant old stalwarts Café Sacher and Café Central should be top of your list.

VIENNA, AUSTRIA
512 Take horse lovers to riding school

With its famous Lipizzan white stallions, and a riding hall in a palace, Vienna's Spanish Riding School is quite an experience. You can watch a training session as handlers take younger horses through their paces, or take in a full-blown classic show that includes breathtaking horse ballet: it's inspirational.

TYROL, AUSTRIA

513 Go skiing in family-friendly Serfaus Fiss Ladis

Although there are many great resorts for a family-friendly skiing holiday, Serfaus Fiss Ladis goes out of its way to make its child-friendly philosophy stand out. There are dedicated children's slopes, lessons that burst into dance, trails that lead you past giant, wooden creatures, lift facilities that are child-appropriate, plus endless activities off the slopes too, such as soft play and climbing walls.

513 SERFAUS FISS LADIS

SALZBURG, AUSTRIA

514 Explore Salzburg with *The Sound of Music*

If your kids don't know about the von Trapps, they soon will after a joyful guided *Sound of Music* tour of Salzburg and its surrounds. You'll hop from mansions and palaces to gardens on a colorful, themed bus, listening to the movie's soundtrack as you go. Singing along is strongly encouraged.

CARINTHIA, AUSTRIA

515 Kick back at a kid-friendly hotel

The Babyhotel makes it very clear that children are more than welcome. There are bright color schemes, a giant kangaroo mascot, a toddler playroom next to the restaurant, spacious rooms with bunk beds and proper cribs, and hours of free childcare. So you can sit back, relax, and let your children be themselves without upsetting any other hotel guests.

518 POSTOJNA CAVE

POHORJE, SLOVENIA
516 Toboggan in the summertime

Is there a more fun way to get down a mountain than the PohorJet? Imagine a bobsled combined with a personal monorail and you're on the right track. Under-sevens can ride the sled with an adult and enjoy all the adrenaline of sledding down a mountain—without the snow.

SOČA VALLEY, SLOVENIA
517 Explore World War I Walks of Peace

It's quite humbling to see where soldiers lived and fought high up in the mountains of the Soča Valley, where as many as one million men lost their lives in World War I. There are five Walks of Peace trails, which lead you past forts and battlements telling the story of the war.

POSTOJNA, SLOVENIA
518 Visit the largest cave in Europe

At two million years old, Postojna Cave is the largest show cave in Europe. Kids will love the electric train here, which winds through its mighty caverns and halls, past a spectacular collection of stalactites and stalagmites. Who can make the best echo?

MOTOVUN, CROATIA
519 Hunt for truffles

The fairy-tale, medieval town of Motovun is surrounded by thick forests. And in those forests are some of northern Croatia's greatest treasures —black and white truffles. The strong, earthy flavor may be an acquired taste, but kids will love the thrill of the truffle hunt. Take to the woods with a guide and a group of specially trained dogs as they sniff out these underground treasures.

KRKA NATIONAL PARK, CROATIA
520 Swim underneath a waterfall

As the Krka and Čikola Rivers meet in the lush forests of Krka National Park, they tumble over travertine rocks creating a beautiful array of seventeen waterfalls as they do so. The deep, emerald-green pools beneath the waterfalls are fresh and inviting. So jump in and swim under the falls, feeling the power of nature raining down on you as you do so.

520 KRKA NATIONAL PARK

PLITVICE NATIONAL PARK,
CROATIA
521 Wonder at the Plitvice waterfalls

Like a panorama drawn from
a fantasy novel, Plitvice National
Park is home to no fewer than
ninety waterfalls and sixteen
cascading lakes, all connected
with a handy network of wooden
boardwalks and hiking trails.
Kids will love exploring these
magical trails, on terrain that
isn't ever very challenging.

HVAR, CROATIA
522 Take a ride on a speedboat

Hvar has the perfect harbor for
an evening stroll with loads of
swish boats moored up here.
Take it one step further than just
looking and hire a speedboat for
yourselves. Zip across the waves
enjoying a new perspective on
the land, and discover hidden
gems of bays and beaches that
can only be reached by boat.

HVAR, CROATIA
523 Try squid ink risotto

Even the pickiest of young
appetites will be intrigued by
a plate of black rice set in front
of them, while adults and older
children will be delighted by
a Croatian delicacy genuinely
made with squid ink. Often
paired with seafood, this
flavorsome dish is best devoured
while perched on a restaurant
table by the sea.

DUBROVNIK, CROATIA
524 Walk the ancient walls of Dubrovnik

Climb the steep stairs to walk the
tops of Dubrovnik's ancient city
walls, built hundreds of years ago
to protect the oceanfront city
from invaders. Today, the walls
provide impressive views of the
city, mountains, and sea, while
providing a glimpse into the
Middle Ages during times of
war and peace. Walk through
battlements, turrets, and fortresses
built into the walls, with plenty
of opportunities to envision how
soldiers defended this gated city.
For *Game of Thrones* fans, many
scenes were filmed here.

524 DUBROVNIK

LAKE SKADAR, MONTENEGRO
530 Kayak on Lake Skadar

Kayaking the wild, vast expanses of Lake Skadar is balm for the soul. Paddle through pristine waters to reach hidden, freshwater beaches, ancient island monasteries, and carpets of water lilies, while looking out for the incredible birds and reptiles that make this area their home. As long as you can wield a paddle, you're old enough to join in.

MRAMOR, KOSOVO
531 Visit a bear sanctuary

The Bear Sanctuary provides a near-natural home for bears that have been rescued from captivity. The bears are brought back to health and allowed to live in spacious surroundings. You can learn all about bear conservation, hear the animals' individual stories, and see the bears in their huge, wooded enclosures on a walking tour.

BUTRINT, ALBANIA
532 Explore a forgotten Greek city

Send the children off to look for treasure or ghosts among the forest-dappled, peaceful, and little-visited remains of the ancient Greek city of Butrint, in southern Albania. It's one of Europe's finest archeological sites, but also comes with the bonus of quiet, nearby beaches where your kids can build sandcastle recreations of the ruins.

SLOVENIA TO BOSNIA AND HERZEGOVINA
533 Trundle through the Balkans by train

For an adventurous, multi-country journey with older children, take to the rails across the Balkans, where a string of fascinating yet underrated countries await. Kicking things off in the riverside Slovenian capital of Ljubljana, you'll roll past beaches, lakes, and crumbling castles and explore cities including Sarajevo, Zagreb, and Mostar. You'll also pass along the Bar to Belgrade line, which goes high up through the mountains and over the breathtaking Mala Rijeka Viaduct, one of the highest railway bridges in the world. Travel on a tour with Explore Worldwide and you'll have a local guide on hand to give you the lowdown on local cultures and explain the recent turbulent history of this fascinating region.

531 BEAR SANCTUARY

THROUGHOUT LATVIA
534 Celebrate the summer solstice

Latvians go all out for Jāņi—a pagan tradition and celebration of the summer solstice that takes place on June 24. Join the locals and head out to the countryside, where the challenge is to stay up all night for the rising sun—one that most children will gratefully accept. Wearing flower crowns and oak-leaf wreaths is de rigueur, as is picking wildflowers, eating cheese, and singing medieval songs around the fire.

WROCŁAW, POLAND
535 Hunt for dwarfs in Wrocław

A riverside city crammed full of Renaissance mansions, Wrocław is Poland's answer to Venice. But it's also a prime location for spotting pint-sized, bronze statues of dwarfs. There are hundreds spread across town, riding tiny bikes, hailing cabs, and even washing clothes in the river, and kids will love counting how many they can spot. They may be cute, but they also symbolize a time when street art was used as resistance against Soviet rule.

534 SUMMER SOLSTICE

ŻYWKOWO, POLAND
536 Visit a village full of storks

For weird and wonderful wildlife-watching, head
toward the Russian border in northern Poland,
where the tiny village of Żywkowo is home to
almost twice as many storks as humans. They
migrate from Africa each March to breed, making
their homes in huge nests up to 6 ft. (1.8 m) wide,
on rooftops, chimneys, and specially constructed
platforms. You can also catch these gangly creatures
wandering through nearby pastures and wetlands.

CZĘSTOCHOWA TO KRAKÓW, POLAND
537 Go on a castle crawl

A chain of twenty-five castles built to secure
fourteenth-century Poland from invaders, the
Trail of the Eagle's Nests is spellbinding hiking
and biking territory. As you travel, you'll take
in ravines, forest, and mountains, crowned by
some of the most atmospheric ruins in Europe.
If you're going to bring fairy tales to life, this
is a phenomenal place to do so.

536 STORKS IN ŻYWKOWO

PREŠOV REGION, SLOVAKIA
538 Snowshoe in the High Tatras

You don't get much more magical than snowshoeing through the wintery wilderness of the High Tatras, listening to the soft whoosh of your feet gliding through the snow. Kids as young as twelve can pull on some snowshoes for treks along mountain paths, through forests and to faraway villages, where people still live traditional lives.

THROUGHOUT THE BALTIC STATES

539 Get to grips with the Baltic states' history

You can get far off the European tourist trail on a trip through the Baltic nations of Lithuania, Latvia, and Estonia. Several companies can organize tours that will take in UNESCO-listed medieval towns and fill you in on the darkest days of the twentieth century. Visits to a ballistic missile-launch complex, Lithuania's Cold War and KGB Museums, and the Occupation Museum in Latvia are an eye-opening experience for teenage history buffs.

539 LAKE GALVĖ

BUDAPEST, HUNGARY

540 Ride a train staffed by kids

The kids in Budapest don't have to fantasize about working with trains—they actually can at the Children's Railway, where they don uniforms and sell tickets on a temporary, voluntary basis. The train itself trundles uphill through the woods, and you can hop on and off to hike and search for wildlife.

BUDAPEST, HUNGARY

541 Glide around one of Europe's oldest ice rinks

The largest and one of the oldest ice rinks in Europe, City Park has a magnificent setting adjacent to Heroes' Square and underneath nineteenth-century Vajdahunyad Castle. For maximum ambience, come after dark when the castle is all lit up, and you can stop and refuel with hot chocolate or mulled wine.

BUDAPEST, HUNGARY

542 Wallow in a thermal spa

Budapest's thermal waters have been harnessed by everyone from the Romans to the Ottomans, and the city's many spas are open to kids aged fourteen and up. Try the elaborate Art Nouveau Gellért Baths for serious wow factor, or Széchenyi, which has huge, outdoor spa pools where you can play chess on floating boards all year round.

541 ICE SKATING IN BUDAPEST

543 BRAN CASTLE

BRAN, ROMANIA

543 **Go on
a vampire hunt**

With its misty forests and
medieval villages, it's easy to let
your imagination run wild when
visiting Transylvania. And while
the locals aren't particularly
enthused about lurid tales of
vampires and bats, there's no
denying the appeal that stories
like *Dracula* have for kids.
Families with nerves of steel
(and carrying garlic) can visit
Bran Castle, to learn about the
real-life tyrant who inspired one
of the great fictional monsters.

CARPATHIAN MOUNTAINS,
ROMANIA

544 **Visit mountains
full of wolves**

Once, wolves roamed all over
Europe, but now they are only
found in isolated areas. The
Carpathian Mountains in
Romania are home to thousands
of wolves—for now. New roads
and industry threaten their
habitats, but a wildlife holiday
specifically to see them sends the
message that they are valuable.
Feel the goosebumps rise on your
neck as their early-evening howls
reverberate across the mountains.

DNIESTER RIVER CANYON,
UKRAINE

545 **Take a child-focused
rafting trip**

A rafting trip through the
Dniester River Canyon is the
perfect way to slow down your
sightseeing as you paddle a
catamaran-style raft past small
villages, thundering waterfalls,
and old, mystical grottoes.
Tourclub Ternopil organizes
child-focused tours so when you
fancy a swim in the river or a
quiet moment gazing at nature,
the tour guides will engage the
children in fun and games.

548 PELICANS

RHODOPE MOUNTAINS, BULGARIA
546 Go on a forest safari

Hundreds of brown bears make their home in the thick forests of the Rhodope Mountains, alongside golden eagles, gray wolves, and the elusive Balkan lynx. Take your teenagers on a weeklong tour with Balkan Trek, and you can search for bears and other wildlife on foot, learning about Bulgaria's rural and natural heritage as you travel.

KEFALONIA, GREECE
547 Help sea turtles survive

Make a family beach holiday in Greece even more memorable by spending a few days volunteering at a turtle conservation project on Kefalonia. Kids will love joining the nighttime patrols to help turtles lay their eggs safely in the sand, and helping to count tiny hatchlings as they make their way down to the sea.

LAKE KERKINI, GREECE
548 See pelicans swallow fish

Pelicans and their oversize beaks are truly a wonder of the natural world. Watch from the shores as the Dalmatian pelicans—there are eight different species around the world—scoop up fish with their bill and tilt their head back to swallow it whole. Gone.

549 SKOPELOS

SKOPELOS, GREECE

549 Recreate scenes from *Mamma Mia*

With its ABBA soundtrack, and story of young love and free living, *Mamma Mia* is a hit that crosses generations. Take your teens and tweens on a trip to Skopelos and climb the 106 steps to Agios Ioannis, the chapel at the top of a hill. Or find yourselves humming along to "Does Your Mother Know" at the Kastani Beach Bar—sadly, not the one from the film.

DELPHI, GREECE

550 Tell ancient tales of heroes and monsters

Wander the beautifully preserved ruins of Delphi and it's easy to imagine a time when it was the spiritual center of the ancient Greek world. Perched on the slopes of Mount Parnassus and centered around the Sanctuary of Apollo, Delphi once drew in rulers and pilgrims from far and wide to hear the prophecies of the gods. These days its tales of heroes and monsters will keep young children transfixed.

ATHENS, GREECE
551 Bring history to life

Bring the past to life at the Acropolis Museum in Athens. It's home to the world's finest collections of ancient Greek artifacts, and after you've finished inside, head out to be wowed by the might of the Acropolis itself. History lessons will never be the same again.

552 SARAKINIKO BEACH

MILOS, GREECE
552 Explore the caves and cliffs of Milos

Milos has all the emerald seas, fabulous snorkeling, and dreamy, seafront villages you'd expect of a small Greek island. But its volcanic nature brings another side to your family adventure. Explore otherworldly caves, hike multihued cliffs, and visit ancient catacombs that date to the first century. Then marvel at the lunar landscape of Sarakiniko Beach.

THROUGHOUT GREECE
553 Enjoy a family meal in a Greek taverna

A long, family meal at a simple taverna, sampling a parade of fresh, local dishes, is a wonderful introduction to Greek food and culture. Start with a *mezedes*, a selection of small appetizers to share, which will include treats such as *saganaki* (fried cheese), *keftedes* (meatballs), and *dolmades* (stuffed vine leaves).

MYKONOS TOWN, GREECE
554 Hike to windmills on Mykonos

Scramble along the rocky coastline of Mykonos, where a photogenic group of windmills have welcomed guests since the 1600s. A short walk from the town center, the windmills are no longer turning in the breeze, but provide amazing views and an iconic photo for the album.

554 WINDMILLS OF MYKONOS

IONIAN ISLANDS, GREECE
555 Hop around the Ionian Islands

Each of the Ionian Islands has its own special appeal, from the architectural beauty of Corfu to the wild landscapes of Ithaca, the mythical home of Odysseus. Visit several islands by ferry and you'll maximize the fun. There's little more exciting than watching your temporary island home come slowly into view, and wondering what adventures await.

MOUNT OLYMPUS, GREECE
556 Picnic with the gods

It can be hard work persuading teens that hiking up the side of a mountain has all the makings of a fun day out. But tell them that the mountain is Mount Olympus (9,570 ft.; 2,917 m), which according to ancient Greek mythology is home of the mighty Zeus, and they'll embark on an odyssey to the summit.

555 IONIAN ISLANDS

ISTANBUL, TURKEY
557 See one of the world's largest diamonds

Surrounded by landscaped gardens, Topkapi Palace is a glimpse into the imperial treasures of the Ottoman Empire. A series of interior courtyards leads to a building filled with jewels, gathered over the reigns of more than thirty different sultans. Solid gold thrones, bejeweled ornaments, and countless gemstones of global significance fill the rooms here, including one of the largest cut diamonds in the world.

ISTANBUL, TURKEY
558 Try Turkish delight

A warm, aromatic smell hits you as you walk into Istanbul's Spice Bazaar, and a walk through this Ottoman-era market is a heady experience. Stalls sell honeycomb, cheeses, and dried fruits alongside the colorful spices, but most memorable for children are the huge piles of jewellike *lokum* (Turkish delight)—fragrant cubes of dense, sticky jelly, generously covered in icing sugar.

558 SPICE BAZAAR

559 ANCIENT RUINS OF EPHESUS

EPHESUS, TURKEY
559 Explore the ruins of Ephesus

You can feel the power and scale of the ancient harbor city of Ephesus as you wander around the sprawling ruins—some of the best-preserved in the Mediterranean. This was once an important trading center, and it's an evocative introduction to ancient Roman civilization. Visit ruined temples, mansions, and bathhouses, and look carefully at the marble paved streets—you can still see the marks made by chariot wheels many centuries ago.

TURKISH COAST, TURKEY
560 Set sail on a wooden *gulet*

The best way to explore the Turkish coast is on a family *gulet* adventure. You'll spend days out at sea, stopping in quiet bays for snorkeling, swimming, and long, lazy lunches; and on hot summer nights you can sleep out on deck underneath the stars. You usually share the adventure with two or three other families, so it's an ideal holiday for single parents and only children.

PAMUKKALE, TURKEY

561 Bathe in milky waters at Pamukkale

Follow in the footsteps of Cleopatra with a dip in the steamy, thermal pools of Turkey's Pamukkale. This otherworldly geological oasis is steeped in history too. Before hiking out to explore the petrified limestone cascades that overlook the plains, visit the ancient city of Hierapolis, where the well-preserved ruins include a Roman theater.

OLYMPOS NATIONAL PARK, TURKEY

562 Hike to the Eternal Flame

Hike 2 mi. (3 km) up a rocky trail through the wooded slopes of Olympos National Park, and you'll find the Eternal Flame of Yanartaş, a group of small, natural flames that have been burning for hundreds of years. In ancient times, these flames were thought to be the breath of the Chimaera, a fearsome, three-headed monster. Bring a torch and visit at night for maximum atmosphere—the flames blaze so brightly they're visible out at sea.

561 PAMUKKALE

CAPPADOCIA, TURKEY
563 Hot-air balloon at sunrise

The rock formations in Cappadocia create
a stunning landscape of spires and pinnacles.
The town is made even more intriguing because
around Roman times, people started to hollow out
these rock structures to create churches and homes.
Today, you can sleep in a house inside the rock, then
wake up and take a hot-air balloon ride to see the
view from above.

4

AFRICA AND THE MIDDLE EAST

PORTO MONIZ, MADEIRA
564 Bask in natural swimming pools

The incredible natural swimming pools of Porto Moniz were formed by volcanic lava and are constantly refilled by seawater, yet the temperature is always a comfortable 68°F (20°C). The water is crystal clear, and the area is large enough to be relaxing even when its busy. Older kids will love the independence of having their own dedicated "teen" pool, which is watched carefully by lifeguards.

LANZAROTE, CANARY ISLANDS
565 Stay in an eco-yurt

A world away from Lanzarote's brash resorts is Finca de Arrieta, an off-grid hideaway with views toward volcanic mountains and the sea. Plush yurts have private gardens complete with outdoor kitchens and lounges, kids can get active in the solar-heated pool, and there are chickens and donkeys to visit. All this is just a short stroll from the beach and the fishing village of Arrieta.

FOGO ISLAND, CAPE VERDE
566 Hike up a volcano

The haunting, volcanic landscapes of far-flung Fogo Island make for beautiful hiking territory. Teenagers can take on the challenge of Pico do Fogo, the highest peak of Cape Verde, at 9,382 ft. (2,829 m). It's a dusty, slippery slog to the top of this still-active volcano, but the otherworldly views are well worth it.

FEZ, MOROCCO
567 Learn how to cook a tagine

A cooking class is a fantastic introduction to Moroccan culture for kids. There are many available which typically start with a wander through the medina to stock up on fresh ingredients. Next up you'll learn how to prepare your traditional dish. A tagine—an aromatic stew cooked in a domed, clay pot—is a common starting point.

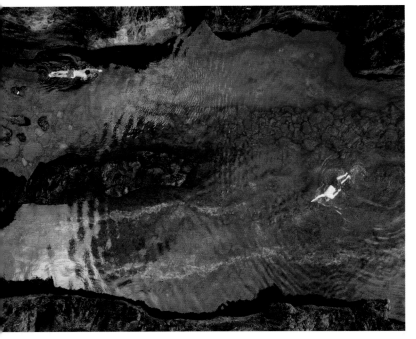

564 PORTO MONIZ

MARRAKECH, MOROCCO

568 Bargain in the souks of Marrakech

Marrakech's central medina buzzes with the smells, colors, and sounds of its different souks (markets)—some selling slippers, others spices, others tableware, others clothing. The narrow alleyways and passing donkeys are all part of the experience, and there's definitely a purchase for every member of the family within the city walls.

569 JEMAA EL-FNA

MARRAKECH, MOROCCO
569 Dine after dark in the Jemaa el-Fna

The Jemaa el-Fna, Marrakech's main square, reaches peak drama after dark. Musicians strike up their instruments, jugglers and storytellers draw in small crowds, and food stalls fire up their grills, filling the skies with smoke. Grab a seat and take in the action while dining on tagines, grilled meats, or peppery snail broth.

ATLAS MOUNTAINS, MOROCCO
570 Trek through the Atlas Mountains

Hike through the snowcapped Atlas Mountains and you'll take in more than just dramatic views. The mountains are scattered with traditional Berber villages, which offer a fascinating insight into rural Moroccan life. Routes range from moderate to challenging, and on guided trips you'll walk with a mule, which little kids can ride if their legs get tired.

ESSAOUIRA, MOROCCO
571 Play soccer on the beach

It's easy to see why the wide, flat, sandy beach in Essaouira is transformed into end-to-end soccer pitches at the weekend. If you see a standard that suits you and your children, ask if you can join a game, or set up your own goals and keep it in the family. Be warned, it can get very windy—look out for curveballs if you're in goal.

ESSAOUIRA, MOROCCO
572 Learn to windsurf

The *alizé* (trade wind) blows fiercely around Essaouira for most of the year—not great for sunbathers, but brilliant for the windsurfers and kitesurfers that come here from across the globe to ride the waves. One of several local windsurfing schools along the beach can show your older child or teenager the ropes.

SOUSS VALLEY, MOROCCO
573 See goats climb up trees

In the countryside of southwest Morocco, you'll see goats using their mountain-climbing skills in a different way—getting up high in the branches of argan trees. It's said that the goats climb the trees because argan nuts are such a delicious treat.

573 GOATS IN TREES

SAHARA DESERT, MOROCCO
574 Cross the Sahara by camel

Camels were once used for trading expeditions from Morocco to the legendary kingdom of Timbuktu. You can follow in the footsteps of traders and explorers on a camel trek through the desert, stopping for mint tea in the shadow of palm trees, and setting up camp underneath the stars. Many tours depart from Ouarzazate, heading straight for the desert and the Erg Chebbi dunes—the highest and most spectacular in Morocco. Camels offer a bumpy ride, so you'll only be in the saddle for an hour or two a day. The rest of the time you'll walk, as the camels trot beside you through the sands. Older children and teenagers will make the most of this challenging adventure.

TINERHIR, MOROCCO
575 Walk through the Todgha Gorge

The Todgha Gorge is one of nature's most spectacular canyons. Walls of rock rise up 1,312 ft. (400 m) from the valley floor which in places is a mere 33 ft. (10 m) wide. Rarely will you have felt so small. There's a bus to the gorge from Tinerhir or plenty of private tours you can join that offer information along the way.

574 SAHARA DESERT

M'HAMID, MOROCCO
576 Sleep in a Bedouin tent

A night spent in the silence and darkness of the desert is a magical experience. And you'll even have proper beds and comfortable Bedouin tents at Camp Adounia, set under the dunes near M'hamid. Friendly staff will help the kids make the most of the desert, including sand boarding, camel rides, and plain old dune climbing, while nights are spent around the communal campfire.

MERZOUGA, MOROCCO
577 Surf the sand in the Sahara

Walking up a sand dune can be a hard slog, especially when you're carrying a wooden board. But it's worth it for the incredible views across the Sahara when you reach the top, not to mention the rush as you come flying back down. The higher you climb, the better the ride down, and you can choose to sit, lie down, or stand, depending on how brave you're feeling.

DAKAR, SENEGAL

578 Teach the kids how to catch a wave

Brought to international attention by 1966 surf documentary *The Endless Summer*, the beaches around Dakar are uncrowded, with consistent swells throughout the year. Add tropical temperatures and a welcoming vibe, and Dakar is perfect for beginner surfers, including kids. N'Gor Island Surf Camp offers small group and private lessons for beginners.

THROUGHOUT THE GAMBIA

579 Learn to play a *djembe* drum

Traditionally carved from a hollowed, hardwood tree then covered with animal skin, the *djembe* drum has been around since the twelfth century. It's an integral part of Gambian life, and hotels and resorts across the country offer lessons and workshops. The best part is that no one is too young to join in.

578 SURF'S UP

580 FREETOWN PENINSULA

FREETOWN, SIERRA LEONE

580 Go beach hopping along a peninsula

The balmy beaches of the Freetown Peninsula are beautiful and blissfully crowd-free. Try Tokeh Beach for clear, blue waters and Caribbean vibes, Bureh Beach for golden sands and surf breaks, or the coastal fishing village of Kent, where you can grab a boat out to blissful Banana Island for some desert-island relaxation.

FREETOWN, SIERRA LEONE

581 Visit a chimpanzee sanctuary

Set in thick rain forest just outside Freetown, Tacugama Chimpanzee Sanctuary aims to rescue and rehabilitate endangered primates. Kids will love seeing the chimps play and feed in large, forested enclosures, as well as learning about their individual stories and the sanctuary's work. If you fancy a longer visit, there are walking trails to follow, as well as a handful of atmospheric huts where you can spend the night.

TIWAI ISLAND, SIERRA LEONE

582 Stay on a rain forest island

Spend time at Tiwai Island Wildlife Sanctuary—one of the last tracts of ancient rain forest in West Africa—and you'll be in the company of eleven species of primate, 135 bird species, and the endangered pygmy hippopotamus. Adventurous teens will love the community-run forest treks, river tours, and nights spent in simple rooms at the research station, listening to the sound of the jungle.

583 TUNIS

TUNIS, TUNISIA
583 Wander through a medina

A maze of narrow lanes lined with ancient mosques, mausoleums, and palaces, the Tunis medina is the beating heart of the city, and a time capsule that takes you right back to the Middle Ages. Immerse yourself in the noise and color of the covered souks, which sell everything from perfume to precious stones.

JEBIL NATIONAL PARK, TUNISIA
584 Glamp in the dunes

After a long drive through the desert by 4x4, Camp Mars appears like something out of a desert fairy tale—a collection of white tents backed by the towering dunes of the Grand Erg Oriental. Tents are lit by candles, and traditional Tunisian meals are served Bedouin-style, including bread cooked underneath the sand.

EL JEM, TUNISIA
585 Go back in time at an ancient amphitheater

The second-largest colosseum in the world after Rome's, El Jem was built in around 30 C.E. and its three magnificent tiers held up to thirty-five thousand spectators. Wander the interior, and it's easy to imagine the roars of the crowd as gladiators and wild animals battled in the arena.

TIMIMOUN, ALGERIA
586 Wear orange and blend in

The whole of the town of Timimoun is the color of ripe peaches—the mud-brick buildings, the dusty streets, and the enormous sea of sand that enfolds the town. Only the searing green of thousands of palm trees stands out from the tumbledown buildings and stroppy camels of this Saharan oasis.

THROUGHOUT ALGERIA
587 Snack on *mhadjeb*

A thin, flaky pastry, stuffed with tomatoes and onions and then fried, *mhadjeb* is a quintessential Algerian snack, found at street stalls and cafés throughout the country. It's often eaten with a side of harissa, a Maghrebi hot chili sauce, and washed down with a glass of sweet mint tea.

M'ZAB VALLEY, ALGERIA
588 Visit a hilltop oasis

Set on the edge of the Sahara, the five hilltop citadels of the M'zab Valley are like something out of a storybook, with sugar-cube houses and date-palm oases. A visit here is a fascinating introduction to the unique culture of the Mozabite people, a Berber group, who call this desert region home.

BATNA, ALGERIA
589 Marvel at the ruins of Timgad

The sheer scale of the ancient Roman city of Timgad will blow the mind of any mini history buff. Stretching across a mountainous plain are hundreds of beautifully preserved ruins, including bathhouses, temples, a huge theater, and a public library, one of only a few built in the Roman world.

588 HILLTOP CITADEL

OUAGADOUGOU, BURKINA FASO
590 Join the fun at an African film festival

The leading lights of the African movie industry descend on Ouagadougou in March for FESPACO, the biggest film festival on the continent, and a celebration of African cultures and stories. Curious teenagers can join the throngs of locals and visitors who come to do deals, spot celebrities, and watch films in outdoor movie theaters.

NYANYANO, GHANA
591 Study drumming on the beach

Set on golden sands along Ghana's west coast, is the KASAPA project, a beach eco-lodge, cultural center, and all-round brilliant place to get acquainted with Ghanaian dance and rhythms. Both adults and kids can sign up for weeklong drumming, dancing, and music workshops, which include excursions to rain forests, cocoa farms, and deserted beaches.

KUMASI, GHANA
592 Learn about the Ashanti Kingdom

Kumasi was once the heart of the mighty Ashanti Kingdom, which covered much of modern-day Ghana, Togo, and the Ivory Coast from the seventeenth to the nineteenth centuries. Visit the Prempeh II Jubilee Museum, constructed to resemble a chief's house, for an introduction to Ashanti history and culture, complete with a personalized tour.

GREATER ACCRA, GHANA
593 Tour a cocoa farm

Chocolate lovers can get back to the source with a tour organized by Easy Track Ghana. You'll head to a working cocoa farm where you can feel, touch, and taste ripe cocoa fruit, and learn how cocoa beans are extracted and dried. Then comes the best part—tasting samples of the finished product.

ELMINA, GHANA

594 Experience history at a former slave fort

Imposing Elmina Castle was once a notorious slave-trading fort. Teenagers can visit the site for an informative tour, taking in the officers' quarters, the cramped dungeons, and the "door of no return"—through which enslaved people caught a last glimpse of their homeland before being forcibly taken across the ocean.

MOLE NATIONAL PARK, GHANA

595 Walk with elephants

Large herds of elephants wander the savanna of Mole National Park, and older children and teenagers can join a walking tour, alongside an armed guide. The park is uncrowded, and it's a real privilege to get up close to these mighty beasts on foot, often without another soul in sight.

OUIDAH, BENIN

596 Learn the secrets of voodoo

Visit the city of Ouidah, the spiritual home of voodoo, and you'll be immersed in this mysterious religion. You'll find markets selling fetishes and herbal medicines, roadside shrines, statues of voodoo gods, and even a python temple. For the best introduction to Benin's voodoo heritage, visit in January for the vibrant Fête du Vodoun.

594 ELMINA CASTLE

599 VALLEY OF THE KINGS

597 Dive into the Red Sea

The Red Sea at Dahab drops down quickly to great depths, so fantastic diving and snorkeling is easily accessible for beginners. Once you're done floating in clouds of colorful fish, you can soak up the vibe of this lively Bedouin fishing village with harborside shops and restaurants.

SHARM EL SHEIKH, EGYPT

598 Swim with dolphins

There are few more thrilling or memorable family experiences than swimming in the sea together with a pod of dolphins. Getting up close to these friendly, inquisitive creatures in their natural environment will make junior conservationists of your kids. Responsible boat captains ensure the dolphins are respected, and also clue you in on their behaviors.

LUXOR, EGYPT

599 Explore the burial chambers of the Valley of the Kings

Stories of the rulers and rituals of ancient Egypt have always fascinated schoolchildren, and a visit to the royal tombs of the Valley of the Kings will bring those stories to life. The hot, dusty valley was a royal burial site between 1550 and 1069 B.C.E., and is home to sixty-three elaborate tombs. Kids will be particularly fascinated by the treasure-filled, underground burial place of Tutankhamun, the boy king. It includes his four thousand-year-old sarcophagus, with an innermost coffin made of solid gold.

CAIRO TO LUXOR, EGYPT
600 Take the sleeper from Cairo to Luxor

The luxury sleeper train from Cairo to Luxor is one of the most magical journeys in Egypt, a nine-hour trip that sees you falling asleep in the land of the pyramids and waking up by the Valley of the Kings. Families can book a private cabin so that, after feasting like pharaohs in the club car as night falls over the desert, you can relax together in your comfortable bunk beds.

GIZA, EGYPT
601 See the Egyptian pyramids

Looming large over both the urban sprawl of Giza and the desert plains beyond, the Giza Pyramids are Egypt's most treasured attractions: three huge pyramid tombs built in turn for the pharaohs Khufu, Khafre, and Menkaure, and filled with all the things they would need in the afterlife. Arrive at the crack of dawn to beat the crowds and feel the true mysterious atmosphere of the site.

601 PYRAMIDS OF GIZA

ASWAN, EGYPT

602 Experience the vibrancy of colorful Nubian villages

When the Aswan High Dam was built to create Lake Nasser in the 1960s, it flooded the lush ancestral land of the Nubians. Nubian people were resettled in villages throughout the region of Aswan where they have kept their culture and traditions alive with brightly painted domed houses, delicious traditional cuisine, and a reverence for the Nile crocodile. Many families keep crocodiles as pets and will invite you in to meet them.

ASWAN, EGYPT

603 Sail the Nile on a felucca

Board a felucca (traditional sailing boat) and you can travel the Nile as people have done for millennia. You'll visit places that larger ships can't, such as villages and camel markets, and the kids will have a true adventure, getting a close-up view of life along the Nile and sleeping on deck underneath the stars.

LUXOR, EGYPT

604 Learn how to make a mummy

Did you know that it wasn't only kings and queens that became mummies, but their servants and even their household pets too? Best suited to older kids and non-squeamish parents, the small but fascinating Mummification Museum in Luxor explains the rituals and processes behind how, and why, the ancient Egyptians preserved the dead.

602 NUBIAN VILLAGE

607 LALIBELA

MEROË, SUDAN
605 Ride a camel to lesser known pyramids

For anyone who has had their interest sparked by ancient Egypt, then the small village of Meroë in Sudan is something special. Here you can ride a camel between silent pyramids, brush the desert sand off ancient hieroglyphics, and watch the sun set over temples hiding secrets we still don't understand.

ADDIS ABABA, ETHIOPIA
606 Taste injera and *wat*

Injera and *wat*, the national dish of Ethiopia, is food made fun. The kids can forget all about using a knife and fork. Instead let them tear off a bit of rubbery injera (like a giant, fermented pancake), wrap it around a spicy morsel of *wat* (like a curry), and pop the whole messy lot into their mouth.

LALIBELA, ETHIOPIA
607 Relive the Biblical age

Legend and reality unite in Lalibela, where one-thousand-year-old, rock-hewn churches were carved into the ground after a heavenly vision. Visit during a Christian festival and this important pilgrimage center will be awash with white-robed Ethiopians praying by candlelight through the night.

GONDAR, ETHIOPIA
608 Be the Queen of Sheba for a day

As you walk around the palaces and castles of the city of Gondar, enthrall the children with tales of the knights in armor who once lived there, the emperors descended from King Solomon and the Queen of Sheba, and the feasts that took place in the castle banquet halls in which it's said that people ate raw meat carved straight from living cows.

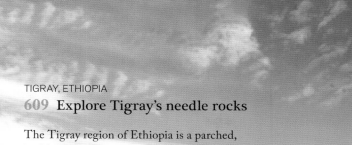

TIGRAY, ETHIOPIA
609 Explore Tigray's needle rocks

The Tigray region of Ethiopia is a parched, highland plateau, soaring out of which are giant needle rocks. Some of these are topped by ancient Christian chapels and monasteries, some of which are still inhabited by monks. Tesfa Tours organize multiday treks across this surreal landscape, with nights spent in village homestays.

PRÍNCIPE ISLAND
610 Get back to nature in Príncipe

A visit to the jungles and beaches of Príncipe will blow the mind of any miniature naturalist. Often referred to as Africa's Galápagos, this lush island is home to just seven thousand people and a whole lot of wildlife. Thick, virgin jungles are home to reptiles, butterflies, and huge numbers of endemic birds; while down at the ocean, turtles nest on white-sand beaches and humpback whales cruise the waters.

LOANGO NATIONAL PARK, GABON
611 Visit great apes in their jungle home

The humid, muddy hike through tough terrain is well worth the endgame: infiltrating the world of a group of western lowland gorillas. Coming up close to a massive silverback, or watching a mother playing with her children, is a wonderful reminder of how close we are to our primate cousins. If you're sixteen or over you can join these treks through Loango National Park, one of Africa's last great coastal wildernesses.

JINJA, UGANDA
612 Ride a raft along the Nile

Jinja is East Africa's adventure-sport capital, and the perfect place for steel-nerved teens to tackle some pretty hard-core rapids along the fast and powerful Nile. If you've younger kids in tow, you can take it easy and float down a slow-moving section of the river, taking in beautiful islands and birdlife.

RWENZORI MOUNTAINS NATIONAL PARK, UGANDA
613 Wander the Mountains of the Moon

Tropical rain forest gives way to mist-soaked, alpine moorland and then snowcapped peaks as you climb through the Rwenzori Mountains, nicknamed the Mountains of the Moon. Walk in the foothills, or go for it and tackle the peak—an activity best reserved for older teenagers.

LAKE MBURO, UGANDA
614 Search for wildlife on horseback

There are few more exciting ways to explore the savanna than on the back of a horse, and older children can join rides around Lake Mburo in search of game such as bushbucks, zebras, and elands. The lack of engine noise means you can blend into the landscape and fully immerse yourself in nature.

612 RAFTING ON THE NILE

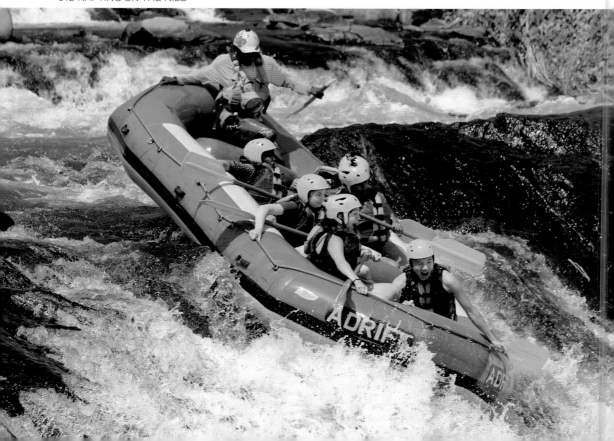

615 Meet Uganda's tree-climbing lions

No one is sure why the lions of
Queen Elizabeth National Park
like climbing up and sleeping in
trees—perhaps to avoid insect
bites or escape the heat of the
day. Book a tour and you might
be lucky enough to spot them
among the branches, scouring
the ground below for prey.

615 RESTING LION

616 Hang out with mountain gorillas

When it comes to visiting
mountain gorillas, Bwindi
Impenetrable National Park
is the cream of the crop and
shelters some four hundred of
these magnificent animals. If
you're fifteen or older you can
hike through the jungle to visit
them and spend an unforgettable
hour in their company.

616 MOUNTAIN GORILLAS

NAIROBI TO LAKE TURKANA,
KENYA

617 Drive through the desert to Lake Turkana

Adventurous teenagers can join a 4x4 expedition to one of East Africa's wildest places—Lake Turkana. It's a long haul from Nairobi along rough, dusty, and often deserted roads, but you'll be rewarded with jaw-dropping landscapes, encounters with pastoral tribes, and Lake Turkana itself, a startling, jade sea in the middle of rocky desert.

NAIROBI, KENYA

618 Navigate Nairobi by matatu

Matatus are a loud and colorful introduction to Nairobi that most kids will love. These privately owned minibuses leave when full from local bus stations, or you can flag them down on the road and jump in. It's best to stick to short rides though—and make sure to check the seatbelts.

NAIROBI, KENYA

619 Ride high in the Eye of Kenya

Step into a glass pod on CK's Eye of Kenya Ferris wheel to enjoy a different view of Nairobi (the CK is for businessman Dr. Chris Kirubi who was the inspiration for the wheel). Taking you to heights of 200 ft. (60 m), you can see the city laid out below you. Come at night to enjoy the lights.

618 RIDE IN A MATATU

631 MAASAI STEPPE

632 WILDEBEEST

MOUNT KILIMANJARO, TANZANIA
630 Climb a mountain for charity

Getting children involved in charitable work gives them pride in being able to make a difference. If you want to aim high, organize a family fundraising trek up Mount Kilimanjaro. Children over ten can take the challenge with adults, but they need to be up for it and fit. It's about an eight-day trek through rain forest, across meadows, and beneath ice fields before you reach the summit at 19,341 ft. (5,895 m) and stand on the roof of Africa.

FROM KENYA TO TANZANIA
631 Cycle across countries

Take the children on a bike ride they'll never forget—from Nairobi in Kenya to Dar es Salaam in Tanzania. An organization such as Escape Adventures can plan all the routes for you (it suggests children are over ten) and arrange campsites or homestays with local families along the way, leaving you to focus on the wildlife and the views.

SERENGETI, TANZANIA, TO MASAI MARA, KENYA
632 Watch the wildebeest migration

Kids of all ages will be wowed by the wildebeest migration—the annual movement of 1.5 million wildebeest between Tanzania and Kenya, and the largest migration of land animals on the planet. Watching an endless stream of grunting creatures crashing through plains and across the Mara River is a spectacle that isn't easily forgotten.

TARANGIRE NATIONAL PARK, TANZANIA
633 Spot wildlife from a swimming pool

If long days out in the bush don't suit your brood, book a lodge where the wildlife comes to you. Sanctuary Swala Camp is so close to the local watering hole that you can watch a constant procession of wildlife as you splash about in the pool.

634 ROCK RESTAURANT

636 SPICE PLANTATION

ZANZIBAR, TANZANIA
634 Eat dinner on a rock

Rising from the sands at the fishing village of Michamvi, on the southeast coast of Zanzibar, is the Rock Restaurant, which sits atop of—you've guessed it—a giant rock. It's most fun at high tide, when you'll need to wade across or be ferried over by boat. The food is almost beside the point but it's excellent in any case—think seafood with Zanzibar's spices.

ZANZIBAR, TANZANIA
635 Soak up Swahili culture

Zanzibar is a melting pot of African, Asian, and European influences due to its former role as a center for spice traders. Base yourself in ancient Stone Town—a tangle of streets peppered with intricately carved doorways and crumbling mansions—and every stroll becomes a lesson in Swahili history and culture.

ZANZIBAR, TANZANIA
636 Tour a spice plantation

The islands off the coast of Tanzania were once known as the Spice Islands, and Zanzibar was the wealthiest of them all. Curious kids will relish a tour of a spice farm, where they can learn about the history of the spice trade and see how spices are produced today. They can touch, taste, and smell the spices, then enjoy them to the full with a spread of curries for lunch.

PEMBA, TANZANIA
637 Bed down in an underwater room

Anchored 820 ft. (250 m) offshore the island of Pemba, Zanzibar's northern island, is Manta Resort's Underwater Room, where you can sleep underneath the ocean and gaze out through panoramic windows at the sea life beyond. If you start to feel claustrophobic, there's an above sea-level living area which has some of the best views in Pemba.

PRASLIN ISLAND, SEYCHELLES
638 Swim with colorful sea life

The calm, clear waters and gently shelving beaches of Praslin Island in the Seychelles are the perfect training ground for mini divers and snorkelers. You can hover above turtles, corals, and clouds of colorful fish while still being close to the shore, so even novice swimmers can join in the action.

CURIEUSE ISLAND, SEYCHELLES
639 Get close to giant tortoises

There are hundreds of Aldabra giant tortoises roaming around Curieuse Island thanks to a conservation program that nurtures them as youngsters, then releases them into the wild. These majestic creatures can live for up to 120 years and weigh up to 550 lb. (250 kg), and seeing them up close is a real privilege.

639 GIANT TORTOISE

LUSAKA, ZAMBIA
640 Go road tripping with a roof tent

Take a road trip in Zambia with a roof tent on top of a Land Rover. You'll drive between national parks and wildlife reserves, following dusty, red roads along the way. At night, your kids can sleep easy knowing they're high above the ground, away from curious critters. What an adventure.

KASANKA NATIONAL PARK, ZAMBIA
641 Watch a massive bat migration

Zambia's Kasanka National Park sees the largest mammal migration in the world, with over ten million bats flocking in from all over Africa between October and December each year. At dawn and sunset, they take to the skies en masse— an incredible sight that will impress the most jaded of teens.

NORTHERN ZAMBIA
642 Explore prehistoric landscapes

Take in the woodland, grasses, and whaleback hills of Mutinondo Wilderness and you'll feel as if you've gone back thousands of years. Families are free to roam this wild landscape without a guide for a true, old-fashioned adventure: swimming in clear rivers, hiking to waterfalls, and sleeping in a simple campsite with astounding views.

LIVINGSTONE, ZAMBIA
643 Float past hippos

Gliding along the Zambezi is a fantastic way to gain a new perspective on the river and its wildlife. Young children should stick to the larger boats, but with teens in tow you could try a canoe and feel your heartbeat race as you paddle right past elephants and pods of hippos.

643 HIPPOS

644 NYIKA NATIONAL PARK

NORTHERN MALAWI

644 Camp in the African highlands

The grasslands and heather-strewn hills of Nyika National Park have earned it comparisons with the Scottish Highlands, but you'll find zebras and antelope here instead of deer and shaggy cows. Active kids will love hiking and biking their way around this stunning patch of wilderness, as well as listening out for the sound of hyenas after dark.

LAKE MALAWI

645 Travel Lake Malawi by ferry

The legendary MV *Ilala* ferry transports people and goods along the length of Lake Malawi. Jump on board for some of the journey and you'll take in fabulous scenery, experience a slice of Malawian life, and have a proper family adventure. If you're after the latter, hiring mattresses and sleeping on deck is the way to go.

LAKE MALAWI

646 Get below the surface of an African lake

Lake Malawi's clear, warm waters offer fantastic opportunities for beginner snorkelers and divers. Just underwater are swarms of colorful cichlid fish, and there's no threat of swells or sharks to dissuade nervous newbies. Cape Maclear and Nkhata Bay are excellent starting points, with dive schools offering scuba classes for kids aged ten and up.

LIWONDE NATIONAL PARK, MALAWI

647 Spot wildlife on the Shire River

Set alongside the wide Shire River, Liwonde National Park is the perfect setting for a water-based expedition with older children or teens. Boat safaris will get you up close to large crocodiles, hippos, and riverine birds, and you'll spot elephants coming down to the riverbank to drink.

648 ETOSHA NATIONAL PARK

650 FUR SEALS

ETOSHA NATIONAL PARK, NAMIBIA

648 Take a guided safari

Family-friendly safaris in Namibia's wildlife-rich Etosha National Park take into account shorter attention spans. It's thrilling to admire animals in their natural habitat, from lions and elephants to zebras and cheetahs, but the wildlife wonders are even more memorable when you're in the company of expert guides. They're skilled at keeping kids entertained while making sure everyone comes away having learned something new.

KUNENE REGION, NAMIBIA

649 Visit a Himba settlement

Namibia is home to some of Africa's oldest tribal communities. Among them are the Himba, a seminomadic tribe famous for the red ochre paste called *otjize*, with which women cover their hair and bodies. A responsible, community-led visit is a fantastic opportunity for children to experience a world that's far removed from their own. They'll be able to go inside a traditional hut, and learn about daily life in a Himba settlement.

WESTERN NAMIBIA

650 Travel the Skeleton Coast

The untamed landscapes of the Skeleton Coast take their name from the shipwrecks and animal bones that lie scattered along the shore. You can drive its length via the C34 Highway, a haunting and unforgettable road trip taking in lunar landscapes, deserts, and coastal wildlife, including one of the world's largest fur seal colonies.

651 SWAKOPMUND

SWAKOPMUND, NAMIBIA
651 Ride a quad bike into the desert

If you want to hurl yourself down sand dunes, jump out of a plane, or thunder across the beach on a quad bike, Swakopmund, the self-styled adventure capital of Namibia, is the place to be. If you've got tots rather than teens, try dolphin or whale watching, or a trip to see fur seals.

DAMARALAND, NAMIBIA
652 Get the kids into conservation

Children aged eight and over can join a family conservation project in the Namibian desert, organized by The Perfect World Travel. Participants work with local communities to help track and monitor wild desert elephants, and nights are spent in basic camps, a world away from modern life.

CHOBE RIVER, NAMIBIA
653 Sleep on a houseboat

Drifting down the Chobe River spotting wildlife from the deck is as laid-back a safari as possible. Sleep on a houseboat and you'll take it to the next level. Floor-to-ceiling windows let you take in the views from your bed, and the sounds of the river and the bush will be your morning wake-up call.

654 OKAVANGO DELTA

OKAVANGO DELTA, BOTSWANA

654 See the Okavango Delta from above

The Okavango Delta is stunning at ground level, but it's up in the air that you'll really appreciate its scale and grandeur. Take to the skies on a scenic flight and you can watch elephants and buffalos make their way across the landscape in a scene so dramatic it looks as if it's straight from a nature documentary.

OKAVANGO DELTA, BOTSWANA

655 Teach the kids how to track game

Children can learn how to track game and make traps at a hands-on, four-day Young Explorers safari at Footsteps Camp. The emphasis is respecting the wilderness and the animals that live there, in the hope that they return home as budding conservationists.

MASVINGO, ZIMBABWE

656 Wander an ancient kingdom

Your kids know about ancient Egypt, but the ruins of Great Zimbabwe, once the center of a wealthy empire, will be a revelation. Crumbling, curved, stone structures up to 36 ft. (11 m) high are spread over a 1,800 ac (728 ha) site. Hire a local guide, who'll help bring the ruins to life.

HWANGE NATIONAL PARK, ZIMBABWE
657 Hang with the superherds

Hwange's forty-four-thousand-strong elephant population is impressive enough, but it's the fact that they run in superherds that will really spark young imaginations. Here, groups of up to three hundred and fifty elephants live together in packs, making those trips to the watering hole an incredible sight to witness.

MOSI-OA-TUNYA NATIONAL PARK, ZIMBABWE
658 Feel the spray at Victoria Falls

You'll hear, smell, and even feel the thundering waters well before you lock eyes on Mosi-oa-Tunya. Also known as Victoria Falls, this mile-long curtain of water is nothing short of spectacular, and there are many ways to enjoy it, from kid-friendly hikes to scenic flights, to testing your mettle at the precarious Devil's Pools.

658 VICTORIA FALLS

BARRA BEACH, MOZAMBIQUE
659 Camp out by the sea

Family camping holidays are a quintessential childhood experience, and many of Mozambique's lodges offer space for camper vans and campers, complete with access to their pools, restaurants, and stretches of paradise beach. At Faraway Lodge by Barra Beach, you can pitch up underneath palm trees just a short stroll from the ocean.

BAZARUTO ARCHIPELAGO, MOZAMBIQUE
660 Sail far-flung islands by sunset

The best way to take in the beaches and islands of the dreamy Indian Ocean is to follow in the footsteps of fishermen, explorers, and ancient Arab traders, and board a traditional wooden dhow. You can sit back while the captain entertains the kids with tales of adventures at sea, stop for swimming and snorkeling, and take a turn at sailing the boat. Plus there's always a chance of spotting sea turtles, pelicans, dolphins, and the elusive humpback whale.

NORTH WEST PROVINCE, SOUTH AFRICA
661 Beat the mosquitos at a malaria-free game reserve

The lack of malaria, plus easy access from Johannesburg, makes Madikwe Game Reserve an excellent choice for young children, and family-friendly lodges add to the appeal. At Tau Game Lodge, you can watch wildlife from the comfort of your own deck, while Bush House has expansive lawns and a private nature trail.

661 MADIKWE GAME RESERVE

664 RIDING IN THE DRAKENSBERG

LIMPOPO, SOUTH AFRICA
662 Ride the rails from Pretoria to Kruger

There are few better ways to arrive at Kruger National Park than by the luxury Blue Train. The nineteen-hour overnight journey takes you through some of South Africa's finest scenery, before stopping at Hoedspruit for transfers to your safari lodge of choice. The refined atmosphere means this one's for older kids.

JOHANNESBURG, SOUTH AFRICA
663 Join the locals at an artisan market

Set just outside Jo'burg in the beautiful Modderfontein Reserve, Fourways Farmers Market pulls in visitors from across the city to browse dozens of artisan food and craft stalls each weekend. There's live music, a fun family-friendly atmosphere, and plenty of space for the kids to run free—including a hay-bale picnic lawn.

DRAKENSBERG, SOUTH AFRICA
664 Horse ride through the Drakensberg

Forming a dramatic boundary between South Africa and Lesotho, the Drakensberg is a wonderland of jagged cliffs, canyons, and valleys thick with pine forest—a perfect backdrop for horseback riding. Rides can be tailored to the needs of your family, ranging from day-long treks to simple pony rides for little ones.

OUDTSHOORN, SOUTH AFRICA

665 Make friends with an ostrich

A visit to one of Oudtshoorn's ostrich farms is a real treat for young children. At Safari Ostrich Farm, you can ride on a tractor, visit an incubator room, and even help feed these giant birds. If you're not too squeamish, you can tuck into an ostrich steak at the restaurant afterward.

CAPE TOWN, SOUTH AFRICA

666 Feel the history at Robben Island

When you take the kids to South Africa it's important to acknowledge the country's apartheid history, and a tour of Robben Island is a great place to start. Nelson Mandela was incarcerated here for twenty-seven years, and you'll visit his tiny former cell, as well as the old limestone quarry where prisoners toiled under the hot sun.

CAPE TOWN, SOUTH AFRICA

667 Soak up the flavors of Cape Malay food

You can learn about the food and culture of Cape Malays on the Bo-Kaap Cooking Tour, which explores Cape Town's most colorful neighborhood. After visiting local food stores, it's time for a cooking lesson. Anything from samosas and chicken curry to kid-friendly *koeksisters*, a traditional sticky doughnut, could be on the menu.

CAPE TOWN, SOUTH AFRICA
668 Get playful with penguins

Calm waters, rock pools, and sandy coves make
Boulders Beach perfect for children. But the icing
on the cake is the resident penguins: this is one of
the few land-based penguin colonies in the world, as
well as a protected part of Table Mountain National
Park. Playing on the sand while penguins preen and
waddle around you is an unforgettable experience
for kids. Just remember not to try and feed them—
they bite.

CAPE TOWN, SOUTH AFRICA
669 Feel the rhythms of live jazz

Tens of thousands of music fans descend on
Cape Town each March for the Cape Town
International Jazz Festival, one of the greatest
jazz events in the world. Teens can dance the night
away to international and South African names at
the main indoor stages, while younger children can
enjoy their first taste of jazz at free outdoor concerts
around the city.

668 BOULDERS BEACH

CAPE TOWN, SOUTH AFRICA
670 Reach the top of Table Mountain

There are several hiking trails that will take you to the top of Cape Town's iconic Table Mountain, including Platteklip Gorge, the easiest route to navigate with kids. It's a steep two-hour climb up, so you'll need a good level of fitness, but you'll be rewarded with the best views in town—and the prospect of a much easier cable car ride back down.

WESTERN CAPE, SOUTH AFRICA
671 Follow the garden route

An outrageously beautiful 124 mi. (200 km) stretch from Mossel Bay in the west to Storms River in the east, the Garden Route is one of the world's most famous road trips. Take it slowly over a couple of weeks, stopping off to watch whales, kayak with dolphins, wander windswept beaches, and hike, bike, and safari in patches of stunning wilderness.

WESTERN CAPE, SOUTH AFRICA
672 Join a junior ranger program

Gondwana Game Reserve goes out of its way to welcome families, including with their Junior Ranger Program. As well as special family game drives, children can go fishing, look for animal tracks, and search for bones and minibeasts. They'll also learn how to identify mammals, birds, and even stars.

WESTERN CAPE, SOUTH AFRICA
673 Take a family-friendly vineyard tour

Picture a day spent wine tasting and it might not involve children. But many South African wineries have a family-friendly vibe. You'll find everything from playgrounds and on-site farms to chocolate-tasting experiences to keep the kids happy while you try out the local vintage.

HARTBEESPOORT DAM, SOUTH AFRICA
674 Volunteer at a monkey sanctuary

Turn the cuteness dial up to one hundred when you bring the family along to volunteer at a monkey sanctuary. Everyone gets a different little rascal to look after, and besides preparing meals and cleaning out cages, your main duty is cuddling. Kids as young as eight can take part in this deeply rewarding holiday.

670 CAPE TOWN FROM TABLE MOUNTAIN

671 THE GARDEN ROUTE

Ostriches

Suspension bridge in Tsitsikamma National Park

Wildlfowers in Kirstenbosch Botanical Gardens

Knysna turaco

676 CHAMELEON

677 ALLÉE DES BAOBABS

MALOLOTJA NATURE RESERVE, ESWATINI

675 Take a zip line through a wildlife park

The zip-line tour of Malolotja Nature Reserve gives you the chance to appreciate the mountain scenery like never before—as well as an epic adrenaline buzz. Ten zip lines pass through the canopy, and one 164 ft. (50 m) long suspension bridge crosses the Majolomba River.

THROUGHOUT MADAGASCAR

676 Watch a chameleon change color

There are more than seventy species of chameleon in Madagascar, ranging from smaller than your fingertip to as long as your arm. They are fascinating to watch, with their glitchy walking style and independently swiveling eyes, but seeing them change color as they meet a friend or foe will bring smiles to everyone's faces.

MENABE REGION, MADAGASCAR

677 Marvel at the baobabs

The Allée des Baobabs is framed by dozens of soaring *Adansonia grandidieri* baobabs. Famed for their thick, swollen trunks and stubby, gnarled branches, they're almost otherworldly in appearance, especially if you come at dawn, when the color of the trees deepens, and long shadows lend an eerie air.

SOUTHEAST MADAGASCAR
678 Go on a family wilderness adventure

A trip around Madagascar offers the opportunity for the ultimate family adventure. You can explore rain forest, desert, mountains, and mangroves; meet weird and wonderful wildlife, including ring-tailed lemurs; and kayak the Manananantanana River in search of crocodiles. Distances and difficulty mean this is best-suited to teens and tweens and organized tours keep things simple.

SOUTHERN MADAGASCAR
679 Get up close to lemurs

There are 111 species of lemur in Madagascar, ranging from the tiny pygmy mouse lemur to the sizable indri, with most of them living in the country's protected parks and reserves. See them in the surreal, prehistoric landscapes of Isalo National Park, or in the spiny forests of the Berenty Reserve. Here, both the sifakas and the ring-tailed lemurs are semihabituated to people, and they'll often wander right in front of you.

NOSY BE, MADAGASCAR
680 Snorkel off a desert island

The small and rugged island of Nosy Be, a short way off the north coast of Madagascar, doesn't seem real. Here, you can snorkel in crystalline waters over coral gardens filled with fluorescent fish, whale sharks, and turtles, and then crawl out onto ribbons of powdered sand surrounded by a multitude of tropical flowers.

679 RING-TAILED LEMURS

THROUGHOUT RÉUNION ISLAND

681 Eat creole cuisine in Réunion

One of the best ways to get to know a culture is through its food, and Réunion's creole cuisine has plenty of delicious eats for kids. Try samosas, *bouchons* (steamed dumplings), or *bonbons piments* (tiny spiced doughnuts), before moving on to some spiced sausage stew and perhaps some cassava cake for dessert.

MAFATE, RÉUNION ISLAND

682 Hike around a natural amphitheater

Set at the bottom of a collapsed volcano, and only accessible on foot or by helicopter, Cirque de Mafate is full of lost-world atmosphere. Follow trails through rain forest, sugarcane fields, and twisted, lunar landscapes, and sleep in one of several tiny villages called *ilets*, where local people can trace their lineage to the original settlers.

MOKA, MAURITIUS

683 Explore colonial history

A beautifully preserved creole mansion backed by mountains and waterfalls, Eureka was built in the nineteenth century by a sugar producer and slave owner. The house is filled with lavish furnishings and photos, and provides an excellent opportunity to teach older children about the island's slave-owning and colonial past.

682 RÉUNION

PORT LOUIS, MAURITIUS
684 Take a Mauritian street-food tour

Vibrant Port Louis is a kaleidoscope of cultures thanks to years of immigration from Europe, Africa, India, and China. A street-food tour will take you around markets and ethnic quarters, tasting treats such as *dholl puri*, a traditional flatbread, and *anana confit*, chili salted pineapple. Visits to both French- and Chinese-style bakeries will please any sweet-toothed kids.

ÎLE AUX AIGRETTES, MAURITIUS
685 Meet wildlife on a coral island

You can wander through ancient coastal forest and get up close to endemic wildlife at Île aux Aigrettes, a tiny coral island and former military base. Boats from Pointe Jerome will whisk you across the ocean for half-day tours, where there's a chance to spot Aldabra giant tortoises and endangered pink pigeons, as well as take in the lush landscape of rare palms, ebony trees, and wild orchids.

685 PINK PIGEON

PORT LOUIS, MAURITIUS
686 Get the lowdown on sugar

Set in a historic sugar mill, on the Beau Plan Sugar Estate on the island of Mauritius, is L'Aventure du Sucre, where you can learn about the history of the sugar industry as well as how sugar is made today. The chance to cut and eat sugarcane, and taste a selection of unrefined sugars, sweetens the deal for children.

BEIT GUVRIN NATIONAL PARK, ISRAEL

687 Dig for ancient artifacts

The Dig for a Day program allows children of all ages to take part in the actual excavation of an ancient archeological cave system. Led by the Israel Antiquities Authorities, the scheme has been running for forty years and many of the finds are now in museums. Let your children join in and feed their inner archeologist.

THROUGHOUT ISRAEL

688 Spend the night at a kibbutz

You can enjoy collective community life for a night at an Israeli kibbutz, which function more like eco-hotels today than the hippy communes they started out as, and there's no work required from guests. Instead, you can get stuck into rural life, following hiking and biking trails, eating food from organic gardens, and letting the kids run wild.

NABLUS, PALESTINE

Tour a soap factory

Kids might shy away from soap on bath nights, but ask them how they think it's made and you'll soon have their attention. Nablus has been at the center of olive oil soap production for thousands of years. Tour the Albader factory in the Old Town to find out how this natural soap is made.

WADI RUM, JORDAN
690 Camp out in the desert

You'll start your overnight camping adventure in a jeep, racing along red roads and over dunes to get to your desert camp—whether that's under canvas or a geodesic dome is up to you. Then it's time to watch the sunset over the sands, before dinner and traditional music around the campfire. A night under the silent desert skies wraps up an incredible experience.

690 WADI RUM

MOUNT NEBO, JORDAN
691 Cycle to the Dead Sea

If you can deal with the heat and the desert wind, getting around Jordan by bike is a workout for both the legs and the soul. Most spectacular is the 15 mi. (24 km) descent from Mount Nebo to the Dead Sea. You'll get incredible views of the Jordan Valley, and there's nothing like floating in the salty ocean to clear off the dust and sweat. Teens might be up for the challenge.

DEAD SEA, JORDAN
692 Cake yourself in healing mud

Book into a resort by the Dead Sea and you'll have plenty of excitement on your doorstep. Floating on the hot, salty water is a unique experience, but the kids might prefer slathering themselves in warm, sulfurous black mud. As well as getting gloriously messy, they'll be left with wonderfully soft skin.

JERASH, JORDAN
693 Watch gladiators do battle

The Roman ruins of Jerash are among the best in the Middle East, but kids will be most impressed with the daily reenactments, which take place in the restored hippodrome. You'll see chariots racing around the arena, legionaries in battle gear, and gladiators wielding swords for heavily choreographed fights. It's loud and incredibly fun.

695 DESERT SAFARI

DUBAI, UAE
694 Eat fresh dates

Fresh dates are like a little piece of nature's candy—sweet, succulent, and moreish. There are more than two hundred varieties of dates, which will come as no surprise on a visit to Deira's souks, where they are piled high on silver platters. Most sellers allow you to taste before you buy, but that still might not help you choose.

DUBAI, UAE
695 Take a desert safari in a 4x4

A desert safari is where you really need the 4x4-capabilities of your vehicle. Deep sand, steep inclines, and rocky paths—you'll find it all in Dubai's desert and you'll put that vehicle to the test. As well as stunning views over golden dunes, there are often opportunities for sand boarding and quad biking on them too.

DUBAI, UAE
696 Ride a traditional *abra*

Dubai Creek winds through the city's oldest and most atmospheric districts, and the best way to explore is by *abra*, a traditional, wooden ferry boat. You can jump on a scheduled service, or hire your own and head upriver. Either way, it's a great way to show the kids a world away from the Dubai bling.

DUBAI, UAE
697 Take an elevator up the world's tallest building

Step into the elevator at Dubai's Burj Khalifa and you'll be whisked up to the 125th floor of this 2,717 ft. (828 m) tall building, the world's tallest. But you won't stop there—there's an outdoor observation deck on the 148th floor. There are mountains lower than this.

DUBAI, UAE
698 Go over the top at the world's biggest shopping mall

Dubai Mall might have 1,300 stores, but for kids they're the least of its attractions. There's plenty of fun to be had at the giant aquarium, the ice rink, and the Virtual Reality Park. And if you head to the Grand Atrium, you'll find yourself in the presence of a genuine dinosaur skeleton.

DUBAI, UAE
699 Gorge yourself at a Dubai brunch

Brunch is a Dubai institution, but the locals won't make do with eggs and an orange juice. The best action takes place at upscale hotels, where opulent, all-you-can-eat buffets are the standard, including plenty of child-friendly treats. There are often children's entertainers on hand, so you can enjoy your champagne and seafood platters in peace.

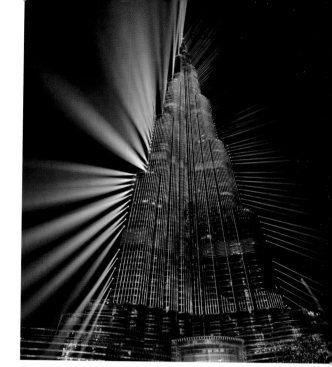
697 BURJ KHALIFA

698 DINOSAUR SKELETON AT DUBAI MALL

ABU DHABI, UAE
700 Explore a wild and wonderful waterpark

Emirati-themed Yas Waterworld has come up with all kinds of ways to get a water-based adrenaline rush. There's a six-person tornado water slide, the world's largest, surfable, artificial wave, and a roller coaster with onboard water pistols. In short, it's a watery paradise for kids.

ABU DHABI, UAE
701 Watch a camel beauty pageant

Every year Emiratis celebrate their culture at the Al Dhafra Festival. Often billed as a camel beauty contest, that is certainly one of the popular events, but it runs alongside falconry, horseracing, saluki dog racing and sheep beauty contests too. The stakes are high, with cash prizes and 4x4s for the winners.

BAHLA, OMAN
702 Eat halwa

The Omani national sweet is *halwa*—a sticky treat made from sugar, water, corn starch, and ghee (clarified butter). If ever there is a celebration—or even if you just go round to someone's house—there will be *halwa*. Enjoy it in the courtyard of Old Bahla Souk, surrounded by traditional pottery from the area.

700 YAS WATERWORLD

THROUGHOUT OMAN
703 Play in the sand dunes

Sand boarding, dune bashing, and camel rides are all very well, but sometimes it's the simple pleasures that are the best. If you're driving through the desert, pull over and let your kids go crazy on the dunes. All kids love a sandbox, and the desert is the largest and wildest sandbox there is.

THROUGHOUT OMAN
704 Wild camp on a deserted beach

Wild camping is allowed almost everywhere in Oman, and the far south has the best and quietest beaches in the country. White sand, turquoise waters, and wandering camels are a common occurrence. And at night it's just you, your brood, and a sky full of glittering stars.

703 PLAY IN THE DUNES

705 Watch endangered turtles lay their eggs

Endangered green sea turtles return year after year to lay their eggs by the fishing village of Ras Al Jinz, now a protected reserve. Come between June and September to see females lay their eggs in the sand, or watch hatchlings scrabble across the sands for their first dip the water.

WAHIBA SANDS, OMAN

706 See the sun setting over dunes

The dunes reach as high as 330 ft. (100 m) at Wahiba Sands, a vast swathe of saffron desert a few hours' drive south of Muscat. Huddle up as a family to watch the sun sink slowly into the horizon, as the temperatures drop and the first stars appear in the sky.

706 WAHIBA SANDS

707 SOCOTRA ISLAND

SOCOTRA ISLAND, YEMEN
707 Explore alien landscapes

Untamed and relatively unknown, Socotra
Island is crammed full of endemic species and
otherworldly landscapes, and getting here is an
adventurous journey that's best reserved for older
teens. Organized tours will take you from pristine
lagoons and hidden caves to dragon's blood forests,
where ancient trees spring from the rocky ground
like giant mushrooms. Nights will be camping at its
most basic—but who needs modern comforts when
you've got a blanket of the brightest stars?

CENTRAL IRAN
708 Live like the locals

Head into the mountains of central Iran for
a village homestay. Once completely nomadic,
many of the people here, the Qashqai, are now
settled in villages, and you can join them in their
daily activities such as herding cattle and sewing
carpets. Immersing yourself in family life, and
helping to cook the meals, gives a true insight
into another culture.

5

ASIA

7O9 HIGHLIGHTS OF THE SILK ROAD

The ancient city of Khiva

Charyn Canyon

Camping under the stars

709 Travel the Silk Road

Join a group tour along the Silk Road and you'll take in the landscapes and cities once visited by traders as they made their way from Europe to Asia and back. Wander around ancient cities such as Khiva and Samarkand in Uzbekistan, hike the vast wilderness of Charyn Canyon in Kazakhstan, or the snowcapped Fann Mountains of Tajikistan, and visit remote villages and nomadic communities along the way. This is an eye-opening expedition for teenagers, and there are some great travel companies that can help you plan it.

710 Ride a legendary railway

The most fabled train journey on the planet, the Trans-Siberian Railway takes you from historic cities to the grasslands of the steppe and through wild Siberian terrain. You can tailor your journey according to the ages (and stamina) of your kids, but it's your time on board that might be the most memorable. Linger outside your carriage, chat with your fellow travelers, and learn about the different peoples that inhabit this part of the world.

711 Investigate ancient stone spirals

Up in the White Sea, the Solovetsky Islands offer beautiful rugged nature, forests, lakes, a huge monastery (that has also served as a prison and a labor camp), beaches—and thirty-five intriguing stone spiral labyrinths. Known locally as "Babylons," it is thought the labyrinths were built to trap the souls of the dead so that they didn't disturb the living. Can you walk through them without crossing the lines?

712 Tour St. Petersburg by boat

With ninety-four waterways flowing through the city, St. Petersburg is crying out to be toured by boat. Russia's first emperor, Peter the Great, decreed that all important buildings had to face the water, so it's by far the best way to see the stunning architecture. Set children the challenge of counting bridges—there are more than three hundred crossing the city's rivers and canals.

713 Dodge the spray of gilded fountains

In the formal gardens of the vast Peterhof Palace—"The Russian Versailles"—sixty-four fountains and two hundred bronze statues line the great stairway leading to Peter the Great's creation. Elsewhere in the gardens are more unusual fountains, including a set designed as a chessboard and—every child's favorite—the "joke" fountain that only goes off when someone unexpectedly stands on a certain paving slab.

714 Admire art in the Hermitage Museum

Indisputably one of the world's greatest art museums, the State Hermitage Museum has over three million items in its collection, from ancient urns to Impressionist masterpieces. The majority of the collection is housed in the opulent Winter Palace, the former residence of the tsars, which lies along the banks of the Neva River.

714 THE HERMITAGE

715 Tuck into traditional Russian cuisine

Russian cuisine makes the most of local ingredients, with potatoes, cabbage, and meat forming the basis of many dishes. Borscht (beetroot soup) and pelmeni (meat dumplings) are national favorites, both served with a dollop of *smetana* (sour cream). At breakfast, savor blini, delicious, crêpe-like pancakes enjoyed with a variety of different toppings.

715 RUSSIAN CUISINE

MOSCOW, RUSSIA

716 Snap a selfie in front of a world-famous landmark

For a family selfie that captures Russia in a single image, line up in front of St. Basil's Cathedral. One of the greatest churches on Earth, this crazy confusion of styles, shapes, and colors was laid down by none other than Ivan the Terrible. And if that name doesn't grab a child's attention, then nothing will.

716 ST. BASIL'S CATHEDRAL

MOSCOW, RUSSIA

717 Go to the Bolshoi ballet

Nowhere does ballet quite like Russia. Even if your child has never pirouetted in their life, they will be transfixed by an evening at the Bolshoi Theater—a building as extravagant as a wedding cake. Performances here of *Swan Lake* or other classics are mesmerizing—you'll probably have little people clamoring for ballet lessons afterward.

719 SUZDAL

720 ICE SCULPTURES

MOSCOW, RUSSIA

718 Ice-skate on frozen paths in Gorky Park

When the cold weather sets in, Moscow's largest park becomes a veritable winter wonderland. Slip your ice skates on and glide along its frozen paths, which form one of the largest open-air ice rinks in Europe. Food and drink kiosks line the route, perfect for a quick pit stop to enjoy a warming hot chocolate.

SUZDAL, RUSSIA

719 Visit one of the Golden Ring towns

Lying northeast of Moscow is a cluster of beautifully preserved, old Russian cities that form part of the Golden Ring of Russia. One of the most attractive is Suzdal, with a Kremlin fortress, monasteries, and delightful onion-domed churches. You can explore the town on a horse-drawn carriage, the clippety-clop of horses echoing through the streets.

TOMSK, RUSSIA

720 Marvel at an ice-sculpture festival

When it comes to building a snowman, standards are high at Crystal Tomsk, an ice sculpture festival in the Siberian city of Tomsk. Highly skilled teams spend days building ornate sculptures out of blocks of ice. The result is a sparkling winter-wonderland show lit by subtle lighting and backed by a huge Christmas tree.

YAKUTSK, RUSSIA
721 Meet a woolly mammoth

For the ultimate in offbeat—
and off the beaten track—family
adventure, head to the remote
eastern Russian city of Yakutsk,
where all the buildings are raised
up on stilts so they don't sink into
the melting permafrost. Venture
into an ice tunnel to see icy
woolly mammoths and ice
sculptures of celebrities.

KRONOTSKY NATURE RESERVE, RUSSIA
722 Look out for Russia's national animal

About as far east as you can go
in Russia, the Kronotsky Nature
Reserve offers a sanctuary for
wildlife amid epic scenery. There
are twenty-five volcanos, a valley
of geysers, thermal lakes, ancient
forests, and stunning waterfalls.
You can stay in the park at camps
and lodges, and there are guides
who will take you on tours that
give the best chance of seeing the
wildlife, such as Russia's national
symbol, the brown bear.

LAKE BAIKAL, RUSSIA
723 Cross a lake by dogsled

The deepest lake in the world,
Lake Baikal freezes over in
winter, its waters transforming
into solid blocks of ice that
can reach up to 4.6 ft. (1.4 m)
thick—look down and you'll
see beautiful patterns of cracked,
dark blue ice. Hop onto a sled
and let frisky Siberian huskies
whizz you across the lake as
you take in views of Siberia's
frozen wilderness.

722 BROWN BEARS

724 TBILISI

TBILISI, GEORGIA
724 Wander a historic Old Town

A beguiling mix of Asian and European influences, Tbilisi is a hit with any young history buffs—and wandering the atmospheric Old Town is the best way to experience it. Winding streets are lined with carved, wooden verandas, narrow shopfronts, and street stalls selling fruit and spices, and there are plenty of places to stop for coffee, tea, or mint lemonade. Head to Mtatsminda Park for the quirky, stacked upside-down home.

THROUGHOUT GEORGIA
725 Attend a traditional feast

Georgians love to host *supra*—a coming together of family and friends for food and conversation. Here you'll be plied with an endless selection of Georgian dishes, such as salads, dumplings, grilled meats, and flaky *khachapuri* (see 726). Key to it all are the *tamada*—heartfelt toasts in honor of your presence, long life, or the Georgian nation, which may involve spontaneous polyphonic singing.

THROUGHOUT GEORGIA

726 Savor *khachapuri*, Georgia's culinary specialty

Rich, hearty, and filling, Georgian cuisine bursts with flavors that delight the senses. *Khachapuri* is a firm favorite: an exquisite, boat-shaped bread with a heart-filled center that oozes with melted cheese. This traditional bread serves as an accompaniment to most dishes and comes in many varieties. You'll find Adjarian khachapuri, served with an egg baked at its center, and Megruli khachapuri, similar to a traditional khachapuri but loaded with even more cheese. Simply heaven.

CAUCASUS MOUNTAINS, GEORGIA

727 Hike in the Caucasus

The snow-covered peaks of Georgia's Caucasus Mountains are some of the highest in Europe, and a paradise for hikers of all ages and abilities. Follow the trails and you'll come across glaciers, waterfalls, and traditional stone villages, and take in views that stretch across to Russia. How far you go is up to you. Day-long walks might work for younger kids, while teenagers could tackle multiday hikes, with nights spent wild camping or in homestays.

727 THE CAUCASUS MOUNTAINS

BUKHARA, UZBEKISTAN
728 Stroll through medieval streets

A major stop along the famed Silk Road, Bukhara is one of central Asia's most beautifully preserved medieval centers. Tucked away along its maze of narrow streets are intricately adorned, onion-domed mosques and madrassas. At the city's bustling central bazaar, you can stock up on all manner of exotic items, from colorful spices to handwoven rugs and scarves.

THROUGHOUT UZBEKISTAN
729 Try Uzbekistan's most famous dish

Plov is the culinary staple of Uzbekistan, a warming, aromatic dish made with long-grain rice, onions, carrots, and lamb. It's traditionally prepared in a large, cast-iron *kazan* (a wok-style casserole) on an open fire. An irresistible smell of meat wafts through the air, tantalizing the taste buds.

THROUGHOUT UZBEKISTAN
730 Stay with an Uzbek family

Warm hospitality lies at the very heart of central Asia, and there's no better way to delve into Uzbekistan's culture than by overnighting at a traditional homestay, learning about local customs. There are plenty of families keen to open their homes to visitors, sharing traditions and favorite foods with their guests.

728 BUKHARA

734 TRADITIONAL YURT

TYURATAM, KAZAKHSTAN
731 Watch a rocket take off

Many kids dream of going into space; give their imaginations a rocket boost and witness an actual rocket launch at the Baikonur Cosmodrome. Before takeoff, guided tours of the spaceport (where Yuri Gagarin once worked), its museums, facilities, and memorials make for a fascinating introduction to the history, and future, of the Russian space program.

ASTANA, KAZAKHSTAN
732 Promote peace

Give children a reason to feel optimistic about world peace with a vist to Kazakhstan's Palace of Peace and Reconciliation. This impressive 203 ft. (62 m) high glass pyramid was built to represent all the world's faiths and reflect the essence of Kazakhstan, where people of many cultures and nationalities live together in peace and harmony.

GOLUBAYA BAY, KAZAKHSTAN
733 See the sea that could be a lake

Political disputes rage about whether the Caspian Sea is a sea or a lake. Five countries border the world's largest inland body of water, and its legal definition affects what share of the coastline they get. Whether it's a sea or a lake, it provides beautiful sunset-watching opportunities at Golubaya Bay (Blue Bay) along the coast from Aktau.

SONG KOL LAKE, KYRGYZSTAN
734 Help herders with their daily life

Staying in a yurt camp in the high-altitude, alpine surrounds of Song Kol Lake is a magical experience. These are the summer pastures of choice for nomadic Kyrgyz people, and kids can spend days horseback riding, hiking, making *kumyz* (fermented mares' milk), or just running, climbing, and scrambling to their hearts' desire.

736 ASHGABAT

735 Hike to the valley of flowers

The alpine scenery around Jeti-Ögüz is beautiful. It is a straightforward two-hour hike from the town to the Valley of Flowers (Kok Jayik) which, as its name suggests, is filled with blossoming wildflowers each spring. It's worth the walk all year, with its towering mountain surrounds—and there are yurts you can rent in the valley if you wanted to spend a night surrounded by the hills.

736 Marvel at a modern city

Ashgabat is an intriguing city. It is described as a cross between Las Vegas, Dubai, and Pyong Yang, and is a curious mix of state buildings—almost always built of white marble and gold—and weird monuments. It appears in the *Guinness Book of Records* four times with entries along the lines of "largest indoor Ferris wheel" or "largest building in the shape of a star." Children will be suitably impressed.

737 Buy a carpet in Turkmenistan

Carpet-making is such an integral part of Turkmenistan's culture that carpet patterns feature on the country's national flag, it has a National Carpet Day at the end of May, and there is even a Ministry of Carpets that has to give its approval to any carpet over a certain size that is bought for export. Visit the Turkmen Carpet Museum to see an astounding amount of carpets, including one the size of a house, or head to Tolkuchka Bazaar to buy one to take home with you.

FANN MOUNTAINS, TAJIKISTAN

738 Soak up the beauty of a mountain lake

The Fann Mountains in western Tajikistan have almost a hundred peaks and countless stunning turquoise lakes. There are hiking options here to suit all types of trip lengths and levels of family fitness. One of the highlights of the area is Iskanderkul Lake near the village of Sarytag. Its vibrant blue waters contrast with the reddish peaks surrounding it. Its name translates as "lake of Alexander the Great," and while there's no evidence that he ever went there, there are many fabulous tales about why the lake was given his name. Take a short trek around the lake, to waterfalls, viewpoints, or other lakes such as Snake Lake—so called because it is home to a large number of water snakes.

KARAKORAM HIGHWAY, PAKISTAN
739 Travel the Karakoram Highway

Follow in the footsteps of traders, pilgrims, and poets along the legendary Karakoram Highway, which winds its way through India, Pakistan, and China. You'll sweep through dramatic mountain scenery, visiting markets, ancient temples, and holy cities, as well as hiking and biking in remote wilderness. This is a true expedition suited to older teenagers. Try joining a small group tour with an operator such as Wild Frontiers.

RISHIKESH, INDIA
740 Find your family zen

Surrounded by the lush, green mountains and peaceful valleys of the Himadri, Ekattva Yogshala yoga school has one thing in mind: helping you and your family to relax and unwind. You can introduce the kids to yoga, meditation, and spirituality, and time away from the studio can be spent soaking up the glorious green of your surroundings.

OLD DELHI, INDIA
741 Go sightseeing by rickshaw

Weaving through chaotic traffic in a rickshaw is a stimulating and bumpy way to take in Old Delhi, and enormous fun for kids. You'll race down narrow lanes, past markets, and to iconic sights such as the Red Fort. And because you're not sealed off in an air-conditioned automobile, you'll feel like part of the unfolding scenery.

NORTHERN INDIA
742 Tour the Golden Triangle

Join other like-minded families on a group tour of the Golden Triangle—a popular tourist circuit taking in New Delhi, Agra, and Jaipur. Traveling with Explore Worldwide, you can go on game drives in search of tigers, visit the Taj Mahal at sunrise, and see a glorious parade of historic forts and palaces.

VARANASI, INDIA
743 Drink a lassi

Lassi, the yogurt-based drink of India, must surely have been created for the culinary delight of children. For the best, head to the legendary Blue Lassi Shop in the holy city of Varanasi, which has been mixing and whipping perfect lassis for over seventy years, and has a menu with around a hundred different types to choose from.

RAJASTHAN, INDIA
744 Live like royalty

Rajasthan is crammed full of elegant palaces and dramatic hilltop forts, and you can live like a maharaja and spend the night in one. From lakeside *havelis* (large traditional houses) complete with wandering peacocks to atmospheric suites set in the walls of Nagaur's magnificent fort, it's the perfect way to inject some fairy-tale magic into your vacation.

744 *HAVELI*

RAJASTHAN, INDIA
745 Get colorful at Holi

You'll get gloriously messy at the festival of Holi, a technicolor
introduction to Hindu culture and a celebration of the coming of
spring. There are bonfires, folk musicians, and dancing, but it's most
famous as a festival of colors. Venture into the streets and you'll
quickly get doused in a rainbow of shades, as people throw colorful
powder and dyed water. Put on some old clothes and join in the fun.

745 CELEBRATE HOLI

RAJASTHAN, INDIA
746 Search for tigers and sloth bears

Once the Jaipur maharaja's hunting ground, the wild jungles of Ranthambore National Park are a wildlife haven for tigers, hyenas, and sloth bears, and a dream destination for young nature buffs. The magic is ramped up further by the presence of temples, *havelis*, and the beguiling tenth-century Ranthambore Fort.

THROUGHOUT INDIA
747 Go upscale on the rails

Riding the rails across mountains, through deserts, and into storied cities is the most romantic way to see India, especially if you bag a suite on a luxury train. Services such as the Maharajas Express, Deccan Odyssey, and Palace on Wheels offer butlers, fine dining, and organized excursions —a fantasy excursion for pampered teens.

750 PUSHKAR

THROUGHOUT INDIA
748 Dig into curry by the roadside

Dhabas, or rustic roadside eateries, are an essential part of life for India's truck drivers and travelers, and joining them is the best bit of any road journey. These are no-frills, open-air joints, but the curry is fresh and delicious, and a sweet cup of chai or a creamy fruit lassi will win over any fussy eaters.

JAIPUR, INDIA
749 Fly a kite above rooftops

On January 14 each year, people flood into Rajasthan to flaunt their kite-flying skills at the Jaipur Kite Festival, which marks the day when winter turns to summer. Join local people on their rooftops and balconies as they launch their kites into the sky. The sight of thousands of colorful kites dancing above the city is truly mesmerizing.

PUSHKAR, INDIA
750 Visit a camel fair

For a few days in November, tourists join locals and traders for the epic spectacle of the Pushkar Camel Fair, on the edge of the Thar Desert. Some fifty thousand camels, horses, and cattle are brought in from across the state and some serious haggling ensues, while musicians, poets, and comedians entertain the crowds.

AGRA, INDIA

751 Take a family portrait at the monument to love

Ask a child to tell you something about India and it's almost a given that the Taj Mahal, the world's most famous monument to love, will be near the top of the list. So imagine the thrill of gathering for a family portrait with this most exquisite of buildings in the background.

751 TAJ MAHAL

DARJEELING, INDIA
752 Stay on a tea estate

There are soul-stirring Himalayan views at
Glenburn Tea Estate, a working plantation in
1,600 ac (647.5 ha) of forest and hills, where you
can see how tea is grown. There are posh suites in
the original colonial mansion, but kids might prefer
riverside, lamplit living at the rustic, off-grid lodge
and campsite.

ALLEPPEY, INDIA
753 Sleep on a houseboat

The backwaters of Alleppey are a tranquil maze of
canals, small rivers, and lagoons fringed with palm
trees and paddy fields. Cruising through these on a
traditional Kerala houseboat (they come in various
styles: some are more toddler friendly than others)
is a beautiful experience, with bird-watching and
sunsets, and village life passing you by on the banks.

753 ALLEPPEY

THEKKADY, INDIA
754 Spot the stripes of a tiger

Finding tigers in their natural habitat is never easy,
but at the Periyar Tiger Reserve your chances are
increased by having groups of six or less people (over
twelves only), and treks are led by former poachers,
now protectors, who know the area and animal
behavior better than anyone.

NORTHWEST SRI LANKA
755 Look out for leopards

You won't find masses of jeeps at Wilpattu National Park—just an expanse of forests, scrub, and wetlands, where you can experience the wild in relative peace. Elephants, leopards, and sloth bears are the region's heavy hitters, but there's just as much wonder to be found encountering herds of deer and colorful, endemic birds.

CENTRAL PROVINCE, SRI LANKA
756 Climb a rock fortress

A visit to Sigiriya is like a storybook come to life. This 669 ft. (200 m) high hulk of rock rises sharply from the central plains, and soars to a flat summit, crowned by the ruins of a fortified, fifth-century palace. It's a strenuous 1,200 steps to get to the top, but the reward is more than worth it: spellbinding views over jungles and lakes, and across to the faraway Knuckles Mountains.

ELLA, SRI LANKA
757 Make the perfect Sri Lankan curry

Sri Lankan curry is a food genre all to itself, and children will love them. Let them grate their own coconut, mix the spices, and simmer the chicken on a family-friendly cookery class in the lovely, cool, green hilltown of Ella.

755 LEOPARD AT A WATERHOLE

756 SIGIRIYA

ELLA, SRI LANKA

758 Take your toddler up a mountain

It's a 3 mi. (4.5 km) round trip through lush, green tea plantations up to Little Adam's Peak from the base, along a safe and well-marked trail that can be tackled by the littlest of legs. Once you reach the top, you'll be rewarded with views out over mist-soaked hills and waterfalls, made even more special if you time your hike to coincide with sunrise or sunset.

EASTERN SRI LANKA

759 Sleep in luxury beachside tents

You can live like an upscale Robinson Crusoe on the golden beaches of Sri Lanka's east coast, where Karpaha Sands offers laid-back luxury tents among the coconut groves. The kids can get stuck into snorkeling, stand-up paddleboarding, and swimming, or just hit the wide, deserted beach and run and run and run.

758 LITTLE ADAM'S PEAK

CENTRAL PROVINCE, SRI LANKA

760 Cycle through an archeological wonderland

Take your miniature history buffs to Sri Lanka's central plains, where you'll find the colossal remains of Polonnaruwa, the country's royal seat between the eleventh and thirteenth centuries, and one of the highlights of the Cultural Triangle. Getting around by bike is all part of the fun. You'll whizz between beautifully preserved palaces, temples, and giant Buddha carvings with ease—and it's an excellent way to keep the kids engaged.

762 SURF IN WELIGAMA

KANDY TO BADULLA, SRI LANKA
761 Sightsee by train

The train ride from Kandy to Badulla is one of the
most beautiful in the world, carving its way from
Sri Lanka's spiritual capital through emerald tea
plantations and steamy tropical forest. The full trip
takes seven to eight hours, but if you're short of time
book in for the final section from Ella to Badulla—
the valleys and ravines make it the most dramatic
section of the trip.

WELIGAMA, SRI LANKA
762 Learn to surf in Weligama

With bathtub-warm water, ever-present sunshine,
and small and gentle waves breaking onto a long
stretch of palm-dotted sand, Weligama has to be
one of the best places imaginable to first take to
a surfboard. Masses of surf schools and camps, as
well as patient and experienced instructors, will
ensure you and your kids are hanging ten by sunset.
Just be aware that you might never get them to leave
the beach again.

764 THE ANNAPURNA FOOTHILLS

765 INDIAN RHINO

KATHMANDU, NEPAL
763 Volunteer at a Nepalese school

Volunteering in a Nepalese community will reap huge benefits for you, your kids, and your hosts. You'll work in a local school while your children take classes and make new friends. Nights are spent at a homestay for a fully immersive and unforgettable experience. Volunteering Journeys can get you started.

NORTH-CENTRAL NEPAL
764 Trek in the Annapurna foothills

Children of all ages can walk in the Annapurna foothills, especially on an organized trip with the likes of Swiss Family Treks and Expeditions. You'll take in stunning Himalayan scenery and visit traditional Gurung villages—and porters and ponies can help carry your bags (or your child).

CHITWAN NATIONAL PARK, NEPAL
765 Go scouting for rhinos

Royal Bengal tigers are the headline act at steamy, subtropical Chitwan National Park, but you're more likely to spot endangered one-horned Indian rhinos. Weave your way through the jungle in an open-topped jeep or feel your heart race on a walking safari—either way, these gnarled, almost prehistoric beasts will take your breath away.

THROUGHOUT MONGOLIA
766 Explore the steppe on horseback

There are epic adventures to be had in the wild, vast landscapes of Mongolia, where mountains, forest, and rolling steppe collide. Outdoorsy kids will be in their element here, particularly if they like to ride. Local operators will help you live like the herders and jump on a horse, a wonderful way to explore the grasslands.

GOBI DESERT, MONGOLIA
767 Search for fossils in the desert

You'll feel like a real-life Indiana Jones in the remote reaches of the Gobi Desert, where the parched landscape hides a host of paleontological discoveries. Nomadic Expeditions can get you out to Tugregiin Shiree, to see a fossil of a protoceratops and velociraptor locked in combat, and to the Flaming Cliffs, a fossil-rich hunting ground.

THROUGHOUT MONGOLIA
768 Ride on a yak cart

Yak carts are part of Mongolian herder culture, and an excellent means of slow travel. Book a trip with Eternal Landscapes and you'll follow a steady pace through the countryside, both riding in the cart and walking alongside your yak. This isn't about ticking off sights, but about soaking up local life and the landscapes around you.

BAYAN-ÖLGII, MONGOLIA
769 Attend a Golden Eagle Festival

The Kazakh eagle hunters of Mongolia put on a thrilling show for the crowd at their tourist-friendly festivals in March, September, and October. Kids will be rooted to their seats with excitement as the horseback riders demonstrate their falconry skills, as well as an impressive ability to communicate with these powerful and beautiful birds of prey.

767 GOBI DESERT

769 KAZAKH EAGLE HUNTER

HARBIN, CHINA
770 Chill out at an ice festival

The scale of the Harbin International Ice and Snow
Sculpture Festival is immense. It's like a small town,
with replicas of famous buildings built from blocks
of ice and beautifully illuminated. It's impressive
yet charming to wander around, but there's also
plenty of fun to be had from ice sliding and
sledding to watching ice hockey matches and
dance performances.

ZHANGJIAJIE, CHINA
771 Take a ride in the Bailong Elevator

Deep within the stunning Wulingyuan Scenic Area
there is a viewing option with a difference: three
double-decker glass elevators are bolted onto the
cliff face, taking you from the valley floor 1,070 ft.
(326 m) up to the clifftop in just two minutes. Now
there's an alternative to a two-hour trek.

770 ICE FESTIVAL

YA'AN, CHINA
772 Volunteer at a giant panda sanctuary

High up in the beautiful Bifengxia mountain range is the Bifengxia Giant Panda Base, home to some forty pandas and a hard-working team of conservationists. They welcome volunteers aged ten and over to help secure a positive future for these beautiful yin-yang bears. You'll help with feeding, making panda food, cleaning enclosures, and monitoring behavior.

772 GIANT PANDA

BEIJING, CHINA
773 Eat authentic Peking duck

A former imperial cuisine created for the Yuan Dynasty, Peking (or Beijing) duck tastes better in the Chinese capital than anywhere else. Crisp, crackly skin and tender meat is served with sweet bean sauce, cucumber, scallions, and pancakes, and is hugely popular with kids—especially since they can get hands-on and roll them up themselves.

BEIJING, CHINA
774 Be wowed by Chinese acrobats

The kids will "ooh" and "aah" at the dramatic displays at Beijing's Chaoyang Theater. It may be touristy, but it's top of the charts when it comes to acrobatics, featuring some of the best troupes in China. You'll see stunts involving bicycles, catapults, and barrels, and of course, there's plenty of flying through the air.

774 AMAZING ACROBATICS

BEIJING, CHINA
775 Wave at the astronauts from the Great Wall of China

We all know you can see the Great Wall of China from space, don't we? Wrong. Nothing human-made is visible from space with the naked eye. From Earth, however, it is wonderfully seeable as it snakes across 13,670 mi. (22,000 km) from northern China to southern Mongolia. Many visitors (about sixty million a year) head to the section at Badaling, but to avoid the crowds go to Mutianyu, which is still beautifully preserved and offers archetypal views of the wall over mountains in the distance. Once they've had their fill of walking on one of history's greatest building projects, children will love jumping on the toboggan which can get them back down.

XI'AN, CHINA
776 Stand to attention with Terracotta Warriors

See if the kids can stand to attention like the Terracotta Warriors on display in the city of Xi'an. Created in the third century B.C.E. and lost to the world for over two thousand years, the Terracotta Army is one of the world's greatest archeological discoveries, and what makes it even more impressive is that not one of the soldiers' faces is alike.

775 GREAT WALL OF CHINA

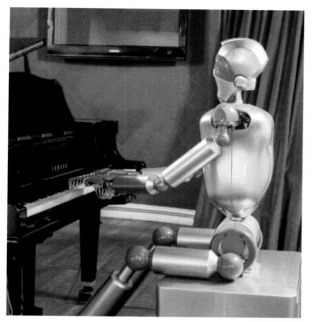
778 ROBOT WORLD

779 WALKING ON PLANKS

XI'AN, CHINA
777 Learn the ancient art of calligraphy

For some hands-on family entertainment, give the children a lesson in the ancient art of calligraphy. They'll learn basic brushstrokes, including how to write their own name, and a takeaway scroll is usually included. Both the Beilin Museum and the Tangbo Art Museum offer classes for kids of any age.

SHANGHAI, CHINA
778 Get hands-on at a science museum

The Shanghai Science and Technology Museum in Pudong is a full-day event. It houses a wealth of interactive, kid-friendly exhibitions on themes such as space travel, biology, and animal kingdoms. Most popular is the interactive Robot World, where you can chat to and play games with animatronic friends.

SHAANXI PROVINCE, CHINA
779 Feel the fear on the Huashan Plank Walk

Be thankful that you're doing the Huashan Plank Walk, a series of wooden planks bolted 985 ft. (300 m) up a sheer-sided mountain slope, in the twenty-first century rather than when it was constructed seven hundred years ago. Today there are chains and safety ropes; back then they just had a sure foot and a lot of faith.

780 KARST HILLS IN YANGSHUO

YANGSHUO, CHINA
780 Cycle through rural China

Yangshuo is ideal for bike rides with kids. Meander along paths past rice paddies, fruit orchards, and grazing water buffalo, into rural villages, all with the splendor of the karst hills looming above you. Pack a picnic and stop on a riverbank for a perfect, relaxed day out.

SOUTHWEST CHINA
781 Hike in a land of leaping tigers

The mountains and valleys of Tiger Leaping Gorge were made famous by the movie *Crouching Tiger, Hidden Dragon*, and they're an incredible setting for a hike with older kids and teens.
You'll need two days to tackle the trail, which will punish your thighs, but reward you with jaw-dropping views of snowy peaks and the Yangtze River below.

GUANGZHOU, CHINA
782 Eat brunch dim sum-style

Guangzhou is the birthplace of Cantonese food, including China's legendary dim sum culture. Once sold from street carts and in roadside teahouses, you can find these bite-size dumplings served in restaurants throughout the city, and they make an excellent family weekend brunch. Top flavors to try include steamed pork buns, turnip cakes, and chicken feet.

784 STAR FERRY

785 DRAGON'S BACK

THROUGHOUT CHINA

783 Join in a Hungry Ghost Festival

On the fifteenth day of the seventh month in the Lunar Calendar, ghosts and ghouls come up from the underworld to roam the earth—or so the legend goes. It's a chance to enjoy the month-long Hungry Ghost Festival, which includes live performances, parades, and offerings of food and money to keep ghostly relations happy.

HONG KONG, CHINA

784 Ride a ferry across Hong Kong harbor

Board one of the famed Star Ferries and travel from Kowloon to Central over the huge Hong Kong harbor. The views of big brash buildings reflected in the still harbor waters and the sense of excitement at arriving in one of the great trade hubs of Asia is palatable for all the family.

HONG KONG, CHINA

785 Hike out of a city

One of the best urban hikes in Asia, and easy to tackle with kids, the Dragon's Back takes you away from the busy city to a peaceful slice of greenery. This 5.2 mi. (8.5 km) trail passes through Shek O Country Park, along the Dragon's Back ridge, and to Shek O Peak, for glorious views out toward offshore islands. Finish your hike at Big Wave Bay, where you can take a celebratory dip in the ocean.

PARO, BHUTAN

786 Learn to shoot an arrow

Budding Robin Hoods can aim for the golden
arrow in Paro, where expert instructors give lessons
in archery. This is the national sport in Bhutan,
the mysterious Himalayan kingdom that puts the
happiness of its people over economic growth. You'll
enjoy plenty of good vibes yourselves as you compete
to see who can hit the bullseye.

PARO, BHUTAN

787 Visit a cliff-ledge monastery

If your kids like fairy stories, then they will love
the Paro Taktsang Monastery in Bhutan. Known
as the Tiger's Nest, this spectacular place nestles
on a cliff face and was built, according to legend,
to commemorate the spot where an eighth-century
guru riding on the back of a flying tiger landed,
bringing Buddhism to Bhutan.

SHAN STATE, MYANMAR

788 Explore by long-tail boat

Stunning nature and fascinating culture collide at
Inle Lake, a peaceful expanse of water framed by
marshland and mountains. A day spent exploring
by long-tail boat is a wonderful adventure for kids.
You'll get to visit the floating villages and gardens
of the Intha people, and see local fishermen rowing
their boats with one leg.

BAGAN, MYANMAR

789 Tour ancient temples by hot-air balloon

Once the heart of a mighty kingdom, Bagan is Myanmar's major drawcard. Some two thousand temples, stupas, and pagodas lie scattered across a vast plain, remnants of the Pagan Empire, which ruled this region from the tenth to the thirteenth centuries. You can explore the temples by car, by bike, or even by horse and cart, but to experience the site's majesty to the full, it's best to get up in the air. Board a hot-air balloon flight at sunrise (eight-year-olds and upward) and you'll float peacefully above the earth, as Bagan's ancient structures emerge slowly from the morning mist. If there's ever a chance to get the kids hooked on ancient history, this is it.

789 TEMPLES OF BAGAN

SAYABOURY, LAOS
790 Watch elephants in the wild

A few hours' drive from Luang Prabang, in Sayabouri, you'll find the Elephant Conservation Center (ECC). Wildlife-loving kids will be able to have an ethical experience watching rescued elephants in the wild, as well as learning about the ECC's conservation challenges and the work that is done by their elephant hospital.

LUANG PRABANG, LAOS
791 Explore the Pak Ou caves

Just a short boat trip along the Mekong from Luang Prabang, the Pak Ou caves have been used as a place of worship for centuries—some say the ancient spirits of river gods inhabit them. Kids love exploring caves, and there's nothing scary here.

LUANG PRABANG, LAOS
792 Go temple hopping

Luang Prabang's riverside setting is seductive enough, but its collection of elegant Buddhist temples makes it even more special. Most enchanting for kids are That Chomsi, a hilltop stupa, and Wat Pa Phon Phao, a monastery surrounded by forest. Be sure to get up early to see hundreds of saffron-robed monks head off to collect alms.

792 LUANG PRABANG

793 GIBBON EXPERIENCE

794 VANG VIENG

NAM KAN NATIONAL PARK, LAOS

793 Take a zip line to your bed

You'll trek for two hours through thick, hilly jungle
to reach the Gibbon Experience destination—a hut
suspended up in the canopy and accessible only by
zip line. From here you can spot gibbons and birds,
and swing through the trees on a purpose-built
cable-gliding network. Kids aged eight and over
can join the adventure.

VANG VIENG, LAOS

794 Ride a river in an inner tube

River tubing in Vang Vieng is a wonderful way to
have fun and relax while connecting with nature.
You simply plop into a big inflatable ring and let the
gentle current of the Nam Song River carry you
downstream. Bring a little cash because there are
restaurants on the riverbanks where you can paddle
over to eat.

LUANG PRABANG, LAOS

795 Watch monks collect their alms

Discover the captivating rituals of monastic life in
deeply spiritual Laos by watching Tak Bat. This
traditional ceremony sees hundreds of monks,
clad in their saffron robes, collect alms from local
Buddhists every morning. It's a moving experience
to watch as the monks walk silently along, their
bowls gradually filling up with sticky rice.

LUANG PRABANG, LAOS

796 Take a Lao cookery lesson

Encourage curious palates (and help in the kitchen
back home) with a cooking lesson designed for
families at the Tamarind Restaurant and Cooking
School. Kids aged ten and up can boost their
confidence by whipping up a few traditional
Lao recipes, including the classic sticky rice, in a
welcoming, supportive atmosphere, before everyone
shares the feast.

798 A BANGKOK NIGHT MARKET

NORTHERN THAILAND
797 Meet hill tribes

It's an eye-opening experience to spend time with Thai hill tribes, living in the foothills of northern Thailand. Choose a responsible, community-based expedition such as those offered by Thailand Hilltribe Holidays and you can stay with a host family, becoming part of village life, and immersing your kids in a lifestyle far removed from their own.

BANGKOK, THAILAND
798 Visit a night market

The Thai capital's street food is legendary, and the best way to sample it is at a night market. Head out in the late afternoon to browse beneath the bright lights, as the traffic is replaced by hungry pedestrians. Kid-friendly options abound, from sizzling plates of noodles and dumplings to meaty, fragrant skewers.

BANGKOK, THAILAND
799 Find the perfect surf

Take the guesswork out of whether the surf is up (and the right size for your experience) at the Flow House, which has a simulated surfing machine. Beginners will love the controlled wave size and soft landing surface it offers. Make a day of it: the center is on the beach and has cafés, restaurants, a pool, and games room too.

BANGKOK, THAILAND
800 Cruise city waterways

Bangkok's energy can be overwhelming for young children, but take to the water and you'll get a more peaceful perspective. Hire a traditional long-tail boat and you can cruise down the Chao Phraya River, checking out the skyscrapers and fancy riverside homes, before branching off into the *khlongs* (canals) to see Bangkok life at its most traditional. You can visit stilted villages and floating markets, spot water birds and giant lizards, and feed fish over the sides of the boat.

KO TAO, THAILAND
801 See a kaleidoscope of coral

Thailand's shores are some of the world's most picturesque, so it's no surprise that they're also home to extraordinary snorkeling and diving experiences. The small island of Ko Tao is the place to go for a family-friendly snorkeling experience, with a kaleidoscope of coral reefs surrounded by lush rain forests and a jagged coastline. Marine and land conservation is at the forefront of the island's focus, offering the whole family an educational experience on top of a world-class underwater adventure.

800 BANGKOK BY BOAT

KOH KOOD, THAILAND

802 Spend your holiday in a bamboo den

Soneva Kiri's eco-luxe villas will suit the pickiest of parents, but it's the kids that are the biggest winners thanks to a whimsical kids' club called the Eco Den. Built from bamboo beneath the lush jungle canopy, it has a drawbridge entrance, a slide exit, and a vibe that's Peter Pan meets desert island.

KO SAMUI, THAILAND

803 Enjoy child-friendly island bliss

You can split your time between building sandcastles, swimming, and gentle jungle hikes on Ko Samui. And the island is big on convenience too. Resorts come with everything from kids' clubs and kids' spas to in-house babysitters, so it's a blissful introduction to Southeast Asia for families with young kids.

802 ECO DEN

803 KO SAMUI

SOUTHERN THAILAND
804 Spot wildlife in ancient rain forest

The evergreen rain forest of Khao Sok National Park is one of the oldest in the world, and it's home to wild and wonderful creatures, including gibbons, hornbills, tapirs, and little-seen tigers and sun bears. Pack your hiking boots and bug spray and you can wander jungle trails, canoe along the river, and explore spooky, bat-filled caves.

SOUTHERN THAILAND
805 Overnight in a raft house on a lake

A slash of green surrounded by soaring, limestone cliffs, Cheow Lan Lake is the perfect base for exploring Khao Sok National Park. Nights are spent in traditional raft houses, which range from basic huts without bathrooms or electricity to comfortable, well-equipped cabins. Either way the kids will get a kick out of sleeping over the water, and you'll be able to swim and boat right from your door.

KRABI, THAILAND
806 Cruise around islands

What better way to explore the many magical islands along Thailand's Andaman coast than by boat. From rocky outcrops and white-sand beaches to steep cliffs and intricate cave systems, these lush, jungle-covered islands are a wonder to be seen. Surrounded by warm, turquoise waters and stunning coral reef, there is also plenty of opportunity for a family-friendly snorkel.

804 SPOT GIBBONS

805 CHEOW LAN LAKE

807 SONGKRAN WATER FIGHT

THROUGHOUT THAILAND
807 Get soaked at Songkran

If your kids want a legitimate reason for
a massive water fight, head to Thailand in April
for Songkran—the exuberant celebration of the
Lunar New Year. Entire towns and cities turn into
aquatic battlegrounds as people spray each other
with water guns and hoses. The more traditional
elements include parades, dancing, and folk singers.

NORTHERN THAILAND
808 Drive a tuk-tuk

Taking the controls of an auto-rickshaw (known
locally as tuk-tuks) and driving your family
along Thai roads might seem terrifying, but book
a guided tour with the Tuk Tuk Club and you'll
travel along quiet roads in a convoy of like-minded
travelers. The lack of doors and windows means
you'll fully absorb the heat, smells, and sounds of
rural Thailand.

KOH PHRA THONG, THAILAND
809 Share an island with wildlife

You'll have miles of golden beaches to yourself at the island resort of Baba Ecolodge, where days of snorkeling, canoeing, and jungle hikes blur into one glorious restorative vacation. There's loads of room to roam, and you'll have hornbills, monkeys, and sea turtles for company.

THROUGHOUT THAILAND
810 Introduce the kids to martial arts

Kids as young as four can sign up for introductory Muay Thai (Thai boxing) sessions, where they'll kick, swing punches, and immerse themselves in an integral part of Thai culture. If you're traveling with older teens, you can sign up for weeklong, rural residential camps, where you'll push yourselves to your limits in a patch of paradise.

SIEM REAP, CAMBODIA

811 Discover Angkor Wat by bike

You can get around the Angkor temples by auto-rickshaw, automobile, motorbike, or even helicopter, but nothing beats the sense of freedom that comes from two-wheeling from temple to temple along a maze of dusty tracks. You'll get from majestic Angkor Wat to farther-flung temples with ease, and tandems and bike seats are readily available, so kids of any age can come along for the ride.

SIEM REAP, CAMBODIA

812 Cycle through the jungle

Rent bikes in Siem Reap and follow a guide into the jungle, pedaling the dirt paths alongside flowering lotus fields, water buffalo, and remote villages. End at a Buddhist monastery, where colorfully-robed monks devote their lives to peace and harmony. Buy a small offering of food outside the temple walls and present it to the monks inside for a special blessing.

SIEM REAP, CAMBODIA

813 Eat spiders, crickets, and snakes

Along the banks of the river near Siem Reap stands an outdoor market filled with exotic wares and unusual food. Spend some time browsing for keepsakes, and sample Cambodian delicacies such as deep-fried crickets or larvae with pepper and spices. Marvel at various foods on a stick, including roasted spiders, snakes, frogs, and more.

811 ANGKOR WAT

813 EAT DIFFERENT

815 BAMBOO TRAIN

NORTHWEST CAMBODIA
814 Visit floating villages

The stilted waterside villages of Tonlé Sap Lake
appear to float on the water's surface during the
wet season, when flood waters swell the lake to five
times its low-water size. Jump on a boat and you can
visit the fishermen and their families, and learn how
they make their living from these fertile waters.

BATTAMBANG, CAMBODIA
815 Travel on a bamboo train

Picture a low bamboo platform with handles at
each end and a small motor at the back. This is
Cambodia's bamboo train—or *norry*. It exists
because of the ingenuity of the local people who
cobbled the transport together after the Khmer
Rouge moved out. Board the train for a thrilling
ride, laced with history.

MONDULKIRI, CAMBODIA
816 See elephants enjoy their freedom

Deep in the northeast of Cambodia, the Elephant Valley Project is a sanctuary for rescued elephants from the logging industry. The welfare of these gentle giants is at the forefront, so there is no riding or bathing. Instead, you will learn about the sanctuary's inspiring conservation efforts, and be able to watch the majestic creatures in the wild.

816 ELEPHANTS BATHING

PHNOM PENH, CAMBODIA
817 Learn about the past

Learning about Cambodia's genocide, and paying your respects to its victims, is important if you're in Phnom Penh with older teenagers. Do so at the Tuol Sleng Genocide Museum, set in a former interrogation and extermination center, which documents the suffering under the Khmer Rouge regime.

817 GENOCIDE MUSEUM

PHNOM PENH, CAMBODIA
818 Dive into Khmer culture

There are over a thousand years of history within the elegant walls of the National Museum of Cambodia, including the biggest collection of Khmer art and sculpture in the world. Ancient Khmers practiced both Hinduism and Buddhism, and children and adults will enjoy this collection, which includes a sixth-century, eight-armed Vishnu and a giant pair of wrestling monkeys.

PHNOM PENH, CAMBODIA
819 Discover the secrets of Khmer cuisine

A cooking class is the best way to learn about Khmer cuisine, and kids will love getting their hands dirty and joining in the prep. Your day typically starts with a wander around a local market to select ingredients, before heading back to base to rustle up tasty treats such as Khmer yellow curry or fish *amok*.

KEP, CAMBODIA
820 Eat bargain crab by the beach

A beguiling fishing village known for its white-sand beaches and ruined colonial villas, Kep has another major attraction—its crab market. For just a few dollars you'll be served a pile of juicy, fresh crabs fried with local Kampot pepper. Breaking into them and getting messy is all part of the fun.

820 KEP–HOME OF CRABS

821 PUPPETS IN WATER

822 RICKSHAW RIDE

HANOI, VIETNAM
821 Go to an underwater puppet show

A Vietnamese tradition for eight hundred years, this is a form of puppetry where the levers that move the figures are submerged in a water tank. Puppeteers stand behind the scenes, manipulating the characters to tell age-old fables and mythical stories. Tales are told in the form of musicians and song, while fire-breathing dragons rage and warriors woo village maidens.

HANOI, VIETNAM
822 Take a rickshaw through Hanoi

Hop on a bicycle-powered rickshaw and tour the historic streets of Hanoi's old town. As you sit under a fringed canopy, see areas of commerce hundreds of years old, where silver goods, household wares, fabric, and other items are offered by local craftspeople. People line the sidewalks selling fresh fruit and vegetables, and preparing meals for sale to passersby.

HANOI TO HO CHI MINH CITY, VIETNAM
823 Ride on the Reunification Express

Pack books, games, and inflatable pillows for a thirty-hour journey on Southeast Asia's most iconic railway. The Reunification Express clanks, judders, and whistles the length of Vietnam past rice paddies, jungle thickets, and picturesque fishing villages. Book family-friendly VIP cabins in advance (kids under five travel free) and prepare for adventure.

HANOI TO HUẾ, VIETNAM

824 Bunk down on a sleeper train

Rumbling along in the darkness on the train from Hanoi to Huế is excitement enough for most kids. Add to that a private cabin with pull-down bunk beds, visits from a food trolley, and dramatic coastal views when you pull up the shutters the next morning—you've had an adventure before the day has even begun.

HA LONG BAY, VIETNAM

825 Spend the night on a junk

The karsts (limestone peaks) and emerald waters of Ha Long Bay are full of otherworldly beauty. To make the most of this stunning seascape, little beats a night or two spent on a traditional wooden junk. You'll watch the sunset over the karsts from the deck, and days can be spent kayaking, visiting waterside villages, and trying your hand at squid fishing.

825 JUNK BOATS IN HA LONG BAY

NORTH CENTRAL COAST, VIETNAM
826 Explore Phong Nha Cave by boat

Entering the vast Phong Nha Cave, in Phong Nha-Ke Bang National Park, sailing gently along an underground river, is like journeying to the center of the Earth. Who will be first to see how the caves' spectacular rock formations such as the Lion, the Buddha, and the Fairy Caves got their names?

HOI AN, VIETNAM
827 Go on a food safari

The ancient port town of Hoi An is known for its wooden houses, pagodas, and delicious regional cuisine. Enlist the help of a tour guide and you'll wander the backstreets in search of the best traditional grub. Dishes such as *bánh mì* (Vietnamese sandwich) and *cao làu* (pork noodles) will go down a treat with younger travelers.

SOUTHERN VIETNAM
828 Stay with a family on the Mekong Delta

You'll pass through thick mangroves and past floating markets, then clamber onto a wooden jetty to get to your Mekong Delta homestay. Accommodation will be simple, but the delicious home-cooked meals and starry skies more than make up for it, as does the chance to learn about life on this vital waterway.

826 PHONG NHA CAVE

829 ROYAL PALACES

SEOUL, SOUTH KOREA
829 Explore Seoul's royal palaces

Hidden among Seoul's shiny, modern skyscrapers and shopping malls are remnants of old Korea, including the city's elegant royal palaces. Lose yourself among the tranquil pagodas and sprawling gardens of fourteenth-century Gyeongbokgung; or soak up the atmosphere at Changdeokgung, built in 1405 and home to a magical Secret Garden, where the king and his courtiers once whiled away their time.

830 CAFÉS FOR KIDS

SEOUL, SOUTH KOREA
830 Take things easy at a kids' café

Kids' cafés are a cultural phenomenon. The hangout of choice for Seoul families, they're a one-stop shop for children's entertainment and range from basic jungle gyms complete with coffee shops to huge affairs featuring gaming rooms, kids' spas, fine dining, and nannies to watch the kids.

832 BUKCHON HANOK VILLAGE

833 BORYEONG MUD FEST

SEOUL, SOUTH KOREA

831 Steam your troubles away at a bathhouse

Jjimjilbangs (bathhouses) are a cornerstone of Korean culture, pulling in everyone from grandmas to young families to unwind in hot and cold baths, saunas, and heated salt rooms, with most open 24/7. Some are like mini-amusement parks, including perks such as karaoke rooms, beauty salons, and even retro arcades.

SEOUL, SOUTH KOREA

832 Soak up traditional architecture

Immerse yourself in Korean history at Bukchon Hanok Village, a bustling district of narrow streets and alleyways that's home to around nine hundred *hanok*—traditional Korean homes with timber frames and curved roofs. To ramp up the fun, you could even borrow a *hanbok* (traditional Korean gown) for some memorable family photo ops.

BORYEONG, SOUTH KOREA

833 Get messy at Boryeong mud festival

Every August, Boryeong becomes a giant mud bath as revelers come from across the country to dive into mud pools, slide down muddy slopes, and even jump around on mud-filled bouncy castles—an absolute dream for kids. Activities take place on the beach, so there's always the option to wash yourself off in the ocean.

NISEKO, JAPAN

834 Sign up for kids' ski school

Niseko's ski slopes have some of the finest powder on the planet, and kids as young as three can sign up for English-language ski lessons, where they'll get all the attention they need to help them tackle the slopes.

THROUGHOUT JAPAN

835 Have a shared bath in a Japanese *onsen*

Not all adults will want to share a bath with strangers, and nor will many children, but in Japan the tradition of communal bathing dates back centuries. *Onsen* are natural mineral baths and are often segregated by gender (children can go with either parent though). Wash first before entering the communal bath, and then sit back and relax.

KOKA, JAPAN

836 Admire the ingenuity of ninjas

Learn about true ninja culture in the Koka ninja house, the last remaining in Japan. Rather than secret assassins, ninjas were far more focused on spying—and getting away alive with their information. This house was built in the seventeenth century and has secret doors, hidden tunnels, and windows that need special tricks to open them.

835 ENJOY A COMMUNAL BATH

MATSUMOTO, JAPAN
837 Spy on snow monkeys

Head to the hills northwest of Tokyo and you'll find one of Japan's best-loved animal attractions—hot-tubbing snow monkeys. At Jigokudani Monkey Park, wild macaques come down from the mountains to bathe in a steaming hot spring whenever there's a chill in the air. Come when the landscape is covered with snow for maximum magical atmosphere.

CENTRAL JAPAN
838 Walk part of a pilgrimage route

Kids can pretend to be samurai warriors, protecting the rest of the group, as you walk the Nakasendo Trail in Japan. The 5 mi. (8 km) section between the historic post towns of Tsumago and Magome is the most family-friendly part of this iconic pilgrimage route. Delicious bowls of ramen and chestnut ice creams await after a few hours of easy hiking.

OBUSE, JAPAN
839 Immerse yourself in the art of Hokusai

Take the kids back in time to Japan's fascinating Edo era by learning about its most well-known artist, Hokusai. Most famous for his *ukiyo-e* woodblock prints, his iconic *Great Wave off Kanagawa,* and *Thirty-six Views of Mount Fuji*, the Hokusai Museum in Obuse has a wealth of his work on display.

837 SNOW MONKEYS

842 GHIBLI MUSEUM

THROUGHOUT JAPAN

840 Learn how to make sushi

There's something for everyone in a sushi-making class—the joy of rolling rice, the precision of chopping ingredients, and the fun of tasting new flavors. Find a course that suits you in Tokyo, and as well as new skills, you'll learn plenty about the traditions and culture of this quintessential Japanese food.

THROUGHOUT JAPAN

841 Stay in a traditional *ryokan*

Once a welcome respite for weary travelers along Japan's ancient highways, *ryokans* (traditional inns) are an atmospheric introduction to Japanese culture and a joy for older kids. Rooms have sliding doors, tatami-mat floors, and low tables, and you'll likely have access to an onsen (hot-spring bath). Multicourse meals of regional cuisine are easily arranged.

TOKYO, JAPAN

842 Be inspired by the Ghibli Museum

You can follow hidden passageways, meet a robot, and board a furry cat bus at the Ghibli Museum, a captivating celebration of the animated movies that have come out of Studio Ghibli. Even the museum's colorful, foliage-clad exterior is an exercise in creativity. When you're done exploring, the pint-size, on-site movie theater puts on a selection of animated shorts.

TOYKO, JAPAN
843 Check out Tokyo's vending machines

Japan has more vending machines per capita than anywhere else in the world, and they offer much more than just candy and soda. You can get almost anything at the press of a button, from fresh eggs and underpants to cuddly toys, and even bags of crunchy roasted bugs.

TOKYO, JAPAN
844 Catch a sumo tournament

A quintessential Japanese experience with ancient roots, a sumo tournament feels like entering another world, complete with elaborately costumed referees, prematch spiritual rituals, and a whole lot of ceremony. The match begins with thigh slapping and intimidating stares before the *rikishi* (wrestlers) launch in. Whoever forces the other to step outside the ring is the winner.

TOYKO, JAPAN
845 Tour Tokyo Fish Market

Rise while the morning is still dark and make your way to the famous Tokyo Fish Market, where fishermen unload their fresh catches into market stalls to sell. The array of different sea life here is impressive—everything from the beautiful to the hideous. The price haggling is fun to witness, and walking the narrow aisles highlights seafood you never knew existed.

TOKYO, JAPAN
846 Ring in New Year at a Japanese temple

For a spiritual New Year's Eve, visit a Tokyo temple for *Joya no Kane*. At midnight, a monk rings the temple bell 108 times in an atmospheric purifying ritual, said to wash your past worries away. Too late for the kids? Take them out for *hatsumōde*, the first temple visit of the New Year.

TOYKO, JAPAN
847 Experience pop culture paradise

Akihabara is an assault on the senses and a dream destination for anime- and manga-obsessed kids. As well as selling all kinds of electronic gadgets, the neon-bright stores of Akihabara are crammed with gaming arcades, anime merchandise, and manga comics stores. You can even don a Mario Bros. outfit and drive go-karts through the streets.

847 AKIHABARA

Pop culture paradise

Bright lights

Anime figures

OYAMA AND SUZUKA, JAPAN
848 Seek out the thrills of a racetrack

Japan has a huge motorsport fan base and plenty of high-octane thrills for miniature speed freaks. Fuji Speedway is the best place to see endurance racing, while the Suzuka Circuit puts on a whole range of exhilarating domestic and international competitions, including Formula One Grand Prix.

SAPPORO, JAPAN
849 Slurp noodles in ramen alley

A narrow passageway lined with tiny eateries, Ramen Alley is the place to head for Sapporo's signature miso ramen, a savory bowl of deliciousness born out of Hokkaido's cold winters. Made with miso broth and springy, chewy, yellow noodles, it's both delicious and fun to eat—and kids can slurp to their hearts' content without worrying about their manners.

KYOTO, JAPAN
850 Handle the secrets of the Samurai

Wannabe samurai will be in their element at Kyoto's Samurai and Ninja Museum. As well as taking in displays of ancient armor, swords, and tools, you can catch a live samurai display, try on samurai gear, and even learn how to use a samurai sword.

YOSHINO, JAPAN
851 Celebrate the cherry blossom

Every spring, the Japanese flock to parks and gardens for *hanami* (cherry-blossom viewing) as the first *sakura* (cherry blossoms) appear on the trees. It's a tradition that's been going for over a thousand years and there are few places more breathtaking to experience it than Mount Yoshino, whose slopes are home to some thirty thousand trees.

851 MOUNT YOSHINO

853 NATURAL SLIDES

852 Ride a bullet train

No trip to Japan is complete without a speedy trip on the impressive Shinkansen, or bullet train. Young train enthusiasts will love the excitement of carefully choosing a bento box (freshly made with local ingredients, of course), watching the train arrive, witnessing the outstandingly precise, seven-minute turnaround service, and then just letting themselves sink into a comfortable seat as they witness Japan's panoramic views pass by at speeds of up to 200 mph (320 km/h).

KYUSHU, JAPAN

853 Slide down a waterfall

Head into the mountains of Kyushu to experience a true natural playground in the form of the Ryumon Falls. Kids (and parents) will love the exhilarating slides created by the smooth rocks at these waterfalls. The natural slides range from tame to adrenaline-inducing high (and fast), making it a perfect day out for families with kids of all ages.

854 SURF IN LA UNIÓN

856 TRADITIONAL POT MAKING

LA UNIÓN, PHILIPPINES
854 Learn to surf in San Juan

Ask any Filipino where to surf in northern Luzon and they'll point you to San Juan, a large bay in La Unión. Waves roll in consistently between September and March, with breaks suitable for beginners as well as more advanced surfers. Hop on a board and ride the waves, then refuel at one of the laid-back beach cafés.

VIGAN, PHILIPPINES
855 Ride on a horse-drawn cart

One of the Philippines's oldest towns, Vigan exudes old-world charm, with pretty, cobbled streets and wonderfully-fine wooden buildings blending Spanish and Chinese architectural styles. Explore town on a *kalesa* (horse-drawn cart) to best soak up the town's bygone atmosphere.

VIGAN, PHILIPPINES
856 Try your hand at traditional pottery

Vigan is famous for its earthenware pottery, known as *burnay*, a craft that dates back to precolonial times, when Chinese immigrants settled in the city to trade. Watch potters at work, then pop behind the wheel to try your hand at creating your own pieces —it's harder than it looks!

BANAUE, PHILIPPINES
857 Trek through rice terraces

Hand-carved into the mountainside thousands of years ago by the Ifugao people, the spectacular rice terraces of the Cordilleras carpet the valleys and hillsides that are dotted with traditional villages. The best way to explore is on foot, trekking through the rice paddies and overnighting in a hut with a local family.

MANILA, PHILIPPINES
858 Explore one of the oldest districts of Manila

Established by the Spanish in the sixteenth century, Intramuros was once the beating heart of Manila. To this day encircled by city walls, the district's buildings are beautifully preserved, with churches, mansions, and museums offering an insight into nineteenth-century life in the capital.

EASTERN LUZON, PHILIPPINES
859 Trek through karst terrain

Nestled in the lush Sierra Madre mountains, the Masungi Georeserve is a conservation area, home to dramatic limestone landscapes harboring endemic species of plants and wildlife. There are trails that crisscross the karst terrain, with hands-on activities designed to help return the land to its natural state.

857 RICE TERRACES

861 DON'T MISS A JEEPNEY

RIZAL, PHILIPPINES

860 Stay overnight in an eco-park

Lying in the foothills of the Sierra Madre mountains, the Mount Purro Nature Reserve is an unspoiled eco-park, where visitors can immerse themselves in nature, with mountain hikes, swimming, and stargazing. Overnight in traditional huts and wake up to the soothing sounds of nature.

THROUGHOUT THE PHILIPPINES

861 Take a ride on a jeepney

Loud, colorful jeepneys—the descendants of American World War II jeeps—are the most common form of public transport in the Philippines, and a much-loved national symbol. Older kids and teens will relish a ride. Either pick one up at a terminal or flag one down in the street, dodging the traffic to jump on.

DONSOL, PHILIPPINES

862 Swim with whale sharks

One of the world's largest concentrations of whale sharks gathers in the waters of Donsol between January and April. Good swimmers will love the thrill of snorkeling with the world's largest fish, watching these gentle giants of the sea glide close to the surface to feed on vast quantities of plankton.

CAMARINES SUR, PHILIPPINES
863 Learn to wakeboard

With scores of activities to keep young watersports enthusiasts entertained, the CamSur Watersports Complex is sure to be a hit. It's one of the top wakeboarding parks in the world, and kids can also try their hand at kneeboarding, waterskiing, and wakeskating, with ramps and obstacles designed to keep them on their toes (and show off a few cool tricks).

ALBAY, PHILIPPINES
864 Experience the thrills of an ATV ride

The most active volcano in the country, Mount Mayon looks deceivingly graceful, with its near-perfect cone and symmetrically smooth slopes. Teenagers can get up close on a thrilling ATV ride, driving across rugged terrain strewn with volcanic boulders and meandering streams—an experience that is guaranteed to get adrenaline pumping.

BORACAY, PHILIPPINES
865 Sail into the sunset

The Philippines's most popular beach resort, Boracay, is famous for its White Beach, a gorgeous stretch of coastline with powdery-white sand lapped by crystal-clear waters. Families can escape the crowds aboard a traditional *paraw* (sailboat) as the sun gently sets, painting the sky in a riot of pink hues.

865 BORACAY

PALAWAN, PHILIPPINES
866 Splash out at an inflatable waterpark

Bounce, slide, and clamber along Kamia Bay Resort's thrilling, inflatable waterpark, which floats on the surface of Palawan's clear blue waters. Obstacles, oversized trampolines, and slides provide plenty of thrills as kids race their friends and family on what is guaranteed to be an epic water adventure.

PALAWAN, PHILIPPINES
867 Explore an underground river

Said to be the longest underground river in the world, the Puerto Princesa Subterranean River carves its way through limestone hills to eventually flow into the South China Sea. You can explore the river by boat, gliding across its tranquil, turquoise waters through vast caverns and narrow passages.

PALAWAN, PHILIPPINES
868 Discover the natural wonders of the Bacuit Archipelago

In the Bacuit Archipelago off the coast of El Nido, limestone outcrops jut out of turquoise-blue waters, harboring hidden lagoons and coves that are best explored on a kayak. Look down to catch a glimpse of the underwater world—the waters are so clear you'll be able to see vibrant coral and shoals of fish.

868 EL NIDO

BOHOL, PHILIPPINES
869 Spot oh-too-cute tarsiers

Cute and cuddly, tarsiers are tiny, nocturnal primates, measuring between 3.5 to 6 in. (9–15 cm) long. Their huge eyes lend them an alien-like appearance, and they're capable of rotating their heads an incredible 180 degrees. Visit the Philippine Tarsier Sanctuary, set up to protect the native population, to spot these extraordinary furry creatures.

THROUGHOUT THE PHILIPPINES
870 Eat, sleep, and dive on a liveaboard

Little beats getting out of bed and jumping straight into the sea for an early-morning swim, or moving from dive site to dive site, spotting whales from the deck as you travel. Book a family cabin on a liveaboard dive boat and you can do just that, with the chance to dive and snorkel with sharks and turtles, and around the area's shipwrecks.

MANADHOO, MALDIVES
871 Slide into the sea

When you wake up in your plush, overwater villa at Soneva Jani, you're faced with some tough questions. Do you jump off the deck into the warm sea, or whizz down into the lagoon courtesy of your own private waterslide? The thrill of the latter will keep the kids going for hours, until they discover the resort's chocolate and ice-cream rooms, or southeast Asia's biggest den, that is.

THROUGHOUT THE MALDIVES
872 Find paradise the local way

Posh resorts aren't the only way to see the Maldives. A local island family could deliver a more authentic piece of paradise. You'll still get stunning, castaway scenery and fantastic snorkeling, but the chance to eat home-cooked Maldivian food while your kids make new pals on the beach will make the experience even more special.

THROUGHOUT THE MALDIVES
873 Sit on a sandbank

As well as the 1,200 permanent islands that make up the Maldives, there are also countless smaller and more transitory sandbanks. With no vegetation and no dwellings, these tiny dots or ribbons of perfect white sand give you a desert island all of your own. Take a boat ride out to one and enjoy splashing in the shallows and building sandcastles, or pack a picnic and make a day of it.

871 SONEVA JANI

RAA ATOLL, MALDIVES
874 Splash in bioluminescence

As night falls on Vaadhoo Island, you might
be treated to a magical phenomenon: the waves
glowing with ethereal blue light due to the presence
of bioluminescent plankton. Take a walk after dark
and watch the surf glitter as it crashes onto the
shore. Dip your feet in and you'll leave a trail of
sparkly footprints on the sand.

SOUTH ARI ATOLL, MALDIVES
875 Swim with whale sharks

If seeing the world's biggest fish is on your wish list,
then head to the whale shark superhighway—aka
South Ari Atoll. For maximum excitement, don
a snorkel, get in the water, and swim alongside
them. Kids as young as six can join in—
just remember to choose a responsible
operator and keep a respectful distance.

GEORGE TOWN, MALAYSIA
876 Indulge in *roti canai* for breakfast

The best thing to do in George Town is fill your stomach. Start at breakfast with local favorite *roti canai*, best eaten at a sidewalk stall or market. The flaky, buttery flatbread, dipped into a plate of aromatic chicken, beef, or mutton curry is great fun to eat, and will set you up for a day of sightseeing.

GEORGE TOWN, MALAYSIA
877 Soak up local history

Drink in George Town's colorful heritage as you walk around its central core, which has played host to Chinese, Malay, Indian, and British cultures. Beautiful 1920s shophouses sit alongside Buddhist temples, Chinese clan houses, and colonial villas, in a beguiling jumble that will enchant any young history or architecture buffs.

877 GEORGE TOWN

879 OVER-THE-TOP RICKSHAWS

LANGKAWI, MALAYSIA
878 Hang out with rescue cats

The first thing you notice when you arrive at Bon Ton Resort is the painstakingly restored, antique wooden villas. Next you might spot one of the furry visitors. The resort owners run a cat sanctuary, and feline friends might join you at the pool, at the bar, or even in your room. It's kitty heaven for kids.

MELAKA, MALAYSIA
879 Ride a fantasy rickshaw

Zipping around on a bicycle rickshaw while exploring a foreign city is exciting enough for most kids. Add an over-the-top, colorful theme and you're onto a serious winner. In Melaka, you'll find rides decked out in everything from Pokémon and Baby Shark to Minions, sometimes blaring out loud pop music for good measure.

881 SUN BEAR

SARAWAK, MALAYSIA
880 Go off-grid in a longhouse

Journeying into the rain forest to spend a night in an Iban longhouse is a dream for young explorers. There are no bedrooms, just a communal living area, with mattresses under mosquito netting, and paraffin lamps to light your way. You're encouraged to join in with cooking, dancing, and singing, in an eye-opening introduction to local life.

SEPILOK, MALAYSIA
881 Spend time with sun bears

The vast patch of jungle around Sepilok is famous for orangutans, but it's also home to a population of sun bears. These endangered bears are the world's smallest, distinguished by the golden patch of fur on their chest. Visit the Bornean Sun Bear Conservation Center and you can watch them feed, play, and climb through the trees.

UMA BAWANG, MALAYSIA
882 Help Indigenous people protect their land

The Uma Bawang community was nearly wiped out by deforestation in the 1990s. It was the international attention brought by the Borneo Project that helped to save it. Visit the longhouse at Uma Bawang, and let your children learn the importance of activism and protecting the rights of Indigenous people.

SABAH, MALAYSIA

883 Take a boat ride through the jungle

You'll get full-on rain forest immersion at Kinabatangan Wildlife Sanctuary, one of the world's richest ecosystems. Hardy, older kids and teens will be up for a river excursion, gliding along through mangrove swamps and jungle backwaters, looking out for crocodiles, hornbills, pygmy elephants, and primates. Opt for a multiday trip and you can spend the night at a riverside lodge, accessible only by boat.

SABAH, MALAYSIA

884 Meet some unusual blooms

Kinabalu National Park is home to birds, mammals, and amphibians, but it's the thriving and varied plant life that's the big draw. While adults are beguiled by the five hundred species of orchid, kids will be drawn to the carnivorous plants and the world's largest and stinkiest flower—the rafflesia—which, when fully in bloom, smells like rotting meat. When you're not gazing at the blooms, forest trails will take you to hot springs and waterfalls.

884 RAFFLESIA FLOWER

SINGAPORE

885 Stroll through botanical gardens

Singapore is known for its
architectural feats, and the
botanic gardens here are a living
example of their design artistry.
Meander along paths both inside
and outside, through a series of
delightful gardens filled with
exotic blooms, tropical greenery,
waterfalls, koi ponds, and more.
Interspersed throughout are
flocks of colorful butterflies,
parrots, and other tropical birds.

SINGAPORE

886 Gawk at a multitude of sea life

The sprawling SEA Aquarium
is home to over one hundred
thousand marine animals, housed
in a series of recreated habitats.
You can experience the Great
Lakes of East Africa and get
spooked by the Shark Seas
Habitat; but best of all is Open
Ocean Habitat, a massive 118 ft.
(36 m) long, 27 ft. (8.3 m) high
aquarium.

SINGAPORE

887 Be dazzled by the Gardens by the Bay

It's pure botanical whimsy at
Gardens by the Bay, where
futuristic Supertrees shoot 165 ft.
(50 m) into the sky, linked by an
aerial walkway with stunning
views over the gardens and
beyond. Below are 250 ac
(101 ha) of sculptures, gardens,
and state-of-the-art biodomes
recreating everything from cloud
forest to Mediterranean climes.

SINGAPORE

888 Fill your belly at a hawker center

There are over a hundred hawker
centers in Singapore—hectic,
open-air food courts selling some
of the best Chinese, Malay, and
Indian cuisine the city has to
offer. Satay, *sio bak* (roast pork
belly), and Hainanese chicken
rice are good contenders for
young taste buds.

887 GARDENS BY THE BAY

889 Go wild at Singapore Zoo

Set on a lush peninsula among 64 ac (26 ha) of greenery, Singapore Zoo gets you up close to all kinds of majestic beasts in both traditional and offbeat ways. There's a River Safari, a Night Safari, and the much-loved Jungle Breakfast with Wildlife, where you can sip your morning coffee in the presence of the zoo's orangutans.

890 Have some good old theme-park fun

Unabashedly commercial, glitzy, and dedicated to fun, Sentosa Island packs a world of kid-friendly attractions into a relatively compact space. There are roller-coaster thrills at Universal Studios and a huge collection of water slides at Adventure Cove Water Park, plus a luge, a 4D experience, a high-ropes adventure course, and even a Madame Tussauds.

890 SENTOSA ISLAND

891 BABY ORANGUTAN

CENTRAL KALIMANTAN, INDONESIA
891 See orangutans in the wild

Borneo's lush and ancient rain forests are among the world's most bio-diverse habitats, and a true delight for families wishing to watch animals in the wild, including the endangered orangutan. Little nature buffs can don their binoculars and head off on an adventure to spot the great apes on a boat safari through Tanjung Puting National Park, or on the Kinabatangan River. Or they can stay on land to watch and learn about the orangutans' plight at the Tabin Wildlife Reserve.

GILI AIR, INDONESIA
892 Roam around a car-free island

Set off the coast of Lombok, the three Gili Islands share stunning good looks, but each has its own personality. With kids in tow, head to the island of Gili Air. The water is warm, calm, and full of colorful sea life, and it's car-free, so you can roam with ease on foot, by bicycle, or by horse-drawn cart.

893 KOMODO DRAGONS

894 MOUNT BROMO

KOMODO ISLAND, INDONESIA

893 Track Komodo dragons

They may not have wings or breathe fire, but Indonesia's Komodo dragons look decidedly mythical. These massive, fork-tongued beasts grow to over 10 ft. (3 m), weigh over 190 lb. (90 kg), and have survived on Earth for over four million years. Trekking with a ranger is the best (and safest) way to see them.

JAVA, INDONESIA

894 Watch the sun rise over a volcano

Watching the sun rise up over the huge volcanic cone of Mount Bromo as it spits thick ash clouds into the sky, and then climbing the flanks of the beast to peer into its crater, is an ethereal experience and a practical lesson in geography that your children will never forget.

BALI, INDONESIA

895 Dine on the food of kings

Originally a meal for royalty, *babi guling* is a whole pig stuffed with onions, chilies, and spices, then roasted over a wood fire. It hails from the town of Ubud, and restaurants across town have their own special version. Wherever you eat, you'll be served chunks of tender meat, crispy shiny skin, blood sausage, rice, and soup.

898 GREEN SCHOOL

BALI, INDONESIA
896 Join a craft workshop

Bali's craft scene is thriving, particularly in Ubud. Signing up for a workshop with a local artist or musician is a wonderful treat for any budding creatives. You could build your own kite, learn how to play Balinese drums, discover the art of puppet-making, or paint using oils and a bamboo stick.

BALI, INDONESIA
897 See many monkey species in one day

Animal-loving kids will love roaming through the rain forest alongside the seven hundred resident Balinese long-tailed monkeys at the Sacred Monkey Forest Sanctuary. The park is a picturesque nature destination in itself, and home to three Balinese Hindu temples. Be warned that the monkeys feel very comfortable with humans, so be prepared to get jumped on.

BALI, INDONESIA
898 Take a tour of Bali's Green School

Set in wall-less bamboo structures deep in the jungle, the Green School pulls in families from across the globe to follow its alternative curriculum, which has a firm focus on innovation and sustainability. If you can't stay for longer, a campus tour will give you a taste of the school's award-winning architecture and progressive ethos.

BALI, INDONESIA

899 Swing above rice terraces

For a fun way to see the famous Tegallalang rice terraces near Ubud in Bali, take to the skies on a swing. Bali's rice terraces are a UNESCO World Heritage Site, intrinsically bound up with the island's culture and Buddhist religion. A swing gives you a stunning bird's eye view of their scale and beauty.

BALI, INDONESIA

900 Hike up Mount Batur for sunrise

Climbing a volcano at sunrise is an unforgettable experience, and the view over Lake Batur is more than worth the early alarm. The trek is light enough that little legs will be able to do it without too many bribes, and the opportunities to see and feed monkeys will help keep little ones entertained.

BALI, INDONESIA

901 Stay in an eco-cottage

Go for a full digital detox in the lush hills of Ubud with a stay in the peaceful Swasti Eco Cottages. This is a little oasis with a true farm-to-table ethos (all dishes are made from ingredients grown on the property), yoga and meditation classes, and a traditional spa if you need that extra kick of relaxation.

899 TEGALLALANG, BALI

900 MOUNT BATUR

6
OCEANIA

904 MILKY WAY COVE

902 Dive with manta rays

The first protected manta ray area in the world lies in Yap, off the coast of Micronesia—a true reef wonder for anyone interested in the underwater world. The whole family will be able to snorkel and swim alongside these beautiful creatures, watching them as they move from the sea into lagoons to feed.

PALAU, MICRONESIA
903 Paddle the Rock Islands

Kayak around Palau's southern lagoon and you'll feel like an adventurer in a hidden world. Hundreds of forested islands rise from the ocean like giant mushrooms, and fertile coral reefs hide some of the richest marine life in the world. A half-day jaunt will suit younger kids, while teens can join longer expeditions, camping on deserted islands overnight.

PALAU, MICRONESIA
904 Slather yourself in healing mud

The creamy, white mud of Milky Way Cove, in southern Palau, is said to have healing and anti-aging powers. It's also an excuse for a giant, squelchy, messy mud bath—a win for kids of all ages. The mud lines the bottom of the lagoon and lies within easy reach. Dive down, grab a handful, and slather it all over your body.

MOUNT HAGEN HIGHLANDS, PAPUA NEW GUINEA
905 See some seriously different birds

The birds of paradise in Papua New Guinea have so many extra quirks that they can't fail to delight. Go with a guide who knows where to find them and marvel at their long, ribbonlike tails, iridescent colors, puffed-out chests, and even, if you're lucky, intricate dance shows.

STARTING IN AUSTRALIA
906 Enjoy each of Australia's three oceans

Australia is surrounded by three oceans: the Indian Ocean, the Pacific Ocean, and the Southern Ocean. Dip your toes in all three, starting with a trip to the Buccaneer Archipelago in the Indian Ocean. Then head to New South Wales for a surf. And finally take a road trip on the Southern Ocean Drive for spectacular scenery.

NORTHERN TERRITORY, AUSTRALIA
907 Explore in a four-wheel drive

"The Gibb" is one of Australia's most iconic outback drives. Running through the heart of the remote Kimberly region, a seven-to-fourteen-day drive will take in spectacular mountain ranges, dramatic gorges, and plenty of rock pools and waterfalls for a refreshing dip.

NORTHERN TERRITORY, AUSTRALIA
908 Marvel at ancient rock art

A sprawl of pristine wilderness in northwestern Australia, the Kimberley region hides some of Australia's greatest wonders. Hidden among the red cliffs, sandstone pinnacles, and river gorges are thousands of ancient rock paintings, including the 17,300-year-old Kimberley Kangaroo, Australia's oldest rock artwork.

CORAL COAST, AUSTRALIA
909 Snorkel Ningaloo Reef

Ningaloo, on Australia's west coast, is one of the largest reefs in the world and home to a hugely diverse range of coral and marine life. These pristine waters offer plenty of different spots to snorkel, suitable for the whole family. Little ones will enjoy spotting different colored fish and even turtles.

906 OCEAN PADDLING

NORTHERN TERRITORY,
AUSTRALIA
910 Learn about the Bungle Bungle Range

Formed over twenty million years ago, the stripy, beehive-shaped rock formations of the Bungle Bungle Range, in the Purnululu National Park, are a sight to behold. Explore with a guide and learn about their spiritual and cultural significance for the Karjaganujaru and Gija people, the traditional custodians of Purnululu.

PERTH, AUSTRALIA
911 Chill and grill on an Aussie beach

Firing up the barbecue for some sun, sea, and sausages is a quintessential family day out, and Perth offers plenty of top options. Serpentine Falls has picnic tables, barbecue facilities, and the odd wandering kangaroo, while at Matilda Bay Reserve you can spot pelicans, herons, or even bottlenose dolphins as you fire up the grill.

ROTTNEST ISLAND, AUSTRALIA
912 Meet the animal with the biggest smile

Rottnest Island is home to one of Australia's cutest animals —a small, furry marsupial known as the quokka. Dubbed the "happiest animals on Earth" because they often look as if they're grinning, these curious creatures love to approach strangers. Just remember that they're wild animals, so while it's OK to snap a selfie, you shouldn't touch them.

910 BUNGLE BUNGLE RANGE

912 A QUOKKA

915 WAVE ROCK

MARGARET RIVER, AUSTRALIA
913 Spot penguins on Penguin Island

Road-tripping from Perth to Margaret River takes you through some of Western Australia's most breathtaking coastline. Vast, sweeping beaches offer world-class surf breaks, and a visit to Penguin Island for, as the name suggests, some penguin spotting, is perfect for little ones.

HAMELIN BAY, AUSTRALIA
914 Get up close to stingrays

Smooth stingrays, black stingrays, and eagle rays visit the shallow waters of Hamelin Bay, a protected part of Ngari Capes Marine Park. Strong swimmers can snorkel with them around the bay. Young kids can stand in the shallows and watch them glide over the sandy bottom as they search for mollusks and crustaceans to eat.

WESTERN AUSTRALIA
915 Be awed by Wave Rock

Children of all ages will enjoy getting their picture snapped inside Western Australia's huge, granite Wave Rock, a natural rock formation in the shape of a breaking wave. And when they've had their photograph taken, there's plenty more to do nearby, including kayaking on Lake Magic, exploring the Humps and Mulka's Cave, and visiting the wildlife park.

917 CAPE LE GRAND NATIONAL PARK

918 LAKE HILLIER

GREAT WESTERN WOODLANDS,
AUSTRALIA
916 Look under a log

Not all adventures are epic;
some come in those micro
moments of discovering that
a whole new world exists in
plain sight. Tip up a decaying log
in the Great Western Woodlands
—the world's largest temperate
woodland, the size of England—
and see what beetles, ants, snails,
millipedes, scorpions, and even
frogs are hiding there.

WESTERN AUSTRALIA
917 Swim in secluded, turquoise bays

Soft, white sand and crystal-
clear waters await you at
Esperance and Lucky Bays,
in Western Australia's Cape
Le Grand National Park, where
bays are safe for families to swim
in. Take a kayak, too, and enjoy
a gentle paddle around these
pristine bays.

MIDDLE ISLAND, AUSTRALIA
918 Fly over a dazzling, pink lake

Visit Middle Island and you'll
take in a startling sight: a surreal,
bubble-gum pink lake. Lake
Hillier gets its hue from colorful
bacteria and algae in its waters,
made even more dramatic by the
surrounding deep-green forests.
The most exciting way to get
there is by light aircraft, taking
in spectacular coastal views along
the way.

921 KAKADU NATIONAL PARK

DARWIN, AUSTRALIA

919 Cheer the sunset at Mindil Beach Market

Half of Darwin descends on Mindil Beach for the twice-weekly sunset market, a family-focused affair that's full of fantastic food and community spirit. Fill your face with anything from kangaroo burgers to Sri Lankan curry, then head onto the sand and join in the applause as the sun disappears into the horizon.

RED CENTER, AUSTRALIA

920 Cross Australia by rail

Take the *Ghan* train for an unforgettable journey that runs between Darwin, in the far north, to Adelaide, in South Australia. A three-day journey will take you right through the breathtaking Red Center of Australia, and includes stops in Katherine and Alice Springs.

KAKADU NATIONAL PARK, AUSTRALIA

921 Hunt for traditional bush-tucker fare

Walk through ancient landscapes and learn hunter-gatherer ways on a bush-tucker safari through Kakadu National Park. Led by an expert Aboriginal guide, gather native tubers, fruit, grubs, and even the odd goanna, before setting up a campfire to cook and eat your haul, washed down with some outback billy tea: cooked in a tin can using gum leaves.

924 ULURU

NORTHERN TERRITORY,
AUSTRALIA

922 Enjoy an Indigenous festival

Over three days every August,
the Barunga people of the
Northern Territory open their
homeland for the Barunga
Festival. Kids will be spellbound
by traditional storytellers and
musicians, and there are art
classes, spear-making, and bush-
medicine workshops to take part
in, as well as exuberant dance
parties run by Barunga teens.

EAST ARNHEM LAND, AUSTRALIA

923 Live life in a First Australian community

It's a long journey to the coastal
home of the Yolngu people, but
it's an unforgettable experience
for older teens. On an immersive
trip organized by Intrepid, you
can join weaving circles with
local women, learn how to hunt
and gather food, and hear about
the history, customs, and
challenges facing one of the
oldest continuing cultures in
the world.

RED CENTER, AUSTRALIA

924 Take a road trip through the outback

You could drive from Alice
Springs to Uluru in five hours,
but turn off the highway and
you've got an epic road trip on
your hands. Go via the West
MacDonnell Ranges or Kings
Canyon, where you can gawk
at gorges, rock formations, and
waterfalls. When you do reach
Uluru, the grandeur of the
ultimate Australian icon will
leave you speechless.

RED CENTER, AUSTRALIA
925 Sleep under the stars

Sleep in the outback and there's no need for a tent. Instead, you can unfurl a swag—a large, canvas sleeping bag with an inbuilt mattress that's an essential part of an Aussie expedition kit. You'll feel like part of the natural landscape as you drift off to sleep with the breeze on your face. Look above and you can count the stars, which come out in full force in the outback night.

COOBER PEDY, AUSTRALIA
926 Search for precious gems

Around 70 percent of Coober Pedy's residents live underground, in order to escape the heat of one of Australia's harshest environments. Kids will love visiting subterranean hotels, churches, and cafés, and learning about what brought people here in the first place—opals. Visit a working opal mine, check out an opal museum, and have a go at "noodling"— sifting through debris for any precious opals inadvertently left behind.

925 CAMP IN THE OUTBACK

ADELAIDE, AUSTRALIA
927 Get down at WOMADelaide

Adelaide's Botanic Park is the setting for one of Australia's most vibrant and diverse music festivals. Over a rocking four days, WOMADelaide (World of Music Arts & Dance) takes over the city center as artists from around the globe play every conceivable type of music. Kids of all ages come to boogie alongside their parents, and there's a special Kidszone, where storytelling, dress-up, and interactive music-making make the experience even sweeter.

CAPE HILLSBOROUGH, AUSTRALIA
928 Watch kangaroos on the beach

The sunrises at Cape Hillsborough are spectacular in their own right. Add some furry marsupials and they're truly magical for young children. The kids can watch as dozens of wallabies and kangaroos hop down to the beach to feed on seaweed and seed pods, silhouetted against a pink and purple sky.

THROUGHOUT AUSTRALIA
929 Relocate a motor home

There's nothing like the thrill of exploring the wilderness in a motor home, especially if you have kids in tow. Drive a motor home for a relocation company and you can do so for free, perhaps with a tank of fuel thrown in too. A delivery date and location are your only restrictions, so a budget adventure is on the cards.

927 WOMADELAIDE

930 DAINTREE RAINFOREST

DAINTREE RAINFOREST, AUSTRALIA
930 Explore the Daintree Rainforest

You'll feel as if you're on the set of *Jurassic Park* as you wander through the ancient coastal wilderness of the Daintree Rainforest, the oldest rain forest in the world. Walk through the treetops along elevated walkways, look for crocs and river birds along the Daintree River, and run along beautiful beaches, where the rain forest meets the sea.

WHITSUNDAY ISLANDS, AUSTRALIA
931 Stay in an underwater hotel

If you love fish and are feeling flush, then check out Reefsuites Underwater Hotel in the Whitsunday Islands. What could be better than waking up to the magical view of tropical fish swimming around Australia's magnificent Great Barrier Reef, right outside your bedroom window?

K'GARI, AUSTRALIA
932 Take a night walk on K'gari

A ranger-guided night tour of K'gari (formerly Fraser Island) is a safe and exciting way for the whole family to explore this magical island. From frogs and bats to sugar gliders, when darkness falls there are plenty of creatures to look out for.

GREAT BARRIER REEF, AUSTRALIA
933 See the Great Barrier Reef

Stretching across 1,200 mi. (2,000 km) of coastline, the Great Barrier Reef is the world's largest living organism and a fantastic place to teach the kids about marine life. Pop on some reef-safe sunscreen and you can snorkel, scuba, and sail around the watery wonderland, and learn how climate change is threatening this enormous ecosystem.

NOOSA NATIONAL PARK,
AUSTRALIA

934 Visit a world class surfing destination

Just a short walk along the coastal track from Noosa you'll find Noosa National Park and the globally recognized World Surfing Reserve, Tea Tree Bay. Granite Bay and Alexandria Bay produce perfect, year-round waves, and if surfing's not your thing, jump in the ocean for a dip instead.

GOLD COAST, AUSTRALIA

935 Spend a day at Movie World

Movie buffs and thrill seekers alike will enjoy a day at the Gold Coast's Warner Brothers Movie World theme park. It's a great place for the kids to meet their superheroes, supervillains, and cartoon characters, as well as enjoy shows, ride roller coasters, and buy some souvenirs.

935 MOVIE WORLD

BELLINGEN, AUSTRALIA
936 Hang out in a hippy town

Enjoy a spot of shopping and café hopping in the quaint "hippy town" of Bellingen, in the Mid North Coast of New South Wales. From trinkets and clothes to locally grown food, and of course a hemp store, Bellingen has something for everyone.

BYRON BAY, AUSTRALIA
937 Do the lighthouse walk in Byron Bay

Get the family up early and take on this iconic walk through rain forest, beach, and bushland to the most easterly point of Australia. Take in the sunrise, watch the surfers, and look out for dolphins and whales (May to November) as you explore this stunning part of the coastline.

DORRIGO NATIONAL PARK, AUSTRALIA
938 Take a moment in ancient rain forest

A visit to this World-Heritage-listed rain forest is sure to instill a sense of awe and wonder into children and adults alike. There are rain forest walks suitable for all ages and abilities, as well as a skywalk and lookout with views across the rain forest to the coast.

NEWCASTLE, AUSTRALIA
939 Swim in Bogey Hole

The name of this tidal pool comes from the Indigenous Tharawal language and means "a place to bathe," but its origins are from European colonization, when it was hewn from the rocks by convict labor. On calm days, it is a welcome spot for a dip, and in rougher weather it's fun for stronger swimmers as waves crash over the outer wall.

939 BOGEY HOLE

BLUE MOUNTAINS, AUSTRALIA

940 Spend a long weekend in the Blue Mountains

Just ninety minutes' drive west of Sydney, the Blue Mountains is a must-visit at any time of year. Stay in the sleepy towns of Leura, Katoomba, or Blackheath and spend a few days exploring all that this area has to offer. There are countless walking tracks through the mountains suited to all ages, plenty of breathtaking lookout spots, waterfalls, swimming holes, and caves, not forgetting the many cafés, restaurants, and shops. Little ones will love Scenic World, home of the steepest passenger railway in the world, as well as a walkway, cableway, and a skyway that traverses a huge valley with panoramic views of the mountains.

940 BLUE MOUNTAINS

THROUGHOUT AUSTRALIA

941 Introduce your children to the Tim Tam

Every nation has its chocolate delicacies and party treats, but in Australia, the Tim Tam biscuit is revered with a level of near-worship. Two chocolate biscuits are sandwiched together with chocolate cream, and then coated in chocolate. You might have eaten something similar in your home country, but you can't leave Australia without trying one.

THROUGHOUT AUSTRALIA

942 House-sit for a holiday

A slice of the much-envied Aussie lifestyle can be yours if you skip the tourist hotels and stay in a local home. In exchange for watching pets or watering plants, you'll get a free, family-friendly base, and the chance to experience an Australia that most tourists never see. Aussie House Sitters or TrustedHousesitters can get you started.

SYDNEY, AUSTRALIA
943 Do a gallery hop

Take in some culture with a Sydney gallery hop. Located within easy walking distance of one another, the Museum of Contemporary Art and the Art Gallery of New South Wales are both great spaces for families to enjoy an abundance of art, and have a bite to eat.

SYDNEY, AUSTRALIA
944 See inside the Sydney Opera House

Beautiful from the outside with its organic peaks and shining white tiles, the Sydney Opera House is also a fabulous venue for a performance with its cathedral-like interiors. The event schedule is packed with as much for small children as young adults and their fully-fledged parents.

SYDNEY, AUSTRALIA
945 Walk along the coast at sunrise

No trip to Sydney would be complete without a walk along the stunning coastal track that runs from Bondi to Coogee Beach. Sunrise is one of the best times to go, and little ones will enjoy looking out for dolphins and whales (May to November) as they go.

944 SYDNEY OPERA HOUSE

948 LUNA PARK

SYDNEY, AUSTRALIA
946 Picnic with a view

Packing a picnic and hitting the beach is the stuff family holidays are made of. Add a view of the Sydney Harbour Bridge or Sydney Opera House and things get really special. Try Bradleys Head on the north shore, or the waterside Royal Botanic Garden, where you can look out over the harbor toward distant mountains.

SYDNEY, AUSTRALIA
947 Watch thousands of bats fly from the trees

Head to Sydney's Centennial Park at sunset and watch as the park's bat colony leave their daytime hiding places to find food. It's quite a spectacular site, as these unique, wide-winged creatures move en masse through the twilight sky.

SYDNEY, AUSTRALIA
948 Spend a day on the rides at Luna Park

If you're a family of thrill seekers be sure to check out Sydney's famous Luna Park. Located directly on Sydney Harbour, with views of the bridge and the Sydney Opera House, it has an abundance of fairground rides and activities suitable for all ages.

THROUGHOUT AUSTRALIA
949 Spot a koala in a tree

Spotting a koala in the wild in Australia is something that everyone can enjoy. It's not always easy though—they often sit high up in trees and are somewhat camouflaged—but here are two top tips that will help you: one, look in the forks in branches, as koalas like to nestle in those spots; and two, look for lumps in trees as they often tuck themselves in like a little ball.

CANBERRA, AUSTRALIA
950 Learn about First Nations art

The National Gallery of Australia has a vast collection of Aboriginal and Torres Strait Islander art, and it's a wonderful introduction to First Nations cultures for young kids. Most spectacular is the haunting Aboriginal Memorial, made up of two hundred hollow log coffins commemorating the Indigenous people who have died defending their land.

949 KOALA

951 GHOST TOWN

953 BIOLUMINESCENT PLANKTON

YERRANDERIE, AUSTRALIA
951 Get spooked at a ghost town

Scattered across New South Wales are the deserted shells of former mining towns. Yerranderie Private Town is among the best preserved, with a handsome, clapboard post office, general store, bank, and homes. Follow bush trails and visit the former silver mine. Then feel the spirits of the past as you spend the night at the adjacent campground.

JERVIS BAY, AUSTRALIA
952 Go glamping among eucalyptus

For the ultimate glamping experience, stay a night or two at the peaceful Paperbark Camp on the south coast of New South Wales. Safari-style tents are nestled among eucalyptus and paperbark trees, and the camp's dining room serves top-notch food. Children aged over ten years are welcome.

JERVIS BAY, AUSTRALIA
953 See a glowing sea

Jervis Bay, on the south coast of New South Wales, is one of the few places in Australia that you can witness the natural phenomenon that is bioluminescence, when the ocean lights up at night. Timing is everything; you're most likely to see it during the warmer months.

GUNDAGAI, AUSTRALIA
954 Sleep in a shearers cottage

Spend a night on a sheep and cattle farm on the Kimo Estate, in Gundagai. Choose from traditional, charming shearers' cottages or modern, eco-huts, and unplug for a day or two in this unique and peaceful spot. Children of all ages are welcome.

VICTORIA, AUSTRALIA
955 Climb Hanging Rock

Take the family on the famous Pinnacle Walk to the summit of Hanging Rock, and keep the children entertained by looking out for koalas, kangaroos, echidnas, and the many colorful bird species that nest in the reserve along the way. Don't forget to pack a picnic to enjoy afterward.

VICTORIA, AUSTRALIA
956 Drive the Great Ocean Road

Soak up salty sea breezes and jaw-dropping views as you follow the curves of Australia's Great Ocean Road, one of the greatest drives on the planet. Stretching some 101 mi. (243 km) between Torquay and Allansford, you'll take in beaches and rain forest as you wind your way along the coast, with plenty of active stopovers that will keep the kids entertained. The superstar is the Twelve Apostles, a series of limestone stacks jutting sharply out of the ocean, but you can also hike through Great Otway National Park, hit the surf at Fairhaven Beach, or just find a roadside shack and eat fresh crayfish on the sand.

SOUTH AUSTRALIA
957 Work on a sheep station

For an authentic Aussie experience, little beats a stay on a working sheep station. Set among the mountains and gorges of the Flinders Ranges, Angorichina Station offers hiking, wildlife watching, and the chance to take part in station activities. Nights can be spent in 1850s shearers' quarters, or in a grand family homestead.

TASMANIA, AUSTRALIA
958 Enjoy a festival of the dark

Visit Tasmania during the month of June for Hobart's midwinter festival, Dark Mofo. Created by the Museum of Old and New Art (MONA), this unique event celebrates the dark through public art, live music, performances, and food. Lots of fun for the whole family.

TASMANIA, AUSTRALIA
959 Stay on a wilderness island

For an extraspecial, relaxing family experience away from it all, book a stay at Tasmania's charming Satellite Island. Surrounded by untamed wilderness, you'll have this magical island hideaway all to yourself. Visitors to the island must be ten years old or above.

VICTORIA, AUSTRALIA
960 Walk on Ninety Mile Beach

If you're looking for an off-the-beaten-track beach experience, then Ninety Mile Beach in southeast Victoria is for you. Enjoy swimming, surfing, snorkeling, diving, camping, and boating along this vast stretch of unspoiled coastline, backed only by sand dunes and bush.

956 SIGHTS FROM THE GREAT OCEAN ROAD

Walking in rain forest

Twelve Apostles

Lovely lighthouses

ROTORUA, NEW ZEALAND

961 Experience Māori culture

An immersive, creative, and joyful celebration of Māori people and customs, Tamaki Māori Village is a wonderful place to introduce children to Aotearoa's (New Zealand's) Indigenous culture. Set in ancient forest, it's an authentic recreation of a precolonial village, where you can hear traditional stories and song, be educated about the *haka* (war dance), and eat a delicious *hāngi* (Māori feast).

ROTORUA, NEW ZEALAND

962 Gawk at geysers and bubbling rock pools

Rotorua's volcanic nature announces itself with a whiff of pungent, sulfuric air—a source of much amusement for little (and big) kids. If that's not enough entertainment, there are active geysers, hot lakes, and pools of bubbling mud to visit, and even geothermal steam rising out of the city's drains.

962 ROTORUA

AUCKLAND, NEW ZEALAND

963 See—and taste— honey being made

New Zealand's manuka honey has a reputation that goes even further than the bees that make it. At the NZMA Beekeeping Experience Center, children as young as four can get kitted out in a full beekeeping suit and learn all about the magic of beekeeping—and try the delicious products that are made.

964 WAITOMO CAVES

WAITOMO, NEW ZEALAND
964 Go into a cave full of glowworms

Don a wet suit and helmet before heading underground on a Black Water Rafting tour of the Waitomo Caves. Clambering over rocks, jumping off waterfalls, and floating along an underground river is all part of the deal, and you'll have thousands of glowworms to light your way. It's a fabulous adventure for children aged twelve and up.

THROUGHOUT NEW ZEALAND
965 Eat sea urchins

Children love the idea of knowing about food that's a little bit different—even if not all of them will try it. Kina is a species of New Zealand sea urchin, and its roe is either eaten raw or used as a flavor in dips and other sauces. It's often described as an acquired taste, but one that rolls all the flavors of the sea into one.

966 HOBBITON

MATAMATA, NEW ZEALAND

966 Explore Middle Earth

You don't have to be a fan of *The Hobbit* or *The Lord of the Rings* to enjoy a tour of the Hobbiton™ Movie Set. The half-size houses, with their round doors and grass roofs, will enchant smaller children (it's free for under-nines), while those that know the films will love seeing Middle Earth's real-life locations.

THROUGHOUT NEW ZEALAND

967 Stay in a bach

Kick back and relax in a traditional bach (pronounced "batch") by the sea. These cute beach cottages can be found all around the New Zealand coastline, and give visitors the chance to switch off and return to a simpler way of living.

AUCKLAND, NEW ZEALAND

968 Eat a meal cooked underground

The Māori style of cooking in an underground pit dates back at least one thousand years, with stones being heated in a fire, before being buried under soil with baskets of meat and vegetables, which would slowly cook in the heat. At the Māori Kitchen on Queen's Wharf, traditional baskets have been updated with stainelss steel, but the technique and flavors remain the same.

LAKE TAUPŌ, NEW ZEALAND
969 Take a white-knuckle river ride

Adrenaline-seeking kids will love witnessing Huka
Falls—a gush of water tumbling down 36 ft. (11 m)
onto the turquoise surface of Lake Taupō. Meander
the Waikato River to experience the falls, either on
a relaxing river cruiser or, for a full white-knuckle
ride, on a jet boat that will have you feeling as if
you're in the middle of the falls themselves!

ABEL TASMAN NATIONAL PARK, NEW ZEALAND
970 Kayak a coastal wonderland

Abel Tasman National Park looks more like a
tropical paradise than a slice of Kiwi wilderness,
but true to NZ form, it's ripe for active adventures.
It's known for its coastal walking track, but it's also
a sea-kayaking hotspot, with crystal-clear waters,
hidden coves, and beaches to explore.

SOUTH ISLAND, NEW ZEALAND
971 Ride in the TranzAlpine's open air carriage

The TranzAlpine is New Zealand's most famous
train journey, taking in coastline, bushland, and the
rugged Southern Alps. Wrap the kids up warm and
head to the open-air viewing carriage. Feel the wind
on your face as the train heads into the mountains:
it takes the ride from special to spectacular.

THROUGHOUT NEW ZEALAND
972 Go WWOOFing

A hands-on insight into New Zealand country
life could be just the family adventure that you're
looking for. Sign up with WWOOF (Worldwide
Opportunities on Organic Farms) and you'll live
the rural good life, with food and accommodation
provided in return for help with anything from
composting and planting trees to bread making.

969 HUKA FALLS

AORAKI/MOUNT COOK NATIONAL PARK,
NEW ZEALAND

973 Gaze at the Milky Way

Inspire your young astronomers with a trip to the
Aoraki/Mount Cook region, part of the Aoraki
Mackenzie International Dark Sky Reserve.
There's virtually no light pollution and little need
for specialist equipment. All you have to do is tip
your head upward and take in the brightest stars
you've ever seen.

SOUTH ISLAND, NEW ZEALAND

974 Hike across a receding glacier

It's a ninety-minute walk through a beautiful valley
to reach the base of the rapidly retreating Franz
Joseph Glacier, but for a proper glacier hike you'll
have to go by helicopter, swooping over dramatic,
wintry scenery before coming in to land high up
on the ice, in a scene that wouldn't be amiss in a
James Bond movie. You'll then put on glacier boots,
crampons, and helmets, and head out to explore the
caves, tunnels, and ice formations of this endangered
frozen wilderness. Kids eight years old and up can
take part in what's both an exhilarating adventure,
and a lesson on climate change.

974 FRANZ JOSEPH GLACIER

976 TAKE THE LUGE

QUEENSTOWN, NEW ZEALAND
975 Throw yourself off a cliff

Travel up a mountain by gondola to reach The Ledge bungee jump, a stomach-churning 154 ft. (47 m) drop that can be tackled by steel-nerved children aged ten and up. As you're hooked into your harness, console yourself with the spectacular views over Queenstown, and the knowledge that you'll be buzzing once you've done it.

QUEENSTOWN, NEW ZEALAND
976 Ride the luge in Queenstown

For the most exciting and unique family activity in Queenstown, take one of the world's steepest cable cars to the summit of Bob's Peak, then ride the luge (a gravity-powered go-kart) back down. Thrill seekers aged over fifteen can go solo, while younger kids can enjoy a ride with their parents.

QUEENSTOWN, NEW ZEALAND
977 Enjoy a quirky winter festival

Every year in late June to early July, Queenstown celebrates the first day of winter with a four-day festival featuring a huge firework display, live music, and delicious food and market stalls. Traditionally, it has a slightly quirky mix of entertainment, such as lake-jumping and dog-barking competitions.

QUEENSTOWN, NEW ZEALAND
978 Race through the Shotover Canyon

If you're traveling with miniature speed freaks, forget about fairground rides and strap them in for a ride on the Shotover Jet, which blasts through the steep-sided Shotover Canyon at speeds of up to 56 mph (90 km/h), with plenty of bumps and 360° spins thrown in for good measure.

979 HOOKER VALLEY TRACK

AORAKI/MOUNT COOK NATIONAL
PARK, NEW ZEALAND
979 Do New Zealand's best family friendly hike

Toddlers, teens, and
grandparents can hit the
Hooker Valley Track, a short,
relatively flat route through
Aoraki/Mount Cook National
Park. It may be short, but it's
still spectacular—smooth, gravel
tracks and bouncy suspension
bridges lead past snowcapped
mountains and glacial lakes on
what's often called the best
family-friendly hike in
New Zealand.

THROUGHOUT NEW ZEALAND
980 Sample fish and chips Kiwi-style

New Zealand's favorite takeout
is serious business, with terakihi,
snapper, hoki, and blue cod
among the most popular choices
to be battered and deep-fried.
You'll find it available everywhere,
from restaurants to cafés and
seaside shacks, but it's best eaten
right out of the paper on the
beach, preferably smothered in
tomato sauce.

MILFORD SOUND, NEW ZEALAND
981 Be amazed by Milford Sound

Milford Sound is not only
outstandingly beautiful and
tranquil, the region is rich with
child-friendly experiences.
Explore Eglinton Valley, where
kids can run around surrounded
by towering mountains before
filling their water bottles with
glacier water, and discover the
Sound aboard a cruise, where
curious eyes will be busy trying
to spot penguins and seals.

983 Tackle the Routeburn Track

There's magic, beauty, and plenty of challenge to be had on the Routeburn Track, one of the most dramatic of all New Zealand's great walks. Over two to four days you'll take in alpine rivers, lakes, and mountains, with nights spent in communal hikers' huts. Go in the Kiwi holiday season and you'll see plenty of kids on the trails.

SOUTH ISLAND, NEW ZEALAND

984 Explore by camper van

What better way to explore New Zealand's South Island as a family than in a motor home? Self-contained, fun, and adventurous, a camper van journey will see you cruising through snowcapped mountains, past deep, blue lakes, huge glaciers, and breathtaking sounds, with plenty of child-friendly activities to explore along the way.

DUNEDIN, NEW ZEALAND

982 Power up the world's steepest street

Young *Guinness World Records* fans will enjoy a visit to Baldwin Street—the steepest street in the world, with a gradient of 34.8 percent. Join curious tourists to make the thigh-straining walk to the top of this suburban road. And be sure to photograph the houses on an angle—it creates the illusion that they're sinking into the ground.

986 JET BOAT TOUR

987 SAWA-I-LAU CAVES

LOYALTY ISLANDS, NEW CALEDONIA

985 Get to know Kanak culture

The Loyalty Islands are the stuff of childhood fantasies—all thick forest, emerald lagoons, and underground caves. To make the most of them, stay in a traditional Kanak settlement, where the kids can paddle a traditional *pirogue* (canoe), learn Melanesian myths and legends, and make a gaggle of local friends.

VITI LEVU, FIJI

986 Test your mettle on a jet boat

Get away from the beaches and into the sultry heart of Viti Levu on a jet-boat tour of the Navua River. You'll race at speed through forests and volcanic canyons, getting seriously wet in the process. Stop-offs to hike and swim beneath waterfalls will calm any fractured nerves.

YASAWA ISLANDS, FIJI

987 Swim into caves

Unlike most of Fiji's islands, Sawa-i-Lau is formed from limestone rather than volcanic rock. This has led to some stunning caves being carved out of the softer rock. Swim in to the roofless dome, where the water is always turquoise, clamber on rocks, jump off, and if you're feeling really brave, swim through the underwater passage into a smaller neighboring chamber.

YASAWA ISLANDS, FIJI

988 Travel by seaplane

There are normal transfers, and there are seaplane transfers. Travel with Turtle Airways and you'll board a tiny six-seater craft and watch in awe as the plane soars over a stunning, tropical seascape. Landing on the water is the fun part. You just take off your shoes and jump straight out of the plane into the warm, clear ocean.

KADAVU ISLAND, FIJI

989 Find Fiji's rustic side

There are no five-star hotels or kids' clubs on Kadavu Island, and this jungly idyll is almost entirely road-free. Instead, there's a clutch of low-key resorts reachable only by boat and hidden among rain forest along the pristine coastline. If you're looking for a place where kids can run wild and immerse themselves in nature, this is it.

SIGATOKA, FIJI

990 Explore Fiji via its old railway tracks

Few bike rides are quite as relaxing as the EcoTrax tour from Sigatoka. Your "bike" is mounted on old railway lines so you never have to worry about taking a wrong turn, and it's electric, so it can take the strain on the uphills. The tour passes through rain forests and mangroves to a beautiful beach so you can stop for a swim before heading back.

990 CYCLING ON RAILS

NADI, FIJI

991 **Admire the colorful carvings at the Sri Siva Subramaniya Temple**

The Hindu temple of Sri Siva Subramaniya is a joyful explosion of color, intricately carved with patterns and deities. Children can search for different Hindu gods among the designs while adults can take in the finer details of the Dravidian architecture, which is rarely seen outside of India.

992 WATERSLIDE

995 FUNAFUTI

TAVEUNI, FIJI

992 Whizz down a natural waterslide

It's a short walk through lush palm forest to reach the Waitavala Water Slide—a natural chute of smooth rock and waterfalls that the local children love to slide down. Hardy older kids and teens can give it a go. They might get a few knocks on the way down but there's a soft landing in a natural pool at the bottom, and a high that's greater than any they'd get at a waterpark.

TONGA

993 Watch humpbacks from the shore

Humpback whales visit Tonga from June to October, but there's no need for a pricey boat trip to see these majestic beasts in action. Young kids can stay on terra firma and watch them make their way through the waters right from the shore. Get the best seats on the beach at Uoleva, Foeata, or 'Eua islands.

FONGAFALE, TUVALU

994 Play soccer on an airstrip

When it's not welcoming the country's twice-weekly flights, Tuvalu's unfenced runway acts as a makeshift park, bike track, and even, on sweltering nights, an outdoor sleeping area. It's the perfect place for kids to make friends and join in a game of soccer or volleyball. Just remember, a loud siren signifies an incoming plane.

FUNAFUTI, TUVALU

995 Cycle on an atoll

A slip of land only 7.5 mi. (12 km) long, Tuvalu's main island is easily explored in a day. Hit the road by bike and you'll pass small settlements and farms, before reaching the atoll's narrowest point, a 33 ft. (10 m) wide strip, with ocean closing in on either side—a stark reminder of the threat of rising sea levels.

APIA, SAMOA
996 Ride a colorful local bus

Loud, old, and painted with colorful murals and slogans, Samoa's public buses are a fantastic way for kids to experience local life. Pick one up at Apia's bus station, or flag one down at the roadside. Then take a seat on the wooden benches, and enjoy the music and chat as you rumble along your way.

TUAMASAGA, SAMOA
997 Slip and slide at Papaseea Sliding Rocks

You'll hear excited screams as you approach Papaseea Sliding Rocks, a collection of small waterfalls used as natural waterslides by locals and tourists. Join them and you'll whizz along at speed, tumbling into the cool pool below. You'll have to clamber over slippery rocks, so this one's for older, confident kids.

COOK ISLANDS
998 Climb a coconut tree

The Cook Islands are home to the first ever, world-champion coconut-tree climber, but people of any age and ability can have a go. You'll need to go barefoot, for grip, then shimmy up the trunk with your feet on either side. Choose a tree with a tilt and you'll have a much better chance of success.

AITUTAKI, COOK ISLANDS
999 Wander deserted islands

The Aitutaki Lagoon is the South Pacific of childhood dreams: a smudge of vivid blue ocean scattered with tiny, uninhabited *motu* (islets). The best thing to do is explore by boat, stopping to run across deserted sands, snorkel with turtles and giant clams, and eat fresh fish on the beach.

996 SAMOAN BUS

BORA BORA, FRENCH POLYNESIA

1000 Have an extravagant adventure in an overwater bungalow

Bora Bora's turquoise lagoons, bone-white beaches, and soaring, forested hills are almost absurdly beautiful—and the perfect place for an upscale family adventure. If you really want to make things memorable, stay in an overwater bungalow at Four Seasons Resort Bora Bora for the ultimate in desert-island luxury. Kids can jump straight into the water for outstanding swimming and snorkeling, kayak to shore to explore dry land, or just sit and gaze at colorful fish from the safety of their private deck.

INDEX

IMAGE CREDITS

The publisher would like to thank the following for the permission to reproduce copyright material.

Front cover: Jim Mallouk/Shutterstock
Spine: Michal Hornicky/Shutterstock
Back cover: (top to bottom): Row 1L Yunsun_Kim/Shutterstock; Row 1M ImagoPhoto/Shutterstock; Row 1R rayints/Shutterstock; Row 2L Aerokart; Row 2M donvictorio/Shutterstock; Row 2R Atlantis Submarines (Barbados) Inc.; Row 3L DELBO ANDREA/Shutterstock; Row 3M Ksenia Ragozin/Shutterstock; Row 3R Kobby Dagan/Shutterstock; Row 4L nelle hembry/Shutterstock; Row 4M Captain Al/Shutterstock; Row 4R BBA Photography/Shutterstock; Row 5L saiko3p/Shutterstock; Row 5M Chad-VPixabay; Row 5R fokke baarssen/Shutterstock.

Alamy: 16 Vespasian; 17T Megapress; 22 Danita Delimont; 24 Russ Bishop; 26BL John De Mello; 39 ZUMA Press, Inc.; 59 Danita Delimont; 61 Witold Skrypczak; 78 Hemis; 87 Ron Giling; 116–17 Westend61 GmbH; 129 EMS-FORSTER-PRODUCTIONS; 130 Susanne Masters; 146 Clarissa Debenham; 147 Dan Santillo (Wales); 162 Hemis; 192 Image Professionals GmbH; 193 All Canada Photos; 203 ClickAlps Srls; 207R Juniors Bildarchiv GmbH; 248 Gary Taylor; 257 robertharding; 268 Carrie Thompson/Stockimo; 326 Hemis; 394 Paul Dymond.

Dreamstime: 102 Sl Photography; 359 Bdingman.

Getty Images: 2–3 Chad Wright Photography; 4–5 Heavenli Denton/EyeEm; 8 Buena Vista Images; 10 Kevin Smith/Design Pics; 12 Neil Rabinowitz; 42–3 Nathan Bilow; 48–9 Bill Heinsohn; 54 *The Washington Post*; 56 Erika Goldring; 71 Jacek Kadaj; 73 Michele Westmorland; 81L Mike Tauber; 83 Roberto Machado Noa; 94–5 Westend61; 97 Lisa5201; 98L Wolfgang Kaehler; 98R JOAQUIN SARMIENTO; 101 KenCanning; 115T ruizluquepaz; 132L Feifei Cui-Paoluzzo; 136–7 Chris J/500px; 141 blue sky in my pocket; 145 Peter Cade; 150 Marco Bottigelli; 151, 155 Johner Images;

166–7 Hans-Peter Merten; 168R Peter Lourenco; 172 Stefan Cioata; 175 Juan Naharro Gimenez; 176 Imgorthand; 188–9 Westend61; 204–5 Heavenli Denton/EyeEm; 214–15 Paul Biris; 225 Mariusz Wozniak/EyeEm; 241 Paul Biris; 242 Atlantide Phototravel; 263R ANDREW KASUKU; 267 Westend61; 270L Buena Vista Images; 274 Chad Wright Photography; 282 Maxime Damour/EyeEm; 283 charliebishop; 303 Emad aljumah; 313B Paul Biris; 320 real444; 322 Vincent Boisvert, all rights reserved; 324–5 Nancy Brown; 329 thianchai sitthikongsak; 336B TANG CHHIN SOTHY/Collaborator; 341B Jean Chung; 349 The Asahi Shimbun/Collaborator; 361 Nora Carol Photography; 367R Putu Sayoga; 372 Stuart Westmorland; 379 David Trood; 382 Romilly Lockyer; 396 Matthew Micah Wright.

Pexels: 25 Jess Loiterton; 123T André Ulysses De Salis; 158r Barry Tan; 237 Mehmet Akyuz; 249 Djamel Ramdani; 297 Preeya Innual; 300 bacho nadiradze; 351 Quang Nguyen Vinh; 374L Rachel Claire; 388 Ethan Brooke.

Pixabay: 28 Chad-V.

Shutterstock: 11 Tory Kallman; 13 Stephen Bridger; 14 Regien Paassen; 15L David J. Mitchell; 17B kentaylordesign; 18–19 MetalPrints; 21T EQRoy; 21BL Mia2you; 21BR ImagoPhoto; 23 Maridav; 26T Stephanie A Sellers; 26BR Valentin Martynov; 29 Aleksei Potov; 30 titipongpwl; 31R Kobby Dagan; 32 kropic1; 33l David A Litman; 33R Michael Barajas; 34–5 Sean Pavone; 36 My Good Images; 37 Unwind; 40L Lauren Elisabeth; 40R Kit Leong; 41L Maria_Usp; 41R Brocreative; 44L Jim Mallouk; 44R Autumn Sky Photography; 45 littlenySTOCK; 46–7 Zhukova Valentyna; 50 Dan Hanscom; 51 Allan Wood Photography; 57 amadeustx; 63 Noradoa; 64 R.M. Nunes; 65 Kobby Dagan; 66L Ivan Soto Cobos; 68–9 RabbitHolePhoto; 70L Trish Backburn; 72L Rob Crandall; 76 Inga Pracute; 77 Milan Zygmunt; 79L boivin nicolas; 79R Margus Vilbas Photography; 81R Kristel Segeren; 82 oscar garces; 84–5 Alex Waltner Photography; 86 Lukasz Nycz; 90 Captain Wang; 92 Chiara Magi; 93 Natalia Barsukova;

99R Douglas Olivares; 100 Maridav; 103 Ksenia Ragozina; 105T Robert CHG; 106–7 saiko3p; 109 Catarina Belova; 110L T photography; 110R–111L Antonio Salaverry; 115B Guaxinim; 118L lu_sea; 118R Locomotive74; 119l Gregorio Koji; 119R Ionov Vitaly; 120 Aleksei Potov; 123B R.M. Nunes; 125 buenaventura; 126–7 Olena Tur; 128 njaj; 131 Sergii Figurnyi; 134 Peter Krocka; 135 4H4 PH; 138 Neil Bussey; 140 coxy58; 142L Mark D Bailey; 142R Victor Lafuente Alonso; 143L Tupungato; 143R cowardlion; 144 Pit Stock; 152 NadyaEugene; 154 Inger Eriksen; 156 dotmiller1986; 157 BMJ; 158L laverock; 160–1 Ilyas Kalimullin; 164 Albert Beukhof; 165R kipgodi; 168L prosiaczeq; 170 Greens and Blues; 171T francesco de marco; 171B JHVEPhoto; 174 Jun Hammady; 178 LanaG; 179 pio3; 184 Irina Kzan; 185 travellight; 186 MisterStock: 187 bensliman hassan; 191 Great Pics Worldwide; 194R EWY Media; 195 SusaZoom; 198–9 BBA Photography; 200R Ali Al Zaabi; 201 Tomsickova Tatyana; 202L Venturelli Luca; 202R Elena.Degano; 206R Gennaro Leonardi Photos; 207L lapas77; 208R Migel; 210T Kirill Skorobogatko; 210B Gulcin Ragiboglu; 211 fokke baarssen; 213L Ceri Breeze; 213R Copycat37; 216 Cristian Puscasu; 220 Ajan Alen; 222TL Elizaveta Galitckaia; 222TR varuna; 222B Matej Kastelic; 223 Unfiltered Adventures; 224 Anna Jurkovska; 226–7 asta.sabonyte; 228 andreivladpopa; 229 Adrian Stanica; 231 Yiannis Papadimitriou; 232 siete_vidas; 233T BlueOrange Studio; 233B Alika Obraz; 235 vitaprague; 236 Sharomka; 238–9 rayints; 240 hbpro; 243 Allik; 244–5 DELBO ANDREA; 247 Fabian Plock; 250–1 trevor kittelty; 252 Graficam Ahmed Saeed; 253 Maiza Ritomy; 256 Joaquim Salles; 258 Anil Varma; 259T Claudio Soldi; 259B GUDKOV ANDREY; 260 Philou1000; 262L Martin Mecnarowski; 264 Michal Hornicky; 265R Jane Rix; 266L Bruna Falvo Fugulin; 266R Trombax; 269 Anna Dunlop; 270R–271L LouieLea; 271R Drepicter; 272 Zaruba Ondrej; 273 Eva Mont; 275 Shams F Amir; 278 BlueOrange Studio; 279T Andrea Willmore; 279ML Eva Mont; 279BL Therina Groenewald; 280L NNER; 280R Michail_Vorobyev; 281 Hajakely; 284–5 I AM JIFFY; 287B Nova Photo

414